Society and Social Change in 21st Century Europe

21st Century Europe Series

General Editor: Helen Wallace

Drawing upon the latest research, this major series of concise thematically organized texts provides state-of-the-art overviews of the key aspects of contemporary Europe from the Atlantic to the Urals for a broad student and serious general readership. Written by leading authorities in a lively and accessible style without assuming prior knowledge, each title is designed to synthesize and contribute to current knowledge and debate in its respective field.

PUBLISHED

Andrew Cottey: *Security in 21st Century Europe (2nd Edn)*
Colin Crouch: *Society and Social Change in 21st Century Europe*
Colin Hay and Daniel Wincott: *The Political Economy of European Welfare Capitalism*
Christopher Lord and Erika Harris: *Democracy in the New Europe*
Anna Triandafyllidou and Ruby Gropas: *What is Europe?*

FORTHCOMING

Tom Casier and Sophie Vanhoonacker: *Europe and the World*
Klaus Goetz: *Governing 21st Century Europe*
Ben Rosamond: *Globalization and the European Union*
Dermot McCann: *Political Economy of 21st Century Europe*

IN PREPARATION

Citizenship and Identity in 21st Century Europe

Society and Social Change in 21st Century Europe

Colin Crouch

 palgrave

First published 2016 by
PALGRAVE

Palgrave in the UK is an imprint of Macmillan Publishers Limited, registered in England, company number 785998, of 4 Crinan Street, London, N1 9XW.

Palgrave Macmillan in the US is a division of St Martin's Press LLC, 175 Fifth Avenue, New York, NY 10010.

Palgrave is a global imprint of the above companies and is represented throughout the world.

Palgrave® and Macmillan® are registered trademarks in the United States, the United Kingdom, Europe and other countries.

ISBN 978–1–137–27781–7 hardback
ISBN 978–1–137–27780–0 paperback

This book is printed on paper suitable for recycling and made from fully managed and sustained forest sources. Logging, pulping and manufacturing processes are expected to conform to the environmental regulations of the country of origin.

A catalogue record for this book is available from the British Library.

A catalog record for this book is available from the Library of Congress.

For Joan

Contents

List of Illustrative Material

Boxes

Tables

Figures

List of Abbreviations

Countries

AL	Albania
AR	Armenia
AT	Austria
BE	Belgium
BA	Bosnia-Herzegovina
BG	Bulgaria
BRD	Federal Republic of Germany (Bundesrepublik Deutschland)
BY	Belarus
CH	Switzerland
CY	Cyprus
CZ	Czech Republic
DDR	German Democratic Republic (Deutsche Demokratische Republik)
DE	Germany
DK	Denmark
EE	Estonia
EL	Greece
ES	Spain
FI	Finland
FR	France
GE	Georgia
HR	Croatia
HU	Hungary
IS	Iceland
IT	Italy
JA	Japan
LT	Lithuania
LU	Luxembourg
LV	Latvia
MD	Moldova
MK	Macedonia
MT	Malta
NL	Netherlands
NO	Norway

PL   Poland
PT   Portugal
RO   Romania
RU   Russia
SE   Sweden
SI   Slovenia
SK   Slovakia
TR   Turkey
UA   Ukraine
UK   United Kingdom
US(A)   United States (of America)
USSR   Union of Soviet Socialist Republics

General

CEE   Central and Eastern Europe
EU   European Union
FEE   Further Eastern Europe
FIFA   Fédération Internationale de Football Association
ICTWSS   Institutional Characteristics of Trade Unions, Wage Setting,
         State Intervention and Social Pacts
ILO   International Labour Organization
IMF   International Monetary Fund
ISCO   International Standard Classification of Occupations
ISIC   International Standard Industrial Classification
NATO   North Atlantic Treaty Organization
NNWE   Nordic countries and North-West Europe
NWE   North-West Europe
OECD   Organisation for Economic Co-operation and Development
ONS   Office of National Statistics (UK)
SWE   South-West Europe
TFR   Total fertility rate
UN   United Nations
UNECE   United Nations Economic Commission for Europe
VET   Vocational education and training
WHO   World Health Organization

Acknowledgements

I am grateful to Joan Crouch, Steven Kennedy, Helen Wallace and Stephen Wenham for help in shaping this book and making it readable; and to Laura Leonardi and successive cohorts of her students at the University of Florence, with whom I have developed some of these themes in lectures over past years.

Some sections of Chapter 6, and an earlier version of the statistics on trade unions used there, first appeared in my book *Governing Social Risks in Post-Crisis Europe* (Edward Elgar, 2015). I am grateful to Edward Elgar for permission to reproduce and draw on this material here.

Note

This book went to press before the outcome of the referendum on the United Kingdom's membership of the European Union (23 June 2016) was known.

Foreword

Helen Wallace, 4 April 2016

Debates about the character and changing dynamics of contemporary Europe tend to be focused on the politics and the economics of the subject, not least these days when 'Europe' has become so politically controversial and when its economic achievements have become so contested. Society is too often taken as a given without being analysed carefully. This volume aims to correct this bias by exploring thoroughly the nature of European society and the underlying patterns of social evolution.

This is an ambitious volume and one which synthesises an astonishing range of empirical evidence and analytical insights. There is no simple starting point for a study of this kind. The terms 'social' and 'societal' encompass many different dimensions of what goes on in contemporary Europe. Colin Crouch focuses on some of the more important ones broadly: the demographic, including patterns of migration; the identifiers, in particular religion and ethnicity; the occupational, including consequences both for class and for income (in)equality; the relationships between social position and social power; and some of the implications of class patterns for health, education, opportunities for mobility and political identities.

So far so good. But Europe is a complicated and diverse continent. So which Europe is under discussion? A great deal of the literature – and much of the current debate – starts from an assumption (often only implicit) that our reference point should in essence be *western* Europe. This is after all the most *advanced* part of the continent in terms of nuanced social models or political sophistication or economic modernity. Moreover the literature has traditionally been dominated by scholars from and focused on west European experience. Crouch explicitly takes a broader and more interrogative view – and one which has required a real feat of hard research. Good social science should after all derive from a basis of careful comparison. This study surveys social developments across the continent. It is intentionally not defined by the membership of the European Union or by the particular social policies and practices of the European Union. Easier said than done, however, in that a good deal of the underlying data is perforce culled from Eurostat sources which understandably are more thorough in gathering information on EU countries than on other European countries. Wherever possible Crouch has included evidence on some of those other Europeans, and now and then for further comparison he draws on evidence from beyond Europe.

The result is a rich overview that reveals the variety and fluidity of social developments. I would argue that this kaleidoscopic set of patterns should be a starting point for understanding contemporary Europe and not an afterthought, since so much of the politics and economics is shaped by the underlying social factors.

Chapter 1

Is there a European society?

Many books present the social structures of individual states or more generally those with advanced economies. Far fewer define social structures for world regions, and the exercise might be questioned. That there should be something both coherent and distinctive about an individual country is usually taken for granted, which is why we are not surprised to see studies of the society, politics or economics of particular states. It is usually assumed that the actions of states – government and law – produce certain social characteristics. Taken for granted though it may be, that is in fact quite a strong assumption, as it means accepting that government and law are important in shaping societies. Do states play a part in determining how many children are in the typical family, or the ages at which people typically die? In the next chapter we shall discover that they certainly do, but it is important to recognize that the assumption might at some points be questioned. The nature of that assumption becomes clearer if we ask whether we would expect to find books about the social structure of a geographical entity below the level of the state. There is indeed a more than 1000-page-long sociology of Catalonia, in the Catalan language, *La societat catalana* (Giner, 1998). Catalonia is a very distinctive part of Spain with a high level of political autonomy, and a government able to make its own laws on many social and economic issues within the framework of overall Spanish law. The idea that a political variable is important therefore remains. Similarly, a British person would probably be less surprised to see a study of the social structure of Scotland than one of Yorkshire.

Behind these questions lie some larger ones. Sociologists often use states as synonyms for societies. For example, we might use 'Poland' and 'Polish society' interchangeably. Is that justified? Poland is an important case in point. For two centuries until 1918 the country was completely absorbed into three other states: Germany, Russia and (affecting a smaller part of its territory) the Austro-Hungarian Empire. None of these three entities was itself a simple nation state. Russia had over centuries expanded from a base around Moscow to embrace a vast territory inhabited by people of very diverse ethnic, cultural and religious

1

backgrounds. Was there a Russian society embracing everyone from the coast of Siberia to St Petersburg, from the Arctic Ocean to the Caspian Sea, during that period? The Austrian Empire also included many people from Slav and other linguistic cultures. Meanwhile, Prussia, the German political entity that had also gained control of western Poland, had during the second half of the 19th century constructed, through treaties, trade agreements and war, a state (which it officially called an empire) of all German-speaking regions outside Austria and Switzerland, and the disputed Alsace and Lorraine territories on its border with France. (It captured Alsace and Lorraine after the Franco-Prussian War of 1870–71, but lost them to France after World War I.) When, if ever, did these empires become 'societies'? Did Poland cease to be a society when it no longer had a state?

The Austro-Hungarian, German and Russian Empires all extended their rule over contiguous, if sometimes culturally diverse, territories. Certain western European states constructed far-flung, marine empires across the world: France, Great Britain, the Dutch Republic, Portugal, Spain and (within Africa only) Belgium. Where these were contiguous – as in the case of Ireland when a colony of Britain, or the Near East under French control – there were long-standing attempts by the imperial powers to incorporate them within the imperial state itself rather than to have them as colonies. When the colonies were further afield (in sub-Saharan Africa, the Caribbean, the Indian subcontinent or the Far East) the situation was far more ambiguous. What implications should that have had for the idea of, say, Irish or Algerian as opposed to British or French societies?

After its defeat in World War II, Germany, which had been a single country since only 1870, became two separate states. On one side was the Federal Republic of Germany, with eventually 64 million people, a capitalist economy, parliamentary democracy and closely allied to the other states of western Europe and the United States. On the other side was the German Democratic Republic, with 16 million people, a state socialist economy and dictatorship and closely allied to the then Soviet Union and the other states of central and eastern Europe. Following the collapse of the Soviet Union in 1990, Germany was reunited as a single state, though one should more correctly say 'united', as this is a newly defined Germany: for the first time a unified German state renounced its claims over parts of Poland. Since the early 1990s, the statistics for the whole of Germany have been presented together as those of one country, and for many comparative studies of economy, politics and society we now take it for granted that this relatively new entity constitutes a single unit. Should we do this? Did political unification suddenly create a unified society? Meanwhile, the Czech and Slovak Republics, which until 1993 constituted the single state of Czechoslovakia, now appear as two separate units, the combined population of which is slightly smaller than the old German Democratic Republic. Were those countries that were part of the same society until 1993 suddenly becoming two different ones? Or were they always two separate societies artificially joined by a single state from 1918 to 1993? Similar questions arise elsewhere. The three countries of Scandinavia (Denmark, Norway and Sweden) are three separate states, but for many institutions they are more similar to each other than, say, southern Italy is to northern Italy, or Catalonia is to many other parts of Spain.

If we go back much further in time to the period between the fall of the Roman Empire and the 16th century, we find very few stable political entities and use the term 'state' only as an anachronism. Rulers established a hold over certain territories and retained these, usually by force of arms, for a while; then a neighbouring ruler might conquer them. These patchworks of territory were often not contiguous. It would make no sense at all to ask whether the Aquitaine region of France became part of English society during the times that English kings managed to control it; it is not clear whether English society itself existed in that period. Until the Protestant Reformation in the 16th century it might have been more accurate to speak of a Catholic society extending across the whole of western and most of central Europe, a society that had in some areas existed continuously since before the fall of Rome, but in Nordic lands only from around the year 1000. The Catholic Church regulated a wider range of areas of life than did secular rulers during that period, and in some respects more than states do today. Provided they obeyed the Church, paid their taxes and did not rebel, rulers were not very interested in the lives and welfare of their subjects. On the other hand, beneath the overarching power of the Church the lives of ordinary people were conducted at a far more local level than we experience today. There were virtually no means of transport for them, and unless they could read, they would have little chance of knowing about the world beyond the scope of their nearest market town. 'Societies', with their distinctive customs and ways of life, could be very local indeed.

A major politico-legal change is usually dated from 1648, when the signing of the Treaty of Westphalia in the German cities of Osnabrück and Münster ended the Thirty Years War that had torn apart much of northern Europe in a politico-religious struggle, and the even longer 80-year war between Spain and the Dutch Republic. The treaties asserted the rights of what became known as states to seek self-determination and not to accept the long-standing but ineffective claims to sovereignty over them of the papacy and the German-based entity that called itself the Holy Roman Empire. However, that does not mean that we can date the career of all European states from around that time. Germany and Italy, the two countries at the heart of the papal-imperial system, remained patchworks of small monarchies, dukedoms, free cities and Church-controlled territories until the late 19th century. Further east, beyond the realm of western Christianity and in the land of the Orthodox churches, there was a wide diversity of social groupings, some of which were similar to medieval and early modern western European state formations. Gradually these were conquered by or merged into the two great competing forces in the east: the Muscovite, eventually Russian, state and the Islamic Ottoman Empire in modern Turkey.

More significant social changes occurred from the late 18th century onwards. States were by then inhabiting more or less contiguous territories, though they continued to invade each other from time to time, and some were busy establishing overseas empires. Following the revolution of 1789 and especially during the Napoleonic years (1797 to 1815), the French engaged on a project to build a tightly integrated, modernizing, nationally based state to unite the very diverse populations inhabiting the territory long known as France, in order to forge a population that could provide effective armies and an improved economy. Napoleon Bonaparte then sought to found republics based on the same principles by invading the Netherlands, Switzerland, Spain, parts of Germany and Italy and elsewhere. This set in train rival nation-building processes among its neighbours. The British moved ahead with a process of industrialization and further imperial conquest. The former was primarily a product of private enterprise, while the latter was a state project and required nation-building. British national elites took little interest in the industrial economy until France, Germany and others appeared to rival the country's industries. These rivals, arriving later on to the scene, used state policy to provide an infrastructure, including roads and railways, as well as skills, and eventually (starting in Germany) social policies to stabilize the insecure lives of industrial workers who might otherwise become rebellious. By the late 19th century one can see states as active builders of *societies*, not just of realms and points of military strength. These states were rarely democratic, but they were embarking on a road towards democracy, as elites were becoming increasingly aware of their dependence on the loyalty and active cooperation of the majority of populations, whose lives had so often been ignored under past regimes. It was at the same time that the academic discipline of sociology was established in order to study these processes. It now began to make some sense in certain contexts to use, say, 'France' as a synonym for 'French society'.

When thinking of states as large aggregations of people, as societies, rather than as political entities, it is usual to use the term 'nation state'. I have avoided that term in this book. Behind it lies an essentially 18th-century idea: first that nations exist as real communities in a pre-state reality and second that the boundaries of states should correspond to the boundaries of nations. This idea was extremely powerful in mobilizing European peoples living under what at least some among them regarded as foreign rule to struggle for independence. It was especially important in encouraging independence movements against the Habsburg Empire among Czechs and Slovaks (acting together), Italians (in the parts of that country that had been conquered by the Habsburgs) and Hungarians. The last-mentioned conflict resulted in the compromise formation of the Austro-Hungarian Empire in 1867. The nations identifying themselves in these cases were often based on the possession of a shared language different from that of the imperial power, though Czech and Slovak were separate if closely related languages, and until the end of the 19th century there was no unified form of Italian, rather a set of very diverse dialects. There was also often a past, pre-conquest history of political unity, though in the Italian case that stretched back to the Roman Empire, which had itself seen 'Italy' as only a part of its territory.

Yet the idea that ideally nations should form states failed to recognize that it was often states that had formed nations. France, like Russia, had been formed as a geopolitical centre (in this case around Paris and the so-called Île-de-France) and gradually extended the territory over which it ruled, breaking down local systems of rule, law, custom and – though not until the late 19th and early 20th centuries – language. Fewer countries demonstrate the complexity of relations between nation and state than Belgium, the territory of which was for centuries an important site of major wars, including both 20th-century world wars. Modern Belgium was formed in the 1830s from a territory of the former Austrian Netherlands, parts of which had once been ruled over by the dukes of Burgundy – geographically remote from Belgium and itself notionally part of France. Following succession problems in the Burgundian dynasty, it had passed to the control of the Spanish branch of the Habsburg family and became known as the Spanish Netherlands until, following war between Spain and Austria (and much of the rest of western Europe), the Austrian branch of the Habsburgs absorbed it during the 18th century. Napoleonic France conquered the territory in the early 19th century, but following the fall of Napoleon in 1815 it became part of the Netherlands. However, in 1832 the Belgian elite rebelled against Dutch rule and following a short war established Belgium as an independent state for the first time. Its eventual boundaries were determined by the outcome of conflict, and the territory continues today to be divided into a Dutch-speaking (or Flemish) majority, a large French-speaking minority and a very small German-speaking minority. Has there been a historic Belgian 'nation'?

The joint results of successful national revolts against 'foreign' rule, the collapse of some cross-national states into their composite parts (e.g. Czechoslovakia and Yugoslavia), and the nation-building activities of established states mean that many contemporary European states can be seen as nation states, but there are important exceptions. The United Kingdom formally recognizes four component nations: England, Scotland, Wales and Northern Ireland. The Republic of Ireland does not officially see itself as a nation state, because part of the island of Ireland (Northern Ireland) remains part of the United Kingdom. In Spain, many Basque and Catalan people consider that they constitute separate nations. The population of Ukraine is divided between a majority who see themselves as Ukrainian and a minority who identify with Russia.

Today we might also question the idea of national societies in a different way. The world's most important corporations now operate across a large number of states, with employees often performing different kinds of task in different countries. For example, a firm might have its headquarters (and key managerial staff) in Switzerland, have its design, research and development activities and staff in California, its products manufactured in Brazil and China, its clerical support and customer relations services in India and sell its products (shaping more or less uniform tastes) partly in shops all over the world and partly through Internet sales located nowhere in particular but fiscally based in Ireland or Luxembourg, where business tax rates are particularly low. As we shall see in Chapter 4, the different kinds of work that people do have a considerable impact on their lives in general, particularly by determining their incomes. These activities of global firms lead to different concentrations of different kinds of workers in different countries and world regions. Are there therefore corporate societies as well as national ones? Multinational enterprises seem often to have been more successful than states in integrating people from multiple national backgrounds into their workforces. Should we, for example, speak of 'McDonald's society' as we do 'Italian society'? Do employees of these firms have lives, not just working lives, that are shaped more by the corporation than by the community in which they live? This question will be mainly encountered by those studying Third World countries, where the lives of the employees of multinationals are likely to be very separate from other local people, regulated by a corporate rather than a community timetable, and where they often live in communities formed by corporate compounds, in the manner of European colonialists from the 15th to the 20th century.

These considerations must all be borne in mind as we return to our initial question: Is there a European society? What should we expect from a sociology of Europe? Some authors have attempted to answer these questions, but they usually end by finding more national differences than similarities (e.g. Leonardi, 2012; Mau and Verwiebe, 2010). Such conclusions are not surprising. Is there any point in putting, say, the United Kingdom alongside Slovakia rather than alongside its former colony and fellow anglophone Australia, or France alongside Latvia rather than its francophone neighbours and former colonies in North Africa? Does the similarity of relative geographical closeness make more sense than the closer similarity of average income and stability of political institutions? For the member states of the European Union (EU) there is a stronger potential rationale, in that the EU does form a layer of government that generates laws and policies that might hypothetically be shaping the societies of those states in the same way that we take it for granted that states themselves shape their own societies. This becomes an important hypothesis in its own right, well worth studying: how do the actions of a supranational body of that type compare with the society-forming capacities of states? However, the question is made difficult to answer by the fact that some countries have been members of the EU for 60 years, others for less than ten, with Norway and Switzerland only partial members.

But what if one adds countries to the east of the EU member states: Belarus, Moldova, Ukraine? And those parts of ex-Yugoslavia that have not (yet) become EU members: Serbia, Montenegro, Macedonia, Bosnia-Herzegovina? Or Albania and Turkey, clearly within (or in Turkey's case partly within) Europe as a geographical entity? Would there be any point in a study of all of Europe if the EU did not exist, if there were no state-like institution in the region? Would there be any point in a study of, say, the whole of Asia or Africa, world regions without such an institution? A major issue here is the doubtful reality of these entities. They originated as divisions of the world made by the ancient Greeks, who, especially in the case of Asia, had very little knowledge of the extent of the land masses and islands that lay beyond the small parts they had actually visited. From the 15th century onwards, when Portuguese, Spanish, Dutch, English, French and other explorers embarked on the process of European discovery of the rest of the planet, they took these limited concepts of the world's continents with them, constantly expanding their application. There is therefore no reason at all why we should take these designations of world regions as having any serious meaning apart from convenient ways of indicating very large territories.

Europe's debatable boundaries

The ancient Greeks used the term Europa to designate a small area, part of what they called Thrace, occupying much of today's Bulgaria, part of northern Greece and western Turkey. It was moved northwards and westwards by ecclesiastical writers in Charlemagne's kingdom in the 8th century seeking to designate the zone of western Christianity (and thus excluding the original Greek idea). Today Europe is normally seen as having three reasonably clear physical boundaries, but one very vague one (see Figure 1.1). To the north it is bound by the Arctic Ocean as that sea passes the coast of northern Norway. To the west is the Atlantic Ocean beyond Ireland, except that Iceland further to the north west is usually included, especially as it is culturally and linguistically part of Scandinavia. (Greenland, even further to the north west, is strictly speaking part of Denmark, but its population is very small.) To the south is the Mediterranean Sea, which was not at all a relevant boundary to the Romans, whose empire's southern extent was rather the Sahara Desert. For much of post-Roman European history it has, however, marked a boundary between the Christian and Muslim worlds, which has at times had considerable social and political as well as religious importance. At the southern tip of Spain, the gap between Europe and the region commonly known as the Near East is very narrow indeed, but for centuries its religious significance has been fundamental. This southern border becomes ambiguous at its eastern corner, where it encounters Egypt, Israel, Lebanon, Syria and the large mass of Turkey. It is on that eastern side that the geographical identity

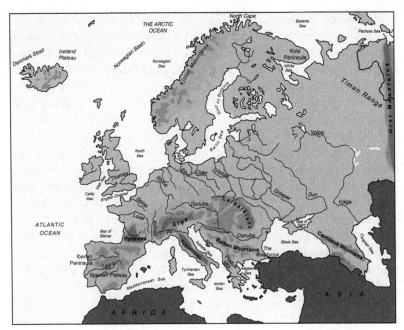

FIGURE 1.1 *Europe, as broadly conceived.*

of Europe becomes difficult. If the boundary is held to follow not the Mediterranean itself but the ancient Greeks' original idea of the flow of water through the Bosphorus and into the Black Sea (placing part of Turkey in Europe and the rest in Asia), then these countries can be defined as constituting the Middle East, outside of Europe except for the western part of Turkey. As the eastern boundary runs north we confront the large question: Is Russia part of Europe? In the 18th and 19th centuries both Russia and the Ottoman Empire, based in modern Turkey, were definitely considered part of the diplomatic world of Europe, but the issue has long been politically contentious within those countries themselves, with changing regimes bringing different perspectives. Looked at purely in terms of physical geography, it is possible and conventional to trace a line running north east from the Black Sea across the north of the Caucasus Mountains, picking up the river Volga where it enters the Sea of Azov and running north with it to the Ural Mountains, which then extend north almost to the Arctic Ocean. This is a boundary that bisects Russia, like Turkey, into a European and an Asian part, a distinction often recognized by Russians themselves.

A sociological study of Russia, which would be partly devoted to identifying possible differences between these two parts, would be an interesting exercise, but it is beyond our present scope. From the time of their conquest in the early 18th century the three small Baltic states (Estonia, Latvia and Lithuania) were part of Russia, but they declared their independence after the fall of the Soviet Union, and are now recognized as independent states with membership of the EU. Outside the EU but within the Volga-Urals definition of Europe are Belarus, Moldova and Ukraine. Within the former Soviet Union, Belarus and Ukraine had been formally independent states, though they remained very closely linked to Russia. South of the Caucasus and continuing east of the Volga-Urals line are other former parts of the Soviet Union and of pre-1917 Russia that are now independent countries, from Georgia to Kazakhstan. World organizations established in the days when the Soviet Union existed – such as the United Nations (UN) and all its associated bodies or the world Association football body, FIFA, and other international cultural and sporting organizations – included the whole of the Soviet Union, and therefore these territories, within an extended idea of 'Europe and Central Asia', the latter being a 19th-century Russian concept. This continues to be their practice today. However, in this book I exclude Russia and Central Asia from the idea of Europe, but Russia itself is included in several discussions as an external comparator.

Defined in this way, Europe has today two troublesome frontiers. The first is this geographically problematic eastern one with Russia. Following the collapse of the Soviet Union, the countries of central Europe, which Russia's political elite had long seen as a buffer between their country and western Europe in general and Germany in particular, joined both the EU and the North Atlantic Treaty Organization (NATO). This brought to Russia's borders NATO, the transatlantic military alliance formed after 1945 under US leadership to counter a perceived military threat from the Soviet Union. The move occurred when post-Soviet Russia was extremely weak. Subsequently the country has developed a strong oil- and gas-based economy and has moved to counter any further moves east by the EU and NATO. The main focus of this concern to date has been on Ukraine, much of the population of which would like to accept the western embrace, but where a minority prefers a closer relationship with Russia. By 2014 this issue had become militarily contested.

Europe's other problematic boundary is that to the south and south east. This has broadly defined the boundary between Christendom and the Islamic world since the ending of Islamic rule over parts of Spain and Portugal and the conquest of Christian Byzantium by the Islamic power that came to be called the Ottoman Empire, both events occurring during the 15th century. The latter brought the territories we now know as Albania, Bulgaria, Romania and the former Yugoslavia (except for the areas now known as Croatia and Slovenia), as well as Greece, under Ottoman rule. Much of the population remained Orthodox Christian, but some converted to Islam, particularly in Albania and Bosnia-Herzegovina. Greece secured independence from the Ottoman Empire in 1832, and parts of the Balkan region had been reconquered by various Christian powers by the 19th century. Following its military defeat in World War I the Ottoman Empire was dismembered, its core in Turkey remaining, however, as a large state formation. The state of Yugoslavia was formed to bring together various parts of the Balkans, a mixture of peoples of Catholic, Orthodox and Islamic origins. It lasted until 1990, when it collapsed in violent inter-communal attempts at 'ethnic cleansing' among the different cultural and religious groups.

Also divided between Greek Orthodox Christianity and Islam is the island of Cyprus. Ruled over by the United Kingdom from the late 19th century until a successful violent struggle for independence ended in 1960, the island was then plunged into conflict between the Orthodox Greek-speaking majority mainly in the south and the Islamic Turkish-speaking minority mainly in the north. The Greek and Turkish governments became militarily involved in the dispute, and in 1974 the island was partitioned. What is today known as the Republic of Cyprus is in effect the southern, Greek part. The Turkish Republic of Northern Cyprus governs the north, but this regime has not been recognized by most international organizations. As a result there are few statistics on that territory, and it has been difficult to include it within the scope of this book. Reference to 'Cyprus' therefore refers to the southern Republic of Cyprus and not to the whole island. (The same applies to our use of 'Ireland' to refer to the Republic of Ireland in the south of that island, the north-western part being included within the United Kingdom of Great Britain and Northern Ireland.)

Relations between some European countries and some parts of the extra-European Islamic world are again contentious and the cause of various kinds of violence. While the problems of this relationship date back to the Crusades, today they are more a by-product of difficult relations between the United States and the Arab world, a theme that is beyond our scope in this book.

Identifying sub-regions of Europe

The definition of Europe is contested not only by geographers, but by actual political conflict. It is a world region containing a wide range of different kinds of society, though with less variation than we would encounter in a study of the whole world. In wealth it ranges from some of the world's richest societies in the north west to some middle-income ones in the east, but with no examples of the levels of poverty that can be found in sub Saharan Africa. Figure 1.2 presents data for

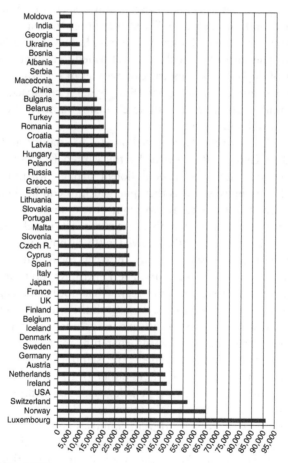

Source: World Bank 2015a

FIGURE 1.2 *Per capita gross national income in purchasing power parities, US$, European countries and various comparators, 2013.*

2014 (the most recent available at the time of writing) for average per capita national income expressed in US$ and calculated by the World Bank to represent purchasing power. That is, rather than just calculate the exchange value of different currencies, which is subject to fluctuations that have nothing to do with varying standards of living, the World Bank relates incomes to prices. The objective is to measure income in terms of the bundle of goods that people living in the country concerned can buy. The figures are expressed as national averages and therefore do not take account of inequalities within countries. This is a topic to which we shall return in later chapters. All European countries are covered, as well as Japan, Russia, Turkey and the United States (our four external comparators), the two largest countries in the developing world, China and India, and some cases of extreme wealth and poverty.

The richest country in the world in 2014 was the small oil-rich Arab state Qatar with US$146,178 per capita. Second was Macao, the small, former Portuguese colony now part of China with US$139,762. The richest European country, again a small one, was Luxembourg at US$91,048, some way ahead of Norway at US$64,893. The world's two poorest countries in 2013 were both in sub-Saharan Africa: the Democratic Republic of Congo with a per capita purchasing power income of US$745 and Burundi at US$770. No European society was anything like as poor as that, though Moldova had a lower income than India, while several countries in eastern Europe and ex-Yugoslavia were poorer than China.

There is a very clear geography to the relative wealth of European (and indeed other) countries. All countries in North-West Europe (i.e. north of the Alps and the Pyrenees and west of the frontier with the former Soviet bloc and ex-Yugoslavia) have higher per capita incomes than the rest of Europe – with the United States ranking alongside the richest European countries. Japan falls between the 'poorest' country in the north west (France) and the richest in the south (Italy). The southern group (Greece, Italy, Portugal, Spain and the two small islands Cyprus and Malta) in general stands ahead of all eastern cases, though Slovenia and the Czech Republic are now wealthier than Malta, Portugal and Greece, while Slovakia, Estonia and Lithuania are wealthier than Greece. Turkey stands lower than all of South-West Europe and several central and eastern European countries. Below we discuss in detail potential geographical groupings within central and eastern Europe. For the present we can note that those in the centre (the Czech and Slovak Republics, Hungary and Poland) and the Baltics are wealthier than all those further east and in ex-Yugoslavia, except for Slovenia among the latter. Those central countries and the Baltic states were the first ex-Soviet countries to be admitted to the EU on the grounds of their relatively advanced economies. The Czech and Slovak Republics, Hungary and Poland are a geographically compact entity and were known as the Visegrád group, named after the castle in Hungary where their leaders met in 1991 to discuss their future within Europe. Russia has a per capita income similar to this group and the Baltic states, but all other eastern countries have lower incomes. Particularly notable are the low levels in the countries of the former Yugoslavia apart from Slovenia. These countries were torn apart by the civil war that followed the collapse of Yugoslavia.

In terms of economic structure, most western and several eastern European countries can be regarded as becoming post-industrial, in that after an extensive period of industrialization growth is now mainly in certain services sectors. Within that generalization there is diversity in the balance between manufacturing and services, while some countries in the central part of the continent are still major industrial producers and a few in the east continue to have large agricultural sectors.

Apart from some doubtful cases in the east, all European countries are at least formally democratic. Several countries in the north west have had democratic traditions for most of the 20th century – the majority uninterruptedly since the end of World War II. Greece, Portugal and Spain ceased to be dictatorships in the 1970s, while most countries of the former Soviet bloc acquired free elections only after 1990. With the exception of Albania and the European part of Turkey all European countries have had mainly Christian pasts, as is discussed in more detail in Chapter 3.

Several major historical fissures have set different parts of the region on diverse paths, and it is these that justify the focus of a sociology of Europe on the identification of both similarities and differences. Given the diversity of the region, it does not make sense to ask if there is such a thing as 'a' European society. It is, however, interesting to ask if Europe consists of 30 or more national societies, each of which is quite distinct, or whether some groups of countries share certain similarities. The questions then become: Can we identify distinct sub-regions of Europe? And what would we gain from seeing Europe in terms of these rather than as a collection of distinct nation-state societies?

Important stereotypes abound, based on major compass points, and we have already used some of these in considering differences in per capita national incomes. There is a popular stereotype of a difference between a north and a south within western Europe: the former being associated with prosperity, a dominance of formal organizations and hard work, a largely Protestant religious background and wet weather; and the south being seen as less wealthy, with a dominant family life, informality and a relaxed approach to work, Catholic and sunny. There is then an east–west division, with the former emerging from Russian domination, poor and disorganized, and the latter wealthy and efficient, perhaps under heavy American influence. A primary objective of a sociology of Europe must be to do better than this, though elements of this crude picture do remain in more sophisticated accounts.

Gøsta Esping-Andersen's (1990) trail-blazing account for this type of analysis was restricted to western Europe only (as well as the anglophone world). It was based not on stereotypes but on struggles that took place among key social groups to gain control of the process of industrialization and modernization from the 19th century:

- Conservative, primarily landed, interests mainly concerned with protecting not only their own privileges, but more generally a hierarchical Christian society. Esping-Andersen saw these as dominant throughout Continental western Europe.
- New capitalist groups with liberal ideas in relation to modernization but at least as hostile to attempts by workers to organize themselves as were conservative landed groups. Esping-Andersen saw these as important in the anglophone world. Within Europe this meant just one state, the United Kingdom, until Irish independence in the 1920s. Most other such countries lie outside Europe: the United States, Canada, Australia and New Zealand.
- The new groups of mainly manual workers being produced by industrialization. They lacked not only the wealth of traditional landed and new industrial capitalist groups, but also the embeddedness in traditional community of many rural workers – though these too were affected by the upheavals of modernization, industrialization and urbanization. These new groups were insecure outsiders, lacking citizenship and other rights, unless they organized themselves into parties and trade unions. They acquired their greatest strength in the Nordic countries.

This threefold division of the opposed forces that through their exchanges and conflicts constructed the industrial world is a familiar and important one. It designates the three great political families that can be found in the party structure of many societies: conservative, liberal and socialist or social democratic. It also lies behind Max Weber's seminal conception of the three forms of social division as being those based on status (traditional elites), class (bourgeois property owners) and party (the organized working class). Esping-Andersen argued that the power balance between these forces varied in different parts of the industrializing world, leading to certain differences in their social structure. This therefore becomes a key hypothesis in accounting for differences among groups of countries in Europe and other modernizing parts of the world, and the general idea behind it will be of importance in subsequent chapters.

Esping-Andersen's main aim in this classification was to account for something narrower and more specific: differences in the kinds of social support offered in different countries to protect workers from insecurity in employment, old age and poor health. The Scandinavian countries and eventually Finland developed the most generous egalitarian systems of social support as a set of universal social rights, releasing workers from their dependence on the labour market (where their position was usually weak) for important aspects of life. This was logically consistent with the particular strength of organized labour in that part of the world. The United Kingdom, the United States and other anglophone countries developed residual systems where workers had to prove destitution to be eligible for help – politically dominant capitalist interests wanting to reduce intervention in the labour market as much as possible. When conservative, mainly rural, elites were dominant, they sought to reproduce in the welfare support system the status-based hierarchies from which they buttressed their own positions. They therefore opted for relatively generous systems of social support, but based closely on employees' work status. Instead of universal schemes as in Scandinavia, conservative elites devised a range of insurance schemes for specific occupational groups. The original and boldest examples of this were introduced in Germany in 1889 under the chancellorship of Count Otto von Bismarck, and occupationally based insurance schemes are usually known as Bismarckian (Palier, 2010).

One might reasonably question whether the design of social support systems provides an adequate basis for a classification of entire societies – surely a case of the tail wagging the dog. But behind this specific application Esping-Andersen's scheme was based on his broader stylized histories of different patterns of class relations. It is these that have given his approach continuing resonance in attempts to find subregions within Europe going far beyond classifications of social policy. Social support systems might be just one outcome of differences in these arrangements, and we might search for others. The potentiality of the class-based account for more general analysis is increased when we see that it is in turn rooted in some other aspects of social structure, in particular the results of the religious conflicts that dominated Europe and produced major divisions across it from the 16th century onwards. The Catholic Church was historically associated with traditional monarchies, even if on occasions specific kings or emperors were at war with it, and the two institutions engaged in mutual defence against newly emerging forces with power bases outside landed wealth, mainly urban and, by the 19th century, industrial property. Logically, the newly emerging bourgeois forces often associated themselves with the Protestant movement. However, in the circumstances of the 16th to 18th centuries it was virtually impossible to establish regimes that were not monarchies, and Protestants found supportive kings and queens in England, Scandinavia and some, especially northern, parts of Germany, as well as in Switzerland and the Dutch Republic (which eventually became a monarchy). Where the Catholic Church dominated, conservative institutions and values prevailed; the impact of bourgeois challenge was blunted. Liberal capitalist groups were often likely to associate with secularist, anti-clerical movements. However, the Catholic Church was deeply entrenched in the minds and lives of the mass of the population, and when by the late 19th century workers began to organize their own movements, the Church was able to establish its own forms of these, challenging the secular ones being set up by socialist movements. With the exception of Calvinism, the Protestant churches were less successful in sustaining the kind of popular loyalty that could sustain mass mobilization and founded few workers' movements.

Presented in this schematic way, we can see how the Esping-Andersen scheme reaches deep into the historical forces that produced the main fault lines in western Europe. Lutheran Protestantism became well established in Scandinavia, and when the labour movement began to organize it experienced no splits based on religion and could develop a united strength. The Continental states that developed conservative social insurance schemes did so on the basis of Catholic ideas as well as post-feudal ones.

However, when we look more closely, the simple threefold scheme begins to fragment. The Nordic story holds up well, and one must remember that Esping-Andersen is Danish, but the two other groups are difficult to sustain. First, why is England, or the United Kingdom, not part of the Nordic group? It had a Protestant monarchy and was indeed the leading modernizing, industrializing country, with a

powerful trade union movement. Also within the anglophone group
if beyond the range of our present study, Australia and New Zealand
had powerful early labour movements. Was Esping-Andersen taking
the United States as the paradigm case of an anglophone group of
countries without deeper inspection of the other cases? The answer
is more complex and more favourable to the Esping-Andersen thesis. In the mid 20th century the United Kingdom (along with Australia and New Zealand) did belong very much to the Nordic model
of welfare states and followed Esping-Andersen's arguments about
the kind of society in which these would develop. Indeed, universal
social benefits systems are often called Beveridgean, after Sir William
Beveridge, the founder of the British universalist social insurance system during World War II. In classifying Britain as a country where an
early-established bourgeois elite was able to resist the labour movement's demands, Esping-Andersen was looking to an earlier 18th- and
19th-century period. However, looking at welfare systems in the late
1980s he found evidence that led him to classify the United Kingdom
as having the residual welfare state that one might predict on the basis
of that earlier history. It was as though British history from 1945
to 1980 had eventually given way to an earlier trajectory, and that
Esping-Andersen's focus on the late 18th century provides a more
accurate guide to the 21st century than does the country's history in
the mid 20th. The British story demonstrates the complexity of trying
to put hybrid cases into classification systems that require them to fit
snugly into a single box; it also raises interesting questions about when
older layers of social relations might be able to reassert themselves over
later developments.

It would seem unambiguous that Germany is the paradigm case
for the Bismarckian system, but here too there are problems. When
Bismarck united the disparate and fragmented regimes of the German
lands into a single state dominated by Prussia, there were parts that
were mainly Catholic and others mainly Protestant. Prussia was predominantly Protestant and imposed a Protestant hegemony on the rest
of the country. This eventually changed; having initially decided that
Catholics, liberals, socialists and Jews were all enemies of the new
German state (*Reichsfeinde*), the regime found it had defined too many
enemy forces and accepted the Catholic Church as one of the friends
of the regime (*Reichsfreunde*). However, the ruling groups remained
primarily Protestant, and it is not easy to see Bismarckian institutions
as the straightforward expression of a European conservatism defined
essentially by a Catholic tradition. Catholicism as such is clearly not

the fundamental variable here. The other countries included in Esping-Andersen's Bismarckian group are rather diverse. Austria and Hungary (formerly united under the Austro-Hungarian Empire) would be better candidates for paradigmatic status among those other countries, as they have had Bismarckian insurance schemes but are predominantly Catholic; the Netherlands and Switzerland, on the other hand, have had an elaborate compromise among Catholic, Calvinist and lay cultures.

Far more problematic have been the southern European Catholic cases with Bismarckian schemes: Italy, Portugal, Spain as well as Orthodox Greece. Most observers (e.g. Ferrera, 1996; Naldini, 2003) have amended Esping-Andersen's scheme by making a separate group of these countries on the basis of the role of the family in their welfare states. German and other North-West European social insurance systems are described by Esping-Andersen and others as 'familist' in that they envisaged a 'male breadwinner' establishing rights that could also benefit his non-working wife and children. In the south, familism has instead meant that the family has primary responsibility for its own social support, leading to lower levels of state social policy than in the north-western cases. As we shall see in Chapter 4, familism in all Bismarckian countries did seem to have delayed the entry into the labour force of married women during the 1970s and 1980s, compared with both the anglophone and Nordic cases, but the difference of emphasis in the meaning of familism between the northern and southern countries has been very important.

More difficult is the location of France in this scheme. It has had a Bismarckian system, but during the formative years of the late 19th and early 20th centuries the country was deeply divided between Catholic and secular forces. Much of this conflict centred on the role of the state, in particular in relation to the family. At that time secularists shared the Catholic aim of keeping women to the role of mothers, but for a different reason: concern over France's low birth rate and a need to resolve it by encouraging motherhood. This difference of motive led to important changes in French policy later in the 20th century, including policies for encouraging mothers to participate in the paid labour force, as will be seen in Chapter 4. For the present we need to note that France does not conform fully to the Bismarckian stereotype.

Esping-Andersen restricted his study to non-communist industrial economies and therefore did not include central and eastern Europe. However, to the extent that his account concerns the formative years of the late 19th and early 20th centuries, it should be possible to embrace those countries that had been part of the Austro-Hungarian or German

Empires (the Czech and Slovak lands, Slovenia, Croatia, Hungary and much of Poland). These have had elements of the Bismarckian system in a way that countries that were either independent or part of the Russian or Ottoman Empires did not. Although the Soviet Union imposed major changes on all these systems, we may make an initial attempt to differentiate within central and eastern Europe by bracketing the 'ex-Bismarckians' together, and provisionally leaving as another group all those cases that were outside Austrian and German influence. Social policy in the Tsarist Russian Empire had been very poorly developed, and after 1917 a communist system was installed and then imported into all countries that were absorbed into the Soviet sphere of interest after World War II. This provided an extensive universal welfare state, limited eventually only by the deteriorating standard of living in the Soviet bloc. It was, however, partly administered by local Communist Party cadres and therefore was not based on citizenship rights as in Scandinavia but on political favours. Poland is complex in this context. It was less industrialized than the other truncated Bismarckian cases, and while Silesia had been within Austro-Hungary and the rest of the western part had been incorporated within Prussia and then Germany until 1918, the eastern regions had been part of Russia until that time.

Other studies have also attempted classifications of countries, mainly on the basis of social and labour policy issues and mostly restricted to western Europe. A comprehensive summary of many of the findings is to be found in the European Commission's report on industrial relations in Europe in 2008 (European Commission, 2009). It was based on a number of studies of comparative European industrial relations and welfare states, including Esping-Andersen (1990) but also making use of Ebbinghaus and Visser (1997), Crouch (1993, 1996), Schmidt (2002, 2006) and Kohl and Platzner (2007). This led it to identify the following:

- North (the Nordic countries);
- Centre West (Germany and the smaller countries of North-West Europe);
- South (the southern countries of the pre-enlargement EU);
- West (Ireland and the United Kingdom); and
- Centre East (the ex-communist EU member states).

This scheme appears purely geographical, but the studies on which it was based were more concerned with power relations within countries – either class relations of the kind proposed by Esping-Andersen (1990)

that are discussed further in Chapters 4 and 5 or long-term state strategies towards organized interests (Crouch, 1993, 1996; Schmidt, 2002,
2006). The Commission's authors then made some changes to their
scheme, based on observations of major institutional differences in
industrial relations organization. They allocated Slovenia outside the
Centre East and put it with Centre West. They also put France with the
South. These were justifiable switches when the focus was on industrial relations systems alone and as they exist now, as opposed to
social policy or earlier political development paths. The authors also
expressed some doubt about the allocation of Finland (ambiguous
between North and Centre West) and Hungary (ambiguous between
Centre East and South).

Since this EU report was prepared, Bohle and Greskovits (2012)
have provided a means of analysing differences among Central East
Europe countries, distinguishing among:

- the Visegrád group, referred to above (Czech Republic, Hungary,
  Poland, Slovakia, to which they provisionally added Croatia);
- the Baltic states, together with Bulgaria and Romania; and
- the lone case of Slovenia, which had been part of Yugoslavia and
  not the Soviet bloc.

All these accounts, being based mainly on EU member states, leave
out the most eastern parts of Europe and most of ex-Yugoslavia. With
the analysis presented in the following chapters there is occasion to
revise and refine these classifications and propose an amended version,
not least because the approach taken so far in the literature does not
take account of the major ruptures since the early 20th century, apart
from the Russian Revolution, and in particular the major changes that
took place after the end of World War I (when the former dependencies
of the Austro-Hungarian Empire acquired independence) and World
War II (when most western welfare states took their predominant
modern form).

However, as a useful starting point the existing literature suggests
we make the following broad and provisional potential distinctions
among European societies. They will be used only as a starting point
and convenient shorthand, and as we proceed we shall challenge and
deconstruct their terms:

- The Nordic countries, with universalist welfare states: Denmark,
  Finland, Norway, Sweden and possibly Iceland. (To form a noun

from Nordic we sometimes use 'Norden'. Strictly speaking the term Scandinavia indicates a language group and therefore does not include Finland, whose language is completely different.)

- The anglophone countries with residual welfare states: Ireland and the United Kingdom, which many observers would expect to find having important similarities with the United States (and also with Australia, Canada and New Zealand).
- North-West Europe (NWE), with Bismarckian, occupationally based welfare states: Austria, Belgium, Germany, Luxembourg, the Netherlands, Switzerland, with a question over the allocation of France.
- South-West Europe (SWE), with Bismarckian, family-based welfare states: Republic of Cyprus, Greece, Italy, Malta, Portugal and Spain.
- Central East Europe (CEE), the ex-state socialist successor states of the Austro-Hungarian Empire: Croatia, Czech Republic, Hungary, Poland, Slovakia, Slovenia, with a question over the allocation of Poland, which had a shared German/Russian and partly Austrian legacy.
- (Highly provisional) Further East Europe (FEE), the previously Russian-dominated states: Belarus, Bulgaria, Estonia, Latvia, Lithuania, Moldova, Romania, Ukraine and possibly Poland.
- (Even more provisional) All of ex-Yugoslavia (ex-Y) apart from Slovenia and Croatia (Serbia, Montenegro, Macedonia, Bosnia-Herzegovina and the Kosovo enclave and possibly – though not part of Yugoslavia and often in conflict with it and some of its successor states – Albania).

These groups make some initial sense in terms of similarities of social history. They are also more or less geographically contiguous (Figure 1.3). This latter point adds to the convenience of using them as recognizable starting points, but it does raise the question of whether physical geography should play such a major part. The primary justification for so doing takes us back to the land-based military foundation of political rule in pre-modern Europe. In some cases it is clear that a dominant power shaped the identity of a wider geographical region: the United Kingdom over Ireland; the Catholic Church over SWE (but not Cyprus and Greece); the Austro-Hungarian Empire over CEE; Russia over FEE. The Nordic countries comprise a geographically distinct part of Europe, have at times come under each other's domination and, with the exception of Finland, have very similar languages. NWE has been dominated at various times by France or Germany, though only

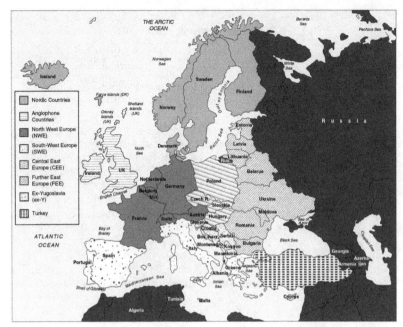

FIGURE 1.3 *Possible regional divisions of Europe.*

for short periods, punctuated by wars, and therefore not as enduringly as with the dominance of major powers in the other listed groups of countries. NWE – the core of the continent – thus remains something of a residual group, a fact which is itself a clue to the difficulty of identifying any predominant form of European society – a question to which we shall return in Chapter 8.

In distinguishing different countries and parts of Europe we have implicitly used a wealth criterion. The countries of Norden and NWE are in general richer than those of SWE, which are, with important exceptions, richer than those in CEE, which in turn are richer than those in FEE or ex-Y. Are the differences between these different sub-regions anything other than a reflection of this fundamental point of difference in national incomes? In the following chapters this question is tested by setting up what is called a null hypothesis. We first assume that there are no differences among groups of countries other than those associated with differences of national income. If some countries have positions that do not seem to be explained in this way, further investigation is presented to determine whether these exceptional cases seem to constitute groups, initially using the sub-regional groups listed

BOX 1.1   Methodological note

When we have a set of statistics on two variables for a number of cases, we can plot one variable on the horizontal (x) axis of a graph and the other on the vertical (y) axis. We can then use statistical techniques to work out the straight line that represents the best fit across the plots. This calculation will also give us an equation in the form $y = mx + c$, where x and y represent the scores on the two variables, m measures the angle of slope of the line, and c the intercept or the point where the line crosses the y access. If the x and y variables are positively related, the line will slope upwards from left to right. If they are negatively related, it will slope downwards and the equation will have a minus sign: $y = -mx + c$.

If there is a strong relationship between the two variables, the plots will all be quite close to the line. An example will be found in Figure 3.2 in Chapter 3, which plots religious belief against attendance at religious services. Not surprisingly, the line slopes upwards, showing us that attendance is higher where beliefs are strong. An example of a weaker relationship is shown in Figure 3.3 in Chapter 3, which plots the percentages of populations that are foreign-born against mean per capita annual income. The line slopes upwards, showing that overall as income rises immigration increases, but the relationship is weak; several countries stand a long way from the line.

We can calculate the strength of the relationship between the variables by calculating a statistic known as the coefficient of determination, which is usually symbolized as r squared (r^2). The higher the coefficient, the more closely related are the two variables. If the relationship is perfect $r^2 = 1$. If there is no relationship at all $r^2 = 0$. In Figure 3.2, $r^2 = 0.7487$. In Figure 3.3, $r^2 = 0.2871$.

⟶

above but approached from a willingness to explore other possibilities if that is where the data lead.

We consider the identification of exceptional cases on an objective basis by using the procedure described in Box 1.1. In brief, this enables us to determine for each case the value it would have on the dependent variable if it were fully determined by the equation of the relationship between the variables for all cases. We can then compare the actual value of the variable for a given case with its predicted value. Countries will be defined as 'exceptional' when their actual value for a variable is + or − more than half the standard deviation for the variable in question across all cases. They will be described as 'very exceptional' when their actual value is + or − more than the standard deviation. These terms are explained in Box 1.1.

⟶

A further way of measuring the spread of a number of cases across a variable is to calculate the standard deviation. This statistic expresses the extent to which the scores of all the cases depart from the mean score. If all scores are close to the mean, the standard deviation will be low. If there is a wide variety, it will be high. The standard deviation is useful to us at a number of points in this book. On many of the variables that we examine we would expect countries' scores to vary according to their national incomes – as with the example from Chapter 3 mentioned above. It is then interesting if a country has a score that is considerably higher or lower than we might expect on this basis. But how do we know whether a country is exceptional, rather than just having a score that is a bit higher or lower than we might expect? For a variable where the r^2 score is weak, we would need a country to have a far more exceptional score before we took notice than for one where it is strong. One way to get beyond a subjective evaluation of this is as follows. Using the equation of the straight line of best fit, we can calculate what score a particular country 'ought' to have on the y axis by applying the equation to its score on the x axis. This is its predicted score. We can then subtract this predicted score from the actual one to indicate how far the actual score departs from the predicted one. We shall be more impressed by the size of a departure the smaller the overall variation in the y scores. To express this, we can divide the gap between actual and predicted score for an individual case by the standard deviation. The result is known by statisticians as the z statistic. In this book we shall follow the rule of thumb of regarding countries as being 'exceptional' on a variable when their actual value for a variable is + or − more than half the standard deviation. They will be described as 'very exceptional' when their actual value is + or − more than the standard deviation.

Conclusion

The main justification for a sociology of 'Europe' is not that it constitutes a coherent group of similar countries, a single 'European society', but that it brings together a fascinating mix of similarities and differences. It is the only part of the world that has experienced a lengthy history of gradual development from subsistence agriculture to an advanced services-based economy within a framework of diverse centres of political and religious power. The only other parts of the world with similarly lengthy histories leading to advanced economies – Japan and possibly China and Russia – lack the diversity of political and religious centres that makes Europe so complex. The other advanced economies, in North America and Australasia, had histories punctuated by abrupt transformations through colonial invasion. Similar points apply to Latin America. It is therefore as a laboratory for the study of long-accumulated patterns of difference and similarity that a sociology of Europe attracts us. The issue remains of whether there is today anything that distinguishes 'Europe', or major parts of it, from other advanced regions of the world. Wherever possible, therefore, comparisons will be made with Japan, Russia and the United States in order to explore whether there really is any European distinctiveness. Where possible, Turkey is also included as a country partly within Europe and partly within 'Asia'.

In each chapter evidence is assembled to answer the questions: Are there groups of European countries or just individual cases, and how do these groups and cases compare with the three main extra-European comparators? If we find groups, how do these compare with the provisional list set out above, and how much do they vary from topic to topic? The aim of each of the following chapters is to cover as many European countries as possible, but this will often mean excluding several of those in the east, for which few comparable data are available. Since it is not possible to discuss more than 40 countries through a set of national narratives, we can achieve comparability only by placing considerable reliance on statistics that summarize a situation across as many countries as possible. This imposes a number of limitations. First, we can use numbers for comparative purposes only if we can be fairly confident that they have been collected on more or less comparable bases. There would be little point, say, in comparing two countries' statistics for religious observance if one source used the numbers of people attending religious services regularly while the other merely asked people if they had any religious beliefs. This mainly limits us to statistics collected by international organizations, such as Eurostat (the statistical agency of the EU), the Organisation for Economic Cooperation and Development (OECD), the World Bank, the International Labour Organization (ILO) and various UN agencies. Even then, one cannot be certain that these bodies have had access to adequate sources, as these are primarily national. The richest data for Europe are produced by Eurostat, but they are mainly concerned with EU member states, though sometimes with associate members, such as Norway, Switzerland, Iceland and Turkey, or candidate members, such as Serbia. Similarly the OECD mainly collects data for its members, the 34 richest nations in the world. This excludes the poorest European states, including some EU members, though it includes Japan and the United States and occasionally provides information on Russia.

A further limitation to a project that tries to cover so many countries on a comparable basis is that not much use can be made of studies of individual, or small groups of, countries. Most of the knowledge that we have of societies comes from research with this more limited geographical scope. We shall try to make use of some particularly strong examples of such work, but much has had to be sacrificed.

A final crucial question concerns the issues that are relevant for a study of social life. This involves a major exercise of subjective judgement. However, an uncontentious starting point is the basic demography of birth and death, as these processes provide the populations that are the main object of our study. This leads us quickly into patterns of marriage and other forms of sexual partnership, the structure of families and immigration. These are the topics of Chapter 2. Such a discussion brings us to religion, as religious belief and authority have so often defined approaches to marriage and childbirth, and to questions of different cultures and ethnic groups, as these are also highly relevant to the demography of a society. These and some other aspects of social identity are considered in Chapter 3.

One might argue that the next most important things that characterize people's lives and differentiate them, that make them who they feel themselves to be, are their leisure pursuits, such as culture and sport. Unfortunately few useful comparative data exist on these; some use is made of what there is in Chapter 8. However, it is not possible to enjoy many cultural and sporting activities without income. Also, for most of their adult life the great majority of people spend the largest single portions of their waking lives in work. I have therefore placed economic activity – the kinds of production being carried out in various countries and the types of occupation that these provide – in Chapter 4. This leads logically to consideration of the different levels of income and social ranking that different kinds of work provide and therefore to the structure of inequality and class. This is considered in Chapters 5 to 7. Finally, Chapter 8 returns to the issues of whether we can identify particular types of European society and whether all or any of these appear distinctive in a wider international perspective.

Chapter 2

The people of Europe

The states of Europe are of very uneven size, with populations ranging from a little over 330,000 (Iceland) to 81,000,000 (Germany). A summary of their population sizes for the years 1990, 2000 and 2015 can be found in the Statistical Appendix (Table A.1, column A). The majority of them are no bigger than some regions of the six largest (Germany, the United Kingdom, France, Italy, Spain, Poland). Even the largest outside that group, the Netherlands, has a smaller population (16,900,000) than the largest region (or *Land*) of Germany, Nordrhein-Westfalen (17,500,000). For much of the time we take for granted that these different countries constitute separate entities that we can compare with each other. For many students of politics this is obvious, because national governments and parliaments are their primary units of study. For all social scientists there is also the fact that many of the statistics we use are produced at the level of states: indeed the very word 'statistics' derives from 'state', as the first uses of calculations of demographic and economic data were those collected for and by governments. For most of this book we shall also follow this practice. But, as discussed at the start of the previous chapter, for sociologists the question must always arise whether the state really is the most appropriate level for exploring data about social behaviour.

Therefore, at certain points we shall look below the national level for the six largest countries within the EU: Germany, the United Kingdom, France, Italy, Spain and Poland. Disaggregation cannot be performed very frequently, partly because often data do not exist at more local levels, and partly because the discussion would become too complex if we did attempt it. The question then arises as to what territorial units should be used if we seek to go below the state level. The European Commission and its statistical agency Eurostat have a classification of different levels of such units, called Nomenclature of Territorial Units for Statistics (NUTS). The largest of these (NUTS 1) comprise what in English are generally known as 'regions', the largest administrative units into which a country is divided for some governmental purposes. We cannot be sure that these statistical units define societies

TABLE 2.1 *Population and gender proportions, world regions, 2012.*

Region	Population (millions)	Males (%)
South Central Asia	1,790	51.34
East Asia	1,612	51.43
Africa	1,084	50.00
Europe	742	48.11
South East Asia	612	49.67
Latin America and Caribbean	610	49.18
North America	352	49.43
Oceania	38	50.01
World	7,080	50.41

Source: United Nations, 2013

or part-societies, but they are the only appropriate levels at which data are collected.

Who are the Europeans as people, and how do they compare with people from other regions of the world? As Table 2.1 shows, Europeans are considerably outnumbered by the populations of each of South Central Asia, East Asia and Africa, using UN definitions of those entities. There are, however, considerably more of them than North Americans (citizens of Canada and the United States), the countries that probably most resemble them in standards of living. Slightly more Europeans are women than men; this is a characteristic that they share with other relatively wealthy regions of the world. In all human populations slightly more boys are born than girls (a ratio of about 105:100), but as they grow older males and females are exposed to different life risks. In many poor societies sons are more prized than daughters, and families reserve the best food and living conditions for them, leading to a higher mortality rate among girls. Women's lives are sometimes rated as of lower importance than men's in religious values and within the operation of legal systems. When it becomes possible to predict the gender of a baby before birth, these values can even lead to the selective abortion of female foetuses. Also in poor societies and those without good modern health services, childbirth is a dangerous experience for women, leading to further female deaths. On the other hand, male babies seem more likely to die than females, men are more exposed to combat in warfare and are often, though not always and mainly in agricultural and early industrializing societies, engaged in heavier and more dangerous work tasks than women. In many societies, including wealthy ones, men are more likely to engage in life-threatening activities outside the sphere of work: drinking excessive alcohol, fighting and engaging in dangerous sports and road behaviour. Particularly in wealthy societies, women are more likely than men to care for their bodies and to eat healthily. This combination of different types of exposure to risk results in different longevity patterns for the two genders in different kinds of society, with the net result that in all wealthy societies, regardless of their cultures, women are in a slight majority, while in poorer ones males predominate slightly.

Life expectancy

Given that slightly more boys are born than girls, differences in the overall proportions of the two genders are primarily determined by differences in life expectancy. As one of the richest regions of the world, Europe as a whole has higher life expectancy for both men and women than many others. Figure 2.1 presents life expectancy data for 2013 for all European countries and certain other large nations, as well as the country currently with the world's lowest life expectancy, Sierra Leone; Japan has the world's highest.

After Japan, western Europe (north and south) has many of the world's longest-living populations, with all countries in that region having higher life expectancy than the United States. Eastern Europe has lower expectancies, with all except Slovenia falling below the United States. In general, CEE countries rank above ex-Y (apart from Slovenia) and in particular FEE cases and Russia. Several of these last have lower life expectancy than Turkey or China.

Appendix Table A.1 (Column C) shows current male and female life expectancy, with male data expressed as a ratio to those for females (i.e. the closer that the ratio is to 1.00, the smaller the gap between the genders; the lower the ratio, the larger is the superiority of female over male life expectancy). Although all wealthy countries have higher female than male longevity, it is clearly the FEE countries, and in particular Russia and its neighbours, that have the lowest relative male longevity. This declined heavily in that part of the world in the immediate wake of the collapse of the Soviet bloc after 1989; since then it has been recovering, but the gender gap remains high.

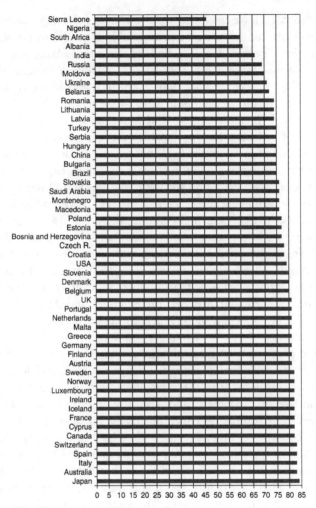

Source: World Health Organization, 2015a

FIGURE 2.1   Life expectancy at age 0, European countries and various comparators, 2013.

Differences in life expectancy across nations and between the genders reflect a variety of factors. We should expect that to a considerable extent differences in national income would be a determinant. Comparing the data for European countries and our four key comparators (Japan, Russia, Turkey and the United States) around 2013 shows a strong positive correlation between life expectancy and per capita national income of $r^2 = 0.4417$. Using the methodology outlined in the previous chapter (Box 1.1), we can identify the following as having exceptionally high longevity (in the sense of considerably higher than predicted by the equation): Bosnia, Croatia, Finland, France, Iceland, Macedonia, Malta, Slovenia, Sweden and the United Kingdom. Very exceptionally high are Cyprus, Greece, Italy, Japan, Portugal and Spain. Apart from Japan these constitute a combination of several northern European countries (including the United Kingdom) and all the middle-income countries of southern Europe (with France). Several countries from ex-Yugoslavia are also on the list, only one of which (Slovenia) counts as medium- rather than low-income. The main explanations that medical scientists have found for the high longevity of most southern countries concern the healthy diet, rich in fruit and vegetables and often fish, that the Mediterranean climate provides. Turkish people do not seem to benefit in the same way. Japanese people have a similar diet, which helps explain their position with the highest life expectancy in the world. People in both regions eat relatively small amounts of red meat.

With exceptionally lower than predicted longevity was the United States and in particular Albania, Luxembourg and Russia. The poor life expectancy, especially among men, in Russia has been partly attributed to alcohol abuse. It is less easy to account for the lower than predicted expectancy in Luxembourg and the United States. It is possible that the relationship between living standards and longevity is not linear; in other words, there may be a point beyond which increments in national income cannot continue to have their usual effect on longevity. This may well account for the position of exceptionally wealthy countries – Norway and Switzerland also underperformed, though less strongly so. Mackenbach and Looman (2013) have shown that large upward shifts in the relationship between longevity and income occurred only before 1960, and were due to rapid declines in mortality from infectious diseases. These shifts accounted for between two-thirds and four-fifths of the increase in life expectancy in Europe as a whole during this period. After 1960, they demonstrate, upward shifts in the relation between national income and life expectancy were much smaller, and contributed only between one-quarter and one-half to the increase in life expectancy in Europe as a whole. During the latter period, the main improvements in longevity that could be attributed to increases in national income were declines in mortality from cardio-vascular disease. Cardiovascular diseases, including stroke and heart attacks, are caused by unhealthy diets, tobacco and excessive alcohol use, and physical inactivity. It seems that these problems are likely to be more prevalent in poor countries.

In general, we have here encountered our first grounds for identifying sub-regions, and they correspond broadly to two of those provisionally identified in Chapter 1: high longevity in the south, low in the far east of Europe, but with diet as a major probable causative factor.

Differences in income also determine important differences in longevity *within* countries. Appendix Table A.2 presents regional mean individual income in purchasing power parities and longevity data for the six largest countries in Europe. The internal differences in per capita income are interesting in themselves. One might have expected Germany to show the biggest variation, given that it comprises what had been from 1949 to 1989 two separate states, but in fact the gap between its poorest and richest regions is the smallest of all six large countries: the income of the poorest region is 61 per cent of that of the richest; in France it is 60 per cent, Poland 53 per cent, the United Kingdom 51 per cent and Italy with the biggest gap at 48 per cent.

Longevity expectations reflect the state of societies in the recent past, so one should not expect a close relationship to regional incomes today. Nevertheless, in each case except for Poland there is a clear positive association between the two variables. The correlation coefficients (r^2) are: Spain 0.6238, Germany 0.5512, the United Kingdom 0.5360, Italy 0.4060, France 0.2825 and Poland 0.0004. There are some puzzles here: why is longevity unrelated to income in Polish regions? Why is life expectancy so much lower than one might expect on the basis of income in Scotland? (Is this a reflection on Scottish people's diet or on the many years of relative poverty before earnings from North Sea oil improved its prosperity?) It is notable that regions around capital cities often have particularly high incomes – the Île-de-France around Paris; the Mazowieckie region in which Warsaw is located; Madrid; London. The exceptions are Germany, where Berlin has only relatively recently been re-established as the capital, and Italy, where Rome is part of the mid-income Lazio region. Although we associate high Italian and Spanish longevity with the Mediterranean diet, the main agricultural regions of those countries, which are poor, have the lowest longevity within the countries. In London and Paris high incomes are not associated with particularly strong longevity. These data hint at variables that are beyond the scope of this chapter, but which we shall encounter in later ones: the importance of inequality of income for life chances; the social characteristics bound up with different geographical regions, across and within countries; and the different kinds of work that people do and its implications for other aspects of their lives – a variable that is partly reflected in the capital city phenomenon.

Birth rates

While Europeans have been living longer than in earlier decades, and longer than people in poorer parts of the world, they have been having fewer children. This helps explain the puzzle presented by Appendix Table A.1 (column B), where some rich countries, notably Germany and Japan, have had declining populations. It is characteristic of wealthy countries to have lower birth rates than poor ones. This is paradoxical, as the wealthier that people are, the more they can afford to look after children. But against this are set various other factors. First is the simple fact that knowledge of and access to contraception are far more readily available in wealthy societies. Yet probably more important are the different attitudes to control over life that people acquire if they emerge from expecting to have just a short span at a subsistence level, constantly prey to misfortune and disaster, to a situation where they have some chance to plan how they will spend a growing number of years. Higher personal incomes and (in many societies) strong welfare states and other government measures that protect citizens against uncertainty and disaster bring life more under control, and it can seem worthwhile to control fertility too. Also, there is a tendency for people in wealthy societies to be less responsive to religious teachings that tell them that it is wrong to try to control fertility artificially. Finally, infant and child mortality must be taken into account. In poor societies larger numbers of people die in infancy (defined as the first year of life) or in childhood. If we assume that parents in poorer and richer societies have similar ideas about how many children they would like to bring through to adulthood, the former need to give birth to more babies in order to realize that same idea.

When immigrant populations come to wealthy societies from poorer ones, they tend to bring with them the birth practices of their country of origin, and have higher birth rates. In this way relatively small numbers of immigrants can contribute disproportionately to population growth. Some European countries, in particular Germany, are virtually dependent on immigrant communities for population increase. Over time, however, immigrants and their descendants begin to conform to the demographic practices of their host society and this difference disappears.

Total fertility rates

There are two ways of looking at birth rates. We might be interested in them as evidence of women's (or families') practices and preferences.

In that case we need data on what is called the total fertility rate (TFR). This attempts to estimate the number of children likely to be born to women in a given society during their childbearing years. On the other hand, we might be interested in birth rates as determinants of population growth, what is called the crude birth rate, expressed as the number of live births per 1,000 population. This figure is determined partly by the TFR, but partly by the age structure of the population. In societies where life expectancy is high, women of childbearing age form a smaller proportion of the population than those where it is low, as there are larger numbers of women past childbearing age (and of course also a larger number of older men). The higher the life expectancy of a population, the lower the crude birth rate that will be produced by a given TFR.

We first consider birth rates from the perspective of TFR, concentrating on women's childbearing behaviour (Figure 2.2). Since calculating TFR involves making assumptions about changes in behaviour, longevity and the balance of emigration and immigration, demographers provide a range of estimates based on different assumptions. We shall here use the medium variant estimates made by the UN for women's TFRs in the years 2010–15. Although, across the world as a whole, the highest birth rates are mainly found in poor countries for the reasons set out above, this generalization does not hold true within Europe. TFRs fell in most parts of the world from the 1960s onwards. In Europe at that stage most countries had scores above 2.0. However, after a lengthy period of general decline, some of the world's richest countries, including several in Europe, saw increases, until they now have higher birth rates than the poorest European countries, suggesting that once the broad historical processes mentioned above, of a move away from subsistence economies, have been completed, the opposite rationale of greater wealth making possible larger families begins to operate. This helps account for the apparent jumble of countries found together in Figure 2.2.

The overall relationship between TFRs and per capita national income in European countries and the key comparators is indeed low ($r^2 = 0.1218$). Also, to the extent that there is a relationship, it is the opposite of that which is expected: there is a weak positive relationship between income and TFR. In some wealthy countries TFR is higher than might be expected: the Nordics, the anglophones (Ireland, the United Kingdom and the United States), France, Belgium and to a lesser extent the Netherlands. In contrast, the three German-speaking countries (Austria, Germany and Switzerland) along with Luxembourg

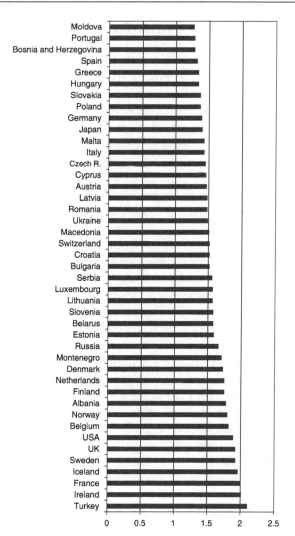

Source: : UN Population Division, 2015

FIGURE 2.2   *Expected total fertility rates, medium variant estimate, European countries and key comparators, 2010–15.*

have considerably lower TFR than might have been predicted. Only two very poor countries (Albania and Turkey) conform to the global expectation of a positive association between low national income and high TFR. All other countries with lower per capita gross domestic product (GDP) than France and the United Kingdom have the TFR that would be expected or a lower level.

Explanation of these patterns is not straightforward. A particularly interesting contrast is between France and Germany. These are two major, wealthy countries, with similar rates of female employment, but with a distinctly higher TFR in the former, even though its economy has been functioning less well than its neighbour's for several years. Research suggests that a key factor is the availability of far more publicly provided childcare in France than in Germany (Ahles, Klammer and Wiedemeyer, 2012; Klammer, 2012). Several other countries with relatively high birth rates, the Scandinavians, also have extensive childcare. The United Kingdom and in particular the United States are exceptions to these trends, having low public childcare provision but a high level of mothers' labour force participation, but these countries have (like the Netherlands and Scandinavia) major part-time work possibilities for mothers, and also extensive private childminding arrangements. These may not always provide satisfactory care, but they do permit women to combine the two roles. There are also important variations among countries in the extent to which fathers share childcare. There may be an important spiral in operation here. Comparative research on the Netherlands, Spain and the United Kingdom suggests that it starts to become accepted that mothers are engaged in paid employment, employers become more likely to make 'family friendly' work arrangements, and fathers start to accept a share in domestic responsibilities (Ibanez Garzarán, 2007). This will be partly affected also by the extent to which an economy generates jobs likely to attract women, which in general means jobs in certain kinds of services. This is a subject to which we shall return in Chapter 4, demonstrating the interwoven nature of aspects of society as apparently unrelated as childbirth and economic activity.

These complex changes have produced a major historical reversal. It used to be the case within Europe that TFRs were high in southwest Europe and Ireland – which were poorer and dominated by the Catholic or (in Greece) Orthodox churches, with their disapproval of artificial restraint of fertility – and low in the wealthier, more secular or Protestant countries of NWE. (Austria is strongly Catholic, as, primarily, was the majority in pre-1990 West Germany.) This has now completely changed, partly because of a changing dynamic of that same church power. Where churches that were hostile to artificial fertility control and also to married women departing from full-time engagement in the sacred role of motherhood dominated both everyday and political life, governments were less likely to introduce childcare policies. But eventually women in such countries became determined to engage in paid work, if necessary at the expense of not having, or having only a small number of, children. This was partly because of the growing availability of services jobs that women found more attractive than manufacturing; in some countries partly because families could afford to buy their own homes if both partners had paid employment; and partly because a general decline in religious commitment reduced the claims that churches held over women's life choices, even while their power remained embedded in the history of social policy. Therefore arose a paradox. The more that governments pursued social policies, and where established institutions preached values that extolled motherhood as a full-time role for women, the more the TFR declined; and the more they projected an idea of motherhood as one among a number of roles that women might occupy, the higher the TFR became – high, that is, within the context of the generally low levels of all wealthy societies.

There had also been extensive childcare provision and a high level of female employment in the state socialist economies of central and eastern Europe, but TFRs had been low. This was probably because of the problems of managing daily life in those countries; however, after 1989 childcare systems collapsed, as did female employment levels, and TFRs declined even further, though in recent years they have begun to recover.

A particularly important case is Poland, where the Catholic Church has been exceptionally strong, with high attendance levels at services even (in fact, especially) during the state socialist regime. The major trade union movement that led opposition to the regime, Solidarność, was in large part a Catholic movement. During the Soviet period female labour force participation had been high, with state-provided workplace nurseries; but despite the efforts of both the socialist state and the Catholic Church in encouraging reproduction, the TFR was low. After the fall of communism, the Church acquired a powerful political role and strongly influenced childcare policy (Glass and Fodor, 2007). Female participation in the labour force declined, but the TFR fell further; church attendance also declined. Other studies suggest that it was an imitation of US social policy, with its generally low levels of public support, rather than the role of the Catholic Church, that produced a post-1990 collapse of TFRs in Poland and right across CEE (Saxonberg and Szelewa, 2007), the declines in childcare policies and in female labour force participation being at least equally strong in the secular Czech Republic.

We have again identified sub-regions with exceptional characteristics: the Nordics, the anglophones and *some* NWE countries with exceptionally high rates and the other, German-speaking NWE countries, and those in CEE and FEE, with exceptionally low ones. This reveals an intriguing difference within the North-Western group.

Crude birth rates

The impact of varying fertility rates on overall population structure is affected by both the proportion of the population comprised of women of childbearing age and the age structure of the overall population (and thus by its longevity). We therefore now turn to crude birth rates. Compared with all other regions of the world, Europe has very low overall birth rates. The UN Population Division (2015) estimated the following rates for the 2010 to 2015 period for the main world regions (expressed as live births per 1,000 population): Africa, 19; Latin America and Caribbean, 18; Asia, 17; Oceania, 17; North America, 13; Europe, 11.

Globally there is clearly a negative relationship between national income and the birth rate, but, as for TFRs, the situation within Europe is more complex. There is no overall relationship between the variables at all, with $r^2 = 0.0118$ – if anything there is a minuscule positive relationship between national income and birth rate. As with TFRs, two different logics are at work within Europe, as two different groups of countries have crude birth rates above the continental mean of 10.8: several wealthy, northern European cases and several poor ones in the east and south east. The United States shares northern European characteristics, and Russia those of the east. Turkey has the highest rates of all, but SWE countries fall below the mean, with all except Cyprus having exceptionally low rates. A combination of the paradoxical consequences today of traditional approaches to mothers' domestic roles (low TFR) already discussed and a healthy diet (high life expectancy and therefore a higher number of women past childbearing age) produces these low crude birth rates in SWE. Also below mean are all CEE cases except the Czech Republic, some FEE countries and most of ex-Yugoslavia. However, the lowest rate of all in Europe is found in Germany. Japan comes in even lower.

The combination of low birth rates and high longevity produces an overall ageing of Europe's population, leading to the frequent tag of Europe as an 'ageing society'. There is considerable debate over the implications of this. For those concerned with the financing of pension schemes and health services it is seen as a problem, as a smaller working population is supporting a large number of pensioners, while health services are used particularly heavily by older people. On the other hand, in ageing societies there is also a decline in demand for spending on schools and on health services for children. Also, since crime, especially violent crime, is often the province of younger people, especially males, ageing societies tend to be less violent than those with lower life expectancy and higher birth rates.

Death rates

Temporarily setting aside the issue of migration, overall population growth is affected by death rates as well as birth rates. The death rate is the proportion of a given population that dies in a given year. Increasing longevity reduces death rates, but the ageing of populations that results from a combination of increased longevity and reduced birth rates leads to an increase in them. Complex patterns result. According to World Bank (2015b) data, national differences are here moderately related to national income, with $r^2 = 0.3123$. Unsurprisingly, similar countries occupy distinctive positions in terms of longevity – it and death rates being related but by no means identical variables. Two high birth rate Islamic countries, Albania and Turkey, have the lowest death rates, as do some other cases of high birth rates, namely Cyprus, Iceland and Ireland. Higher death rates than expected, even given their low national incomes, occur in FEE, especially Russia and its neighbours Belarus, Ukraine and Moldova but also Lithuania, Latvia and ex-Y Serbia, as well as Hungary in CEE.

More important for population growth than death rates as such is the combined impact of birth and death rates. Eurostat has produced data for EU member states alone in 2011, showing the effect of the two factors on overall population change. The countries are shown in Figure 2.3 ranked in ascending order of their natural increase or decrease in population, a figure that is defined as the combined effect of the two variables. Some countries in SWE or NWE owe a relatively high overall natural increase to a low death rate rather than to a high birth rate.

Immigration and overall changes in population size

Two further factors need to be borne in mind when considering these large historical trends in demography: the wave-like nature of population change and migration. In many parts of Europe the 1930s and the subsequent years of World War II saw a sharp decline

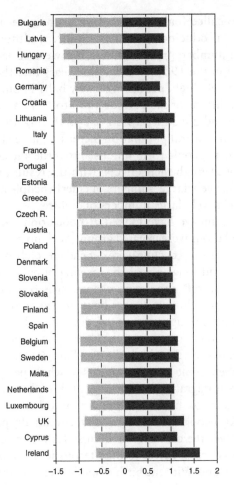

Source: Eurostat, 2015a

FIGURE 2.3   *Crude birth (dark shading) and death (light shading) rates expressed as percentage change in population size, EU member states, 2011.*

in birth rates. There was also major loss of life through war itself in the main combatant countries, including the continuing legacy of differential male death from World War I. This produced a relatively small, young population, which, when it became adult, and to the extent that the TFR remained constant, produced a further 'small' generation, which in turn did the same. However, immediately after the war, peace and rapidly rising mass prosperity produced an increase in birth rates throughout much of the western world, the so-called 'baby boom'. Two or three decades later these 'babies' were producing their own children; although their TFR declined, the numbers in that generation were so large in relation to those born in the 1930s and the war years that their crude birth rate was relatively high, producing a new baby boom. The contrasting living conditions of the periods 1930 to 1945 and from 1945 to 1960 and beyond have therefore been producing alternating waves of low and high natural population increase. These effects will peter out over time, as people form unions across the age cohorts, but we are still living through their effects, with the result that 20 years of producing relatively large numbers of elderly people are followed by 20 years of relatively large numbers of children.

Up to this point we have looked at population change as though national populations were isolated groups, with no one moving among them, and increase and decline were dependent solely on the childbearing behaviour and longevity of the existing population; this is what is known as 'natural' population change. It is of course unrealistic. Throughout history human beings have moved across the surface of the planet, either fleeing war, natural disaster and oppression or just seeking a better life. For most of that history the scale of these movements was limited by the physically gruelling nature of long-distance travel. Even then, some vast movements of whole peoples took place, such as the great migrations that brought the 'barbarian invasion' that led to the collapse of the Roman Empire, or a similar westward wave bringing Turkic people into old Byzantium, eventually producing modern Turkey. Over the centuries modern states began to stabilize their borders and to control access to their territories from outside, mainly for security reasons. With the birth of modern citizenship rights, political democracy and welfare states new questions arose of entitlements to reside in states other than those in which people had been born, and the kinds of rights they might expect to enjoy if they did move. While these factors all tend to restrict population movements, there are countervailing factors that tend to increase them. Vastly improved transport facilities are an obvious factor, but two others are at least as important. First, as markets for products, capital and labour alike have become global, so employers have sought workers with particular skills and aptitudes that will enhance their firms' effectiveness, irrespective of the national origins of the individuals concerned. For states within the EU and its wider European Economic Area, this market preference is embedded in rules guaranteeing more or less free movement within the

EU for their citizens. Second, inequalities between rich and poor countries have been intensifying, while people in poorer countries are able to gain more knowledge of the quality of life in wealthier places. This strengthens their incentive to move from an environment of poverty to one of possible wealth, even illegally.

Migration

The overall process of geographical movement of persons from one place of residence to another, distant, one is called 'migration'. This general term can include major movements within countries, as was the case when people moved from the countryside to towns during industrialization and, today, where there is a move from many towns and cities to the small number of large cities that are becoming the centres of such new leading sectors as finance and information technology. When such movements happen to cross national boundaries we talk of emigration from the places being left and immigration into the countries to which people move. Thus, when Irish people moved to England and Scotland during those countries' industrialization in the 19th century they were just internal migrants moving from one part of the United Kingdom to another. Once Ireland became a state in 1922, such people became immigrants. Germans moving from east to west within their country were internal migrants until the division of Germany into the Federal Republic of Germany and the German Democratic Republic in 1949, after which they became immigrants; after 1961, when following the building of the Berlin Wall by the government of the German Democratic Republic attempts to move west resulted in arrest or death, those successfully making the same move became refugees. For a few months in 1989 and 1990 when the wall was destroyed, movement west became possible again, but the East German state still existed, so such movements again constituted immigration. Following German unification they have become simple internal migration once more.

One might expect migration within a country to be freely available to citizens, while immigration would be controlled by national governments, but there are exceptions to this. Some states control population movements into major cities; this was often the case in state socialist countries. On the other hand, as noted, there is migration free from control among member states of the EU. Strictly speaking therefore emigration and immigration within the EU are just migration. Large waves of such migration were stimulated by the accession of former state socialist countries to the EU and the subsequent extension of the right of free movement to their citizens. Economic prospects seemed so much better in the west that many of them have taken the opportunity to migrate and find work in more prosperous countries. This will be considered further in the following chapter. The immigration of people from outside the EU into European countries is subject to controls, but since the outbreak of major crises and wars in the early years of this century in Europe's neighbouring region south of the Mediterranean there have been important increases in attempts to escape to Europe. Since 2014 war in Syria and Iraq has generated a vast growth in refugees and asylum seekers making dangerous attempts to cross the sea and enter Europe. They are usually seeking a better life in countries such as Germany, Austria and Sweden, though their points of arrival in Europe are the coasts of Greece, Italy and Turkey, and their subsequent moves to the north west involve them crossing Serbia, Slovenia, Hungary and other CEE countries. There has therefore been a large influx of desperate, homeless, penniless people with which all countries affected are finding it hard to cope.

At any one time countries experience both a loss of their existing population through emigration and a gain through immigration. The two figures together provide another for net migration. Figure 2.4 sets this net migration alongside changes in natural population across the three years 2012–14 for EU member states and a number of other European countries. These numbers come too early to include the peak of the wave of refugees and asylum seekers from Syria and elsewhere, but do capture its early stages. It should also be noted that these statistics are not always reliable. Almost by definition, they exclude most illegal immigration, and states do not have reliable techniques for measuring the numbers of their citizens who have emigrated, rather than simply left the country for a period. Countries are ranked in ascending order of their overall change in population. Italy and Germany experienced population growth during the period solely because of positive net migration – their 'natural growth' was negative. A large number of countries in western Europe experienced growth on both dimensions: Luxembourg, Norway, Switzerland, Iceland, Malta, Sweden, the United Kingdom, Belgium, Denmark, France, Finland, the Netherlands, together with Slovenia and the Czech and Slovak Republics in CEE. The same applied to Turkey. Austria had zero natural growth but a rise in immigration, while Ireland had enough natural growth to offset net emigration. All other countries saw net population loss. In Hungary

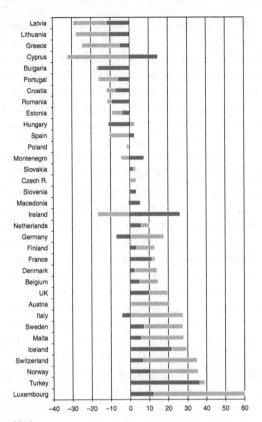

Source: Eurostat, 2015a

FIGURE 2.4   *'Natural' population change (dark shading) and net migration (light shading), per 1,000 initial population, EU member states and associates, 2012–14.*

this was despite a slight rise in immigration, but in all other cases there was decline on both dimensions. This affected all remaining eastern European countries, and also Cyprus, Greece, Spain and Portugal.

'Natural' population growth or decline tends to be fairly stable from one year to the next, as it results from deeply rooted beliefs and practices about how people organize their lives. Migration is liable to more abrupt changes, as it is usually a response to differences in economic conditions, political disturbances and natural disasters. Appendix Table A.1 (column D) shows these fluctuations over the three years already discussed. Cyprus, Greece, Ireland, Portugal and Spain, countries affected strongly by the financial crisis of 2008 and its delayed aftermath in the Eurozone, saw major net emigration, but for another affected country, Italy, this was offset by large numbers of refugees from North Africa. Other heavy losses were incurred by the Baltic states. The main recipient countries of immigrants were the prosperous economies of Luxembourg, Switzerland, Austria, Germany and Scandinavia, but also Italy and Malta, receiving large numbers of asylum seekers because of their location near to North Africa.

Emigration usually sends people from poorer countries to richer ones, which sometimes means sending people from societies with higher birth rates to those with lower – though this is not likely to be the case with intra-European migration, as Europe's poorer countries tend to be among those with the lowest birth rates. Immigrants also tend to be young adults, and therefore to comprise a higher proportion of people of childbearing age than the native population. Over time, as immigrants age and children are born, while some return home, the age structure of ethnic minority populations (as settled immigrants eventually become) comes to resemble that of natives. Over a still longer period of time, if many immigrants marry outside of their minority, the group may disappear as a separate entity within the host population. However, in the early stages of immigration to wealthy European countries, the demographic structure of immigrant populations offsets the tendencies towards ageing in the host populations. Given the self-selected nature of much migration, poor countries losing emigrants tend to lose young, energetic people with low levels of dependency on health and care services; this becomes a concomitant gain for the richer receiving countries. Migration therefore tends to redistribute populations in favour of wealthy countries.

We shall return to some of the issues raised by immigration in the next chapter; we are here interested solely in its demographic implications.

Marriage and family

In discussing the birth of children, whether of native populations or immigrants, we have taken for granted the existence of families, as young human beings cannot survive without a group of adults close to them who look after their welfare. While this can be done in specialized institutions, and for some children who either lose or are abandoned by their parents this is the case, the great majority of children are cared for by parents, or at least by one of them, usually the mother, or some other family relation. Families are therefore important units of social structure, though by no means all of them consist of parents and children. Many people have no children. Some live alone without a partner, perhaps with groups of friends with whom they have no family or sexual relations; in these cases we speak of 'households' rather than families. 'Household' is a more general term to describe groups of people habitually sharing a home, and can be considered to include 'family' as an important sub-type. Other people again have older relatives living with them as well as or instead of children, while in other cases older people are more likely to live alone, perhaps with some care delivered to them by family members, friends or specialized services. In very recent years parliaments in many countries in Europe and elsewhere have made it possible for homosexual couples to solemnize their relationships in marriage. This has further extended the legal meaning of the family in a highly important way, with significant implications for many people who have hitherto had to keep their relationships secret – a circumstance that continues in some European countries. These changes are, however, too recent for us to be able to take account of them in the following detailed discussion.

Taken together, all these factors provide a wide range of possibilities of household (including family) size and structure. It is therefore interesting to note that among most European countries there is not much difference in average household size, the range being from Croatia at 2.8 to Germany and Sweden at 2.0, though in Macedonia it is 3.6. In Turkey it is 3.7 (Eurostat, 2015a). One might expect average household size to vary directly with birth rate, but almost the opposite is the case. To some extent this is a reflection of past birth rates, but other factors are more important. In societies where there is a high level of elderly care, older people are more likely to live alone; in societies where there is higher employment or more generous unemployment pay, daughters and particularly sons are more likely to leave home at younger ages. (In most countries sons leave home on average at a later age than daughters, especially in countries with low levels of employment, as daughters will be more likely to leave home upon marrying.) In general, those states that provide the childcare services that enable women to combine childrearing with paid employment (and therefore maintain relatively high birth rates) are also those that provide high levels of elderly care (enabling older people to live in their own homes), and have typically high levels of employment as well as of unemployment pay. This is the complex set of factors that lead relatively high birth rates to be paradoxically associated with relatively small household size. This shows the complex effects of different kinds and levels of generosity of welfare states.

Nevertheless, there is overall a small negative relationship between household size and national income ($r^2 = 0.1825$); the statistic would be higher but for the exiguous and very small case of Luxembourg, and the extreme cases of Macedonia and Turkey. Ireland is, with Luxembourg, the only wealthy country with higher household size than should be expected. The Nordics cluster with Germany as having particularly low household size. Countries in south-east Europe have an even higher household size than their low incomes would suggest.

Marriage, cohabitation, divorce and separation

Over the long trajectory of European history it was assumed that if a man and a woman formed a sexual union and produced children they would marry, meaning to enter a legally binding undertaking to remain with each other in a mutually supportive relationship, usually sanctioned by a religious ritual and celebration. This norm was by no means universally followed. There were many instances of husbands abandoning wives, and of couples not bothering to legalize their union. This latter was particularly the case among poor people; since the main function of marriage laws was to regulate the division and inheritance of property, persons who owned no property had less incentive to bother with marriage. However, the various Christian churches to which the vast majority of European people at least nominally belonged took a very strong view of the importance of restricting sexual activities and relationships to married couples alone. The same view was taken by the Jewish and Islamic religions to which small minorities of Europeans also belonged. The Christian churches also regarded the marriage tie as indissoluble except in very strictly defined circumstances.

From this circumstance derived some primarily religious definitions of the family and the mutual responsibilities of its members, including for example the discouragement by the Catholic Church of mothers taking paid work, which persisted for a very long time, as discussed above. This situation lasted into modern times despite the various schisms and conflicts among different Christian churches, the many vicissitudes of European history and even the official atheism of the state socialist countries. The great majority of births took place among married couples, and very few marriages ended in divorce. (In countries where the Catholic Church retained a strong political influence, legal divorce was almost impossible.) In more recent decades there has been general and rapid change. The number of births taking place outside marriage has increased everywhere, though with very considerable differences among countries.

In 1990 only two EU member states (both Nordic: Sweden and Denmark) had over 40 per cent of births outside marriage, and 11 had rates below 10 per cent (Eurostat, 2015b). Among these 11, largely Catholic (Malta, Poland, Italy, Lithuania, Croatia, Slovakia, the Czech Republic and Spain) and Greek Orthodox (Republic of Cyprus and Greece) countries predominated, with only mixed-faith Catholic and Reformed Protestant Switzerland being an exception. It is interesting that this religious variable seems at first sight to be more important than whether a country was in eastern or western Europe: for example, Catholic Lithuania differed considerably from the other two, mainly Lutheran, Baltic states (Estonia and Latvia). By 2000, six countries had rates of childbirth outside marriage above 40 per cent, Denmark and Sweden being joined by fellow Baltic countries Estonia, Norway and Latvia, and also by France. Only four now had rates below 10 per cent, two Catholic (Italy and Croatia) and two Greek Orthodox (Cyprus and Greece). By 2012/13, 16 countries from a range of cultural, political and religious backgrounds saw over 40 per cent of babies born outside marriage, and only Greece remained below 10 per cent. Extending the account for the most recent years to European countries outside the EU does not change this picture, though most countries in FEE as well as Russia and ex-Yugoslavia (apart from Slovenia, which has one of Europe's highest rates) have rates below 25 per cent. Turkey has only 2.7 per cent. National sources indicate a figure of 40 per cent for the United States, but only 2.0 per cent for Japan.

A tantalizing mix of variables is clearly at work here, with considerable convergence among countries with different cultural histories, as the fastest rates of growth in this kind of childbirth have been in those where it was low before. This process runs alongside a general decline in the role of churches in Europe, as we shall see in the next chapter.

The increase in childbirth outside marriage becomes part of a general debate about whether marriage is 'declining' in contemporary Europe, another indicator of which would be the divorce rate. This tells us the number of couples that divorce in a country during a specific year, usually expressed as a rate per 1,000 marriages. The average rate for EU member states stood at 2.06 in 1995, the closest date to 1990 for which we have data, and by 2012/13 was virtually unchanged at 2.01, though that average conceals considerable increases in some countries and declines in others (Eurostat, 2015c). Overall there was some convergence across countries, the standard deviation in 1995 being 1.02, but by 2012/13 only 0.71. At the earlier period divorce tended to be higher in largely Protestant countries, though rates were also high in predominantly Catholic Belgium, the Czech Republic and Lithuania. The lowest rates were found in Catholic and both Greek and Russian Orthodox countries. By 2011, Catholic Portugal and Greek Orthodox Cyprus had also joined the countries with high rates, but the low rates tended still to be concentrated among Catholic and Orthodox. Rates in FEE and ex-Yugoslavia tend to be low. Both Japan and the United States have a divorce rate very close to the European mean.

The rise in divorce rates that took place during the late 20th century has stabilized in many countries, but another long-term trend affecting family life has been an increase in the proportions of people cohabiting, that is living together in sexual unions that are not formalized through legal marriage. This trend, initially limited to northwestern Europe, was first noted by Kathleen Kiernan at the start of the present century (Kiernan, 2001). Since that time it has grown more generally. In a study of cohabitation in ten countries from different parts of Europe, Hiekel, Liefbroer and Poortman (2014) identified several different forms of the phenomenon. For some couples it was a stage in the marriage process, while for others it was a clear alternative to marriage. The latter was more common in western and northern Europe. Those intending to marry despite having a generally unfavourable attitude towards it were found mainly in central and eastern European countries.

The most recent (2012) statistics covering cohabitation and other relationship statuses have been summarized by the OECD, as shown in Figure 2.5. It is unlikely that the data are sufficiently recent to be able to take account of homosexual marriages. Unfortunately they also cover only certain OECD member states and therefore exclude non-OECD European countries, as well as some OECD members that did not furnish data to the organization; but the chart also includes some important extra-European comparators. The statistics are expressed as proportions of persons aged 15 and over. They show marriage rates of over 40 per cent for all European countries covered except Estonia, and over 50 per cent for all except the Nordic countries, France, Hungary and Slovenia. Since most Europeans marry considerably later than 15, it is clear that marriage remains the destiny for a majority of them. European marriage rates are highest in Catholic and Greek Orthodox lands. Rates are considerably higher among over-15s in China, India and Japan than those in Europe, but lower in South

Source: OECD, 2013a

Note: Data presented in following order: Proportions married; cohabiting; single; widowed; divorced; separated.

FIGURE 2.5   *Relationship status, all persons aged 15 and over, OECD member states and certain comparators, 2012.*

Africa, while Russia, Canada and the United States fit within the overall European range.

Cohabitation is, unsurprisingly, highest where marriage rates are lowest. Slovakia is the only European country to have a lower level of cohabitation than we might expect on this basis, the other exceptions being outside Europe: South Africa, Russia and the United States. If we combine the figures for proportion married with that in cohabitation, there is far less diversity among countries, particularly European

ones. The standard deviation for proportion married across all countries considered in Figure 2.5 is 9.73; that for married and cohabiting
is only 7.64. Among European countries alone the respective figures
are 6.39 and 3.23, suggesting an emerging distinctive European pattern of relationships in which people are choosing to have a period of
cohabitation, either before or instead of marrying, this pattern being
found mainly but not solely in northern (and therefore wealthier)
European countries.

The third part of the bars in Figure 2.5 gives us proportions that
at the time of the survey had, according to the terminology of the
OECD, 'never been married'; but in fact it also excludes those in
cohabitation (whether homosexual or heterosexual), so it is really a
balancing item after all other categories have been deducted, leaving
us to consider the final bars, the figures for widowed, divorced and
separated. Those for widow(er)s are rather similar across countries,
though the rather high ones for Russia and certain CEE countries
(Estonia, Hungary, Slovakia) should be noted. Statistics for those
'divorced' mean divorced and not remarried, as divorced persons who
have remarried are included among the married. These statistics do
not therefore enable us to gauge the overall effect of divorce on marriage in a particular country, two factors being at work: the tendency
to divorce and the tendency for divorced people to remarry at some
point. Also, the divorced figure needs to be combined with that for
couples who are separated, as the decision whether to divorce or separate often depends on the particular provisions of a country's divorce
law. If we combine the two statistics, Russia emerges as the country
with the highest combined divorce and separation rate, followed by
the Czech Republic, the United States and Finland. The lowest levels
are found in the three Asian countries included here. The categories
that we have been using to distinguish among countries (religion,
region and income) do not enable us to make much sense of the diversity among European countries, reflecting the heterogeneous nature of
the statistics involved.

In a detailed statistical study of (heterosexual) marriage, cohabitation
and divorce across Europe at the end years of the last century, Kalmijn
(2007) reached the main conclusions summarized in Table 2.2: where
female employment was high and the country in Norden, marriage
rates were low and cohabitation and divorce rates high; where religion
was strong (in terms of church attendance), marriage rates were high
and divorce rates low; in Catholic and Orthodox countries cohabitation was also low, but this was not a dominant feature in Protestant

TABLE 2.2 *Factors associated with various predominant patterns of relationships.*

Factor	Marriage rate	Cohabitation rate	Divorce rate
High female employment	Low	High	High
Religion: Protestant	High	Mixed	Low
Religion: Catholic or Orthodox	High	Low	Low
Central Eastern Europe	High	Low	High
Southern Europe	High, but not when young	Low	Low
Northern Europe	Low	High	High

Source: Kalmijn, 2007

lands; in CEE marriage and divorce rates were high, cohabitation rates low; in SWE marriage rates were high, but young people, especially women, were marrying at later ages than in many other countries, while divorce and cohabitation rates were both low. Some of these findings would seem less valid for the more recent years we have been considering, perhaps because of a decline in religious observance during the intervening years.

Kalmijn's findings make use of some variables that we have mentioned here – the region of Europe and religion – but he has introduced a third that we have mentioned but not so far examined in this connection: female employment. This signals something more profound concerning changing gender relations. It raises the more general issue of work and its place in human society, which will also lead us to consider a topic that has been relevant here: differences in levels of income among and within societies. We shall address these issues in detail in Chapter 4. Religion also requires more consideration; we have noted it as a variable, but have not considered why it is important. We shall return to this in Chapter 3.

Age at marriage

A further aspect of changing heterosexual marriage patterns is the mean age at which people first marry. Men's mean ages at marriage

are usually two to three years older than women's, and this relationship does not change much over time. We can therefore concentrate
on women's ages alone. There has been a steady rise in women's age
at first marriage over the years shown here, which in many cases is a
reversion to a pattern found in the first decades of the 20th century, disrupted as they were by war and economic chaos. Then, as life became
more settled after the end of World War II, the age of marriage declined
very considerably, a trend that started to be reversed again in most
countries in the early 1970s. The European mean rose from 24.42 in
1990 to 29.03 by 2011/13, via 26.43 in 2000 (Eurostat, 2015c). The
US figure has risen, but more gently, from 23.9 to 26.6; similarly in
Japan from 25.9 to 29.3; and probably in Russia, where in 1990 the
age stood at 22.6, rising only to 24.9 by 2011.

Women's age of first marriage at the present time correlates moderately closely with national income, with $r^2 = 0.4336$. Marrying
older than predicted are the Nordic countries (except Norway),
southern Europe, Ireland, France, the Czech Republic and Hungary.
Marrying considerably younger are Russia and its associated countries Belarus and Moldova, Poland, the two Islamic countries (Albania
and Turkey), Luxembourg and the United States. Setting the small
case of Luxembourg, and also Poland, aside, the countries with lower
than expected marriage ages are all outside the main body of Europe.
Japan on the other hand fits well into the European pattern. This suggests a distinctive European – and Japanese – late marriage pattern.
Among European countries there is a wider clear split between east and
west, which has not changed much over time. All former state socialist countries except Slovenia have younger ages of marriage than all
western ones. It is interesting to note that the United States resembles
the eastern European cases, while Japan is on the margin between the
two European groups.

The odd pattern we have found among the western Europeans
makes some sense if we plot women's age at first marriage against the
proportion of people living in cohabitative heterosexual relationships.
Ceteris paribus, we might expect that the more people are in such relationships, the more likely is formal marriage to be postponed. This is
broadly the case, though the correlation is very weak ($r^2 = 0.1196$).
We can concentrate on the outliers. High above the line is Sweden,
which is just an extreme case of conformity to the hypothesis; at the
other extreme comes Poland. More interesting are those that conform
on one dimension but not on the other. Below the line in this way is

Estonia, which has a low age of marriage given the high cohabitation rate. Unfortunately we lack data on Latvia and Lithuania for proportions in cohabitation, and cannot tell whether the formerly Soviet Baltic states have a distinctive high cohabitation rate, while sharing the overall young age of first marriage of most other eastern countries. Similar to Estonia are Hungary and Slovenia. These are all former state socialist countries, though others in that category (Slovakia and Poland) have very low rates of cohabitation. At the opposite extreme, with high age of marriage but low cohabitation rates, are Ireland, Italy and Spain, all three countries where there is possibly a conflict between women wanting to participate in the labour force but where there are few opportunities for part-time work and little publicly provided childcare.

Conclusion

In this chapter we have explored the basic demography of Europe. We have seen how Europe compares as a whole with other world regions, noting certain points of similarity binding nearly all Europe together. Among European countries both longevity and TFRs seem related to national income, which is less clearly true of the United States. There might also be an emerging pattern among European countries, but not our extra-European comparators, for couples to have a period of cohabitation before marriage, with a partly associated trend towards a higher age of first marriage for women – a pattern shared with Japan but not Russia or the United States. We have, however, also encountered considerable diversity within Europe. The Nordic countries often cut a distinctive path in matters of family building, elements of which they sometimes share with the anglophone countries, sometimes with France, sometimes with Germany, sometimes with Italy and Spain. It is difficult to draw overall conclusions from this about possible groupings of countries, as the regional scheme provisionally set up in the previous chapter only rarely makes much sense outside the Nordics.

More usefully, we have seen hints of how demographic behaviour and the ongoing human processes of birth, sexual partnership and death are likely to be connected to and influenced by other major elements of social structure, including work, social policy and religion. Certain geopolitical and religious variables discussed in Chapter 1 seem to lie behind several of the differences among European countries, and suggest groupings of nations rather than just a collection of individual cases, though none of these is strongly defined. We must now explore some of these variables in more detail: religion, the cultural implications of migration, and income and wealth. The last, which also includes looking at work and the economy, will occupy us for several chapters. Before embarking on that core theme of this book, we should explore further the 'cultural' issues of religion and migration.

Chapter 3

Identities: religion and ethnicity

Religion and migration were discussed in the previous chapter because they are seemingly helpful in accounting for differences in basic demographic facts. But that is not the only part that they play in the structure of society. Religion and, for immigrants, country of origin are powerful sources of identity, enabling people to answer the question 'Who am I?' in ways that might place them together with some people around them but also perhaps distinguish them from others. It is not possible to study all potential identities of this kind here, even if they might be very important. For example, most people have some idea of the cultural styles with which they identify, and this will affect their taste in clothes, music and other aspects of consumption and culture. For many, participation in a sport or cultural activity, or support for a particular sports team, provides an important sense of who they are. For a smaller number, association with a political party or participation in a voluntary activity provides key answers to this basic question. Personal though they are, such identities can be significant, in giving us strong loyalties, helping us to place ourselves within the general mass of humanity and determining the kinds of goods we buy and events we attend. In societies where religion is declining in importance – which, as we shall see, is the case in most of Europe – identities of these kinds play an increasingly important part.

Meanwhile, status as immigrants or as members of ethnic minorities is unlikely to be available to the majority of people – except for occasional examples of societies made up largely of immigrants, as was the case in the 19th century with the United States, Canada and Australia. Majorities do have available a national identity. Ever since the leaders of states have needed large numbers of men to fight in wars for them, they have encouraged residents of the areas over which they rule to identify passionately with those territories. In modern times two factors have reinforced these passions very considerably. First, as mentioned in the previous chapter, in large areas of the world that were governed by people from different and remote societies, the demand for self-rule by members of a nation was a major rallying cry to throw off foreign domination. Second, national identities can also become a focus for hostility expressed towards ethnic minorities and immigrants.

Unfortunately it is difficult to deal systematically with this broad range of potential strong identities in a study of the present kind. We need comparable studies of at least some countries from each of the main parts of Europe that we have identified in order to draw conclusions about patterns across the continent. We therefore have to remain with those identities where comparative sociological research has provided evidence for us. These are primarily religion, ethnicity and social class. The last identity will be the focus of much of the rest of this book. Another form of identity, gender, is more fundamental than any of these and therefore needs to run through the whole book. In this chapter we concentrate on religion and ethnicity. Some readers may be surprised that religion is being given such prominence given that religious belief and participation are in steep decline almost everywhere in Europe. But its past importance continues to mould many aspects of our lives. Ethnicity is, as we shall see, a problematic concept, but it and the related theme of national identity continue to have considerable mobilizing power.

As recently as the early 1990s the federal state of Yugoslavia fell apart in a series of overlapping civil wars that were partly religious in inspiration, either despite or because the country had been ruled by an atheistic state socialist regime since the end of World War II. Yugoslavia had been formed after World War I from various nations that had been either ruled over by Austria-Hungary and were Catholic (Croatia and Slovenia), were independent and Orthodox after a period of Ottoman rule (Serbia), or ruled by Ottoman Turkey and with a mix of Orthodoxy and Islam (Macedonia, Montenegro and Bosnia-Herzegovina). Because these different groups had been united within one transnational state there had been considerable geographical population movement and even intermarriage across religions. Between 1991 and 2001, as leaders of the different nations sought independence from the collapsing federation, religious and ethnic minorities within them became highly vulnerable. In several cases they were subjected to what became known as 'ethnic cleansing', a combination of mass murder, rape of women and expulsion from their homes. Particularly endangered was the Islamic population of Bosnia-Herzegovina. The wars subsided, with military intervention by the United States and some EU member states, and the different regions of the former federation became separate states, and are treated as such throughout this book. The episode was a reminder of the violent power of religious and national sentiment, half a century after the defeat of Nazism.

In 2014 violence bordering on civil war flared in the Ukraine, following major disagreements within the political class over whether the country should move closer to the EU or retain its close links with Russia. From the mid 19th century onwards the country had been absorbed into the Russian Empire and later the Soviet Union. In general, people in the western part of the country wanted to move closer to the EU, those in the east to Russia. An elected pro-Russian government was deposed in a popular uprising in the capital, Kiev, in western Ukraine. This produced a violent reaction in the east, which now sought either independence or at least extensive autonomy within Ukraine. Russia provided military support to the eastern rebellion and annexed the Crimea – a part of Russia that had been 'given' to the Ukraine in the 1950s by the Soviet leadership. The passions around identity engaged in this struggle are less extreme than those in the collapse of Yugoslavia; Russia and Ukraine have their own variants of Orthodox Christianity, so religion is less strongly engaged. But the conflict is around identity – European or Russian.

Both the Yugoslav and the Ukrainian conflicts can be interpreted in terms of economic interests, both within the countries concerned and among intervening outside interests. But this cannot conceal the major role played by deeply held identities that lead people to feel both considerable solidarity with those they perceive to be like themselves and hostility towards those who are – whether nationally, ethnically, religiously or through a combination of all three – different and therefore in their way.

The Soviet Union, like Yugoslavia but on a far larger scale, had been a transnational state formation that had tried to encourage an identity among its vast population based partly on the state socialist project, but partly and increasingly on a Russian patriotism. Where the people concerned had very distinct linguistic and sometimes religious differences from Russia, as in the Baltic states, this proved highly ineffective, and soon after the collapse of the Soviet Union these countries sought and achieved a national independence that the weakened Russia of that period was unable to prevent. Some predominantly Islamic regions of the Soviet Union have also sought independence in continuing violent conflicts, but these involved the Central Asian rather than European parts of the Soviet Union and are therefore beyond our concerns here. Areas that were culturally, linguistically and religiously closer to Russia, such as Belarus and Moldova, have achieved nation-state independence, but – unlike the Ukraine – have not sought a European identity or an EU relationship.

At a more moderate level one can compare the approach of the western German public to the unification of Germany itself after 1990 with their response to the plight of Greece after 2010. Although in principle Germany had been two separate states since the end of World War II, people on both sides of the divide continued to see themselves as the same German people, forcibly divided. When the Berlin Wall was torn down in 1989 without resistance from the East German authorities and free movement permitted between the two parts of the country again, it would have been possible for the eastern part to continue as a distinct state, as did the other countries in CEE, such as Poland or Hungary. But it was quickly perceived in both parts that there could again be a united Germany. There was reluctance among some West Germans, who realized that there would be a considerable financial cost and economic disruption from incorporating these far poorer eastern regions, but the overwhelming feeling was that this needed to be done, because they were all 'Germans'. Unification certainly required massive transfers of funds from west to east, and for several years Germany declined economically as a result, until bouncing back strengthened in the early years of the new century. When Greece required assistance, primarily from Germany, following its share in the general euro crisis of 2010, the reaction of the German public and political class alike was very different. German identity, like that of many other nations, can be a politically powerful motivating force; there is nothing comparable to this in the sense of a similar European identity. The strength of national identity can be seen in many other cases. Large parts of the population of Denmark, Hungary, Poland, Sweden and the United Kingdom seem uneasy about sharing their national identity with a European one.

There are also important examples within Europe of powerful national identities within states that lead to serious demands for either considerable national autonomy within the larger state or complete independence from it. Yugoslavia has been the most violent and dramatic example of this in recent history. The separation of Czechoslovakia into the Czech and Slovak Republics after the so-called 'velvet divorce' of 1993 was in contrast highly peaceful, but it was based on a widely held if not universal sense of separate national identities within the populations. There had been a combined sense of shared identity in the struggle for independence from the Austro-Hungarian Empire of people in the provinces of Bohemia (Česko), Moravia and Slovakia that finally succeeded after the collapse of that empire during World War I. There are distinct differences between the Czech language spoken in Bohemia and Moravia and the Slovak of Slovakia, though they are mutually intelligible (also with Polish). Slovaks felt themselves to be discriminated against in various ways within Czechoslovakia, and to have certain cultural differences; for example, as will be seen below, they are considerably more religious, closer to Poles than to Czechs.

Disputes over the state membership of 'submerged' nations are not always so amicable. Long-standing demands from members of the Roman Catholic minority in Northern Ireland for separation from the United Kingdom and unification with the predominantly Catholic Republic of Ireland in the south were for many years marked by sporadic violence, as were demands for separation from Spain among members of the Basque population in the north west. The Basque language, the primary identifier of the Basque country, which straddles the Franco-Spanish border, is a completely separate tongue with relations to no others. Also hotly contested, but in a non-violent way, have been demands for the independence of Scotland from the United Kingdom and of Catalonia from Spain. These and other, smaller conflicts testify to the power of senses of national feeling, sometimes, but by no means always, based on religion or language. It is difficult to predict when these will flare up strongly enough to provoke major demands for national independence or even violence.

European religion

Religious identity has been a major theme in the history of European societies, and the continent's major religious divisions have been fundamental to some of the main social differences that we find. A brief look back further in time than is used for most issues discussed in this book will be needed to place the current situation in perspective. Some parts of Europe have been Christian since the founding of the religion in Roman times and its adoption in the 4th century as the official faith of the empire. The former Roman territories south of the Mediterranean became fundamentally separated from Europe during the rise of Islam from the 7th century onwards – as, temporarily, did parts of the Iberian peninsula, France and Italy. During the medieval period European Christian rulers tried to win back the southern Mediterranean lands from Islam, and particularly the 'Holy Land', in the series of military assaults known as the Crusades, but with no lasting success.

On the other hand, by the 15th century they had complete success in reclaiming territory from Islamic rule north of the Mediterranean. Meanwhile Christianity had been spreading northwards and eastwards beyond the boundaries of the old Roman Empire, extending the idea of Europe as it did so. The rulers of these linguistically mainly Scandinavian, western Slav and Finno-Ugrian peoples had all embraced Christianity by the end of the first Christian millennium or had been defeated in battle by Christian armies. These various movements produced a distinctive association between Europe and Christianity; the two entities were virtually synonymous as 'Christendom' until Portuguese and then Spanish explorers started to impose Christianity on the southern Americas during the 16th century.

The old pre-Christian pagan religions had been completely destroyed once the Roman emperors turned from worshipping their gods and persecuting Christians to worshipping the Christian god and persecuting pagans, but the one non-Christian faith that shared with Christians the Jewish Bible – Judaism – persisted in some parts of Europe. Groups of Jews inhabited many different parts of Europe from Roman times onwards, usually kept in special zones and often being expelled, massacred or required to convert to Christianity. They were expelled from their main European base in the Iberian peninsula at the end of the 15th century, though pockets remained elsewhere, especially in eastern parts of Europe. In the same period, Muslims too were expelled from southern Europe or killed, and the few left behind forced to become Christian. Christian domination over Europe was then complete.

Yet Christianity itself had not remained united. From Roman times onwards Christians had passionate disagreements over the interpretation of their faith, debates sometimes being resolved by the losers being put to death. Of particular importance, by the late 11th century it had become impossible to maintain the same church structure in the west and the east. In the west, the pope in Rome retained a religious authority in the midst of a fragmented set of post-Roman political powers; in the east the successor to the Roman Empire based in Greek-speaking Constantinople (later called Byzantium, today located in Turkey and named Istanbul) held together a united political and religious authority over a considerably smaller territory than the Catholic Church had had to contend with in the west. This structural imbalance between east and west was the origin of the division into Roman Catholic and Orthodox branches of Christianity that survive today. Both were to fragment further.

Following the collapse of the Byzantine Empire and its conquest by the Islamic Ottomans in the mid 15th century, the Orthodox Church struggled on as the religion of local people in Greece, Cyprus and parts of the southern Balkans, which all now had Ottoman (Turkish) rulers. The Church sought the protection of various Christian rulers of Slav-speaking peoples to the north and east, who had withstood Ottoman pressure. For centuries Ottoman-occupied Greece and the Balkan lands became the centre of continuing tension and conflict between Islam and Christianity, but the heartland of Orthodoxy now shifted to the growing Muscovite Empire that became modern Russia. Differences developed between Greek and Russian variants of Orthodoxy, with further national divisions among the latter outside Russia itself. However, unlike in the Catholic west, these were rarely doctrinal or intellectual and were mainly a matter of adapting to the requirements of different rulers: lacking a central religious authority after the fall of Byzantium, these churches looked heavily to secular rulers for protection.

Rulers (and therefore, it was assumed, populations) in the west continued to recognize the pope in Rome. The papacy retained its authority over a vast territory despite not being a secular empire by insisting on conformity to a range of beliefs. Deviation from these was defined as heresy, and Christian secular powers supported the Church's authority by punishing heretics, often with torture and death. In exchange, the popes defined the rule of the emperor, kings, dukes and the rest of the aristocratic order as divinely sanctified. This did not, however, guarantee harmonious relations between the papacy and the secular powers. The German princes who assumed the title of Holy Roman Emperor – in theory successors to the Christian Roman Caesars – from time to time made war on Rome; at one point during the 16th century imperial armies laid waste to the city. From the 11th to the 14th centuries much of Germany and in particular Italy were divided by violent conflicts between supporters of the emperors and supporters of the popes. For a lengthy period in the 14th century the kings of France moved the seat of the Church from Rome to Avignon, more or less capturing a succession of popes.

From this curious, centuries-long patchwork of intense collaboration and open war between secular and religious authorities emerged one of the most important contributions of western European civilization: the idea of a separation of powers. The germ of the idea originated in the writings of St Augustine, a North African bishop working in what is now Algeria in the early 5th century, during the years of decline of the Christian Roman Empire. It became necessary to separate the idea of the Church and its divinely ordained power from that of its secular protector that was now clearly collapsing. Augustine therefore set out what we would now define as a division of labour, between what he called the City of God and the City of Man. From this came such ideas as the possibility of a separation of powers, subsidiarity – today used mainly to define the scope of different geographical levels of government, such as the EU, the state and local authorities. These concepts were available to steer medieval churchmen and secular lawyers through their complex relations, and this eventually and much later made possible such practices as the limitations separating government and other social institutions. In no other region of the world did historical regimes develop such ideas and practices of separation among different bases of power. (For a detailed reflection on the full implications of this distinctiveness of the western part of Europe, see Winkler, 2015: 579–611.)

Yet this heritage did not save the united western Church from extreme division. By the late 15th century doctrinal challenges combined with criticism of what was seen by many as the Church's corrupt social behaviour to produce a major protest movement that became known as Protestantism. The movement had several different, sometimes strongly opposed, wings, which often fought among themselves, but the conflicts between them and Catholicism were extreme in their violence. Most prominent among leaders of the protest movement were Martin Luther, a German monk, and Jean Calvin, a French theologian who eventually made his base in Geneva. In general, where secular authorities were critical of the Church and sympathetic to the new ideas, they gave refuge to Protestants or even supported them and persecuted Catholics on their behalf. Elsewhere secular authorities continued to support the Catholic Church and to kill heretics. In 1685 the Catholic French state repealed a commitment to tolerance of Protestantism that had lasted since 1598, expelling all Protestants from the country. From these conflicts emerged a complex religious geography that continues today to have social and political importance. In general and with very important exceptions, the physically closer a secular power was to Rome, the more likely it was to remain Catholic: France, Portugal, Spain and the various dukedoms and kingdoms that made up Italy, including the papacy itself, which was a major Italian political formation. The Holy Roman Empire, based in the German-speaking lands and eventually choosing Vienna as its seat, continued its conflicts with the papacy during this time but remained staunchly Catholic. It supported that faith against Protestant uprisings in the Southern

Netherlands (broadly speaking modern Belgium) and in the Czech and Slovak lands and Hungary, which it controlled.

Further away, in the north, in the Nordic territories, England and Scotland, several parts of Germany (divided like Italy into a mass of small domains) and the northern Netherlands (the Dutch Republic) and Switzerland, local rulers decreed that their countries should adopt one or other of the Protestant faiths, though Catholic minorities, sometimes large ones, persisted in several areas. In general, the Nordic lands and most parts of northern Germany adopted Luther's version of Protestantism; most of Switzerland, the Netherlands and Scotland and some parts of Germany went with Calvin; the English established their own variant, not based on a particular doctrine. There were exceptions to this geography: Poland and Lithuania in the north east and Ireland (though under English rule) in the north west remained staunchly Catholic.

Wars and less violent struggles based on or at least exploiting these religious differences continued, including ongoing conflicts in England, Scotland and Ireland between Catholic and Protestant claimants to the British throne, and the Thirty Years War that engulfed the German and Scandinavian lands until the Treaties of Münster and Osnabrück mentioned in Chapter 1. Gradually rulers, churches and populations became exhausted by conflict, and led by the Dutch, began to accept more or less peaceful forms of tolerance or at least grudging mutual acceptance among Catholics, various kinds of Protestants and also Jews in those countries where they continued to maintain a hold or (for example in England) were welcomed back after an earlier expulsion. By the mid 18th century this characterized most of the western European religious landscape. Among cultural elites it gave rise to the general movement in search of rationality and tolerance known as the Enlightenment.

One paradoxical outcome of the Enlightenment was intolerance of religion in general and the Catholic Church in particular in reaction against its own past record. This had its main practical consequence in the approach to religion during the French Revolution from 1789 onwards. Priests, monks, nuns and religious buildings were among the main victims of the Revolution, which was avowedly atheist. This pattern was continued by the Napoleonic regime, leading to the closure of many religious institutions wherever French power was extended. Following the defeat of Napoleon and the return of monarchical and aristocratic power, the position of the Church in France was also re-established. Yet the country remained deeply divided over religious issues, with largely non-violent political conflicts continuing through-out the 19th century and beyond. From the 1789 Revolution onwards France departed from the solidly Catholic religious geography of south-west Europe to become the continent's first partly atheist or secular country.

Elsewhere in the west the gradual move towards religious tolerance continued. Practitioners of minority religions were typically allowed to hold their rites and services, though they were often excluded from entering professional occupations, attending universities or occupying positions in public life. During the 18th and 19th centuries various waves of dissent at perceived corruption or negligence of religious authorities swept through communities, often mobilizing very large numbers of people, usually those who for geographical, cultural or class reasons felt marginalized in their wider society. These were some-times absorbed within existing Protestant churches, but in many cases, and particularly in the various parts of the United Kingdom, led to the foundation of new Methodist, Baptist, Congregationalist, Presbyterian and other churches, all within the broader framework of Protestantism.

Developments in the east, defined here as the zone of Orthodox Christianity, were completely different. Where there were Christian secular rulers, primarily in Russia, Church authorities supported them strongly and were in turn supported by the rulers. Where there was Ottoman rule the Church sought to maintain the faith and practices of Christian populations – something that most of the time the relatively tolerant Islamic sultans were content to accept, provided taxes were paid, soldiers provided for the imperial armies and that there were no rebellions.

It was, however, from the east that the next major religious disrup-tion to disturb Europe began, in the mid 19th century when the Russian Tsars instituted a wave of violent attacks, called pogroms, designed to kill Jews or at least to expel them from territories where they had long settled – in Russia itself, the Baltic states, the Russian-controlled part of Poland, and Ukraine. Jews fled west in search of hopefully more hospitable lands. This meant an increase in the practitioners of Judaism (though many either secularized or became Christians) in the Austro-Hungarian Empire, France, the Netherlands, Germany, the United Kingdom and elsewhere. Their acceptance ranged from complete integration to constant discrimination and harassment. This complex and varying pattern persisted until the Nazi Party took power in Germany in 1933. The level of persecution of Jews intensified again, first in Germany itself and then in all the territories that Germany conquered militarily from 1938 to 1943, territories that covered most of continental Europe. Some managed to escape to the United States, the United Kingdom, Sweden, Switzerland, Latin America or the Far East; but most European Jews were first transported to slave labour camps and then slaughtered in large masses. What had been a population of around six million was reduced to a very small remnant. Today nowhere in Europe do Jews amount to more than about 0.5 per cent of the population.

The Russia-dominated part of Europe again moved in a completely different direction from the west in 1917, when its communist revolution repeated the French Revolution's atheism and destruction of religious institutions, but with a different subsequent trajectory. On the one hand, the victors of the Russian Revolution were far more thorough than the French in their intolerance of rivals, and no counter-revolution took place. All territories incorporated within the Soviet Union became officially atheist and the Church reduced to the margins of life. However, unlike the Catholic Church, which claimed an international authority, Orthodoxy had always accepted subservience to the secular state. It therefore adapted to this kind of role within the Soviet system. After 1945, when Russian power was extended to the primarily Catholic countries of central Europe, there was more intense conflict between state and Church, especially in Poland, where Catholicism had long been a symbol of national identity against foreign Protestant Prussian or Orthodox Russian domination.

By 1945 western Europe, as a consequence of Adolf Hitler's genocide of Jews, had become more homogeneously Christian again. But changes to modern Europe's religious demography in the opposite direction of greater diversity recommenced in the 1950s, when labour shortages in NWE particularly Belgium, France, Germany, the Netherlands and the United Kingdom led to major immigration from poorer countries, sometimes as part of official labour recruitment plans. Many of these immigrants, especially those into the United Kingdom from Ireland and the former British Empire (now renamed as the British Commonwealth) or of southern Europeans into NWE, were Christians. They therefore had little impact on overall religious structure, except that the emigrant countries in the south were primarily Catholic, entering countries that were (except for much of West Germany) mainly Protestant. But immigrants tend to be more religiously observant than native populations, making their religious identity more important than their overall numbers might imply. Catholicism therefore grew in parts of NWE in a way that it had not done since the 16th century.

The main non-Christian religion of immigrants during this period was Islam, with people coming for example from Pakistan and later Bangladesh and parts of India to the UK, from North Africa to France and Belgium, from Indonesia and Melanesia to the Netherlands, and from Turkey to Germany. There were also Hindus, Buddhists, Sikhs and others, but in smaller numbers. Immigration from these countries has continued, and the first generations have produced children and grandchildren, leading to a growth of their religions within once predominantly Christian Europe. As the gap in wealth between Europe and the Third World has increased in recent years, so further waves of immigration have occurred. Wars and other forms of violence have further provoked large waves of refugees from North Africa and the Middle East to many parts of Europe. Some have started to go to the Scandinavian countries, which until recently have had a reputation for exceptional tolerance, while Greece, Italy and Spain have become convenient short-distance destinations for the poor of North Africa. These movements have all been primarily of Muslims, further strengthening the presence of Islam within Europe. As Spain's prosperity grew, it attracted immigrants from its former colonies in Catholic Latin America, moves with relatively minor religious and cultural implications.

Another major recent wave of immigration with religious consequences has been within Europe, from east to west as the fall of the Soviet bloc and the accession of most central European countries to the EU generated major movements with economic motives. These people have been predominantly Catholic (especially in the case of Poland) or of no religion.

It is not easy to find comparable data on religious observance for different countries, and it is perhaps a significant comment on the present state of religion in Europe that the most recent statistics come only as a by-product of a Eurobarometer report on public attitudes to biotechnology (Eurobarometer, 2010), religion being one of the variables that affect people's attitudes towards certain contemporary scientific developments. The main results of this survey are shown in Figures 3.1a–e, and give a very broad overview of the current outcome of 2,000 years of religious change. The survey covered EU member states and other states in some kind of relationship with the EU, so we lose the further eastern European cases but retain Turkey. It has, however, been possible to secure data for our external comparators, Japan, Russia and the United States, from other sources. Since these are not necessarily comparable with those for Europe, they will be discussed separately.

Across Europe as a whole the Roman Catholic faith continues to predominate, attracting the allegiance of over 50 per cent of the population in about half the countries of interest to us (Figure 3.1a). The pattern continues to follow the outcome of the 16th-century religious conflicts, with the Church being particularly important in southern Europe, Poland, Lithuania, Belgium, Ireland, Austria and some parts of its former empire. It is hardly present at all in the Nordic lands or eastern Europe. Elsewhere, in France, Germany, the United Kingdom and some other countries in western and central Europe, there are large Catholic minorities.

Included with the Protestant faiths in Figure 3.1b are various smaller Christian groups who do not identify with the Catholic/Protestant division. Protestantism dominates the Nordic lands, and is important in Switzerland, Germany, the United Kingdom and the Netherlands – its original 16th-century heartlands, though much reduced. Further east these western European forms of Christianity are very small.

The Orthodox Church is restricted to, but very dominant in, a small number of countries associated with its Greek (Greece and Cyprus) and Russian (Romania and Bulgaria) forms (Figure 3.1c). We should find the same if we had data for Belarus, Moldova, the Ukraine, and those countries of ex-Yugoslavia that use the Cyrillic alphabet (Serbia, Montenegro and Macedonia). The other countries where it has more than a marginal presence (Estonia and Latvia) have important Russian minority populations.

Turkey is one of only four predominantly Islamic countries at least partly within Europe, though since the fall of the Ottoman Empire its state officially has been strongly secular. We have no comparable data on the other three, Albania, Bosnia-Herzegovina and the unrecognized state of northern Cyprus (Figure 3.1d). Muslim, Hindu, Buddhist, Jewish and other non-Christian faiths make up small populations in a number of other countries, mainly as a result of relatively recent immigration.

Finally, a growing number of people declare themselves to be agnostics or atheists, or say that they do not know if they have a religious belief or not (Figure 3.1e). Only in Estonia do the last mentioned account for more than a very small percentage. The countries where non-religion has become important include: some central and eastern European countries where state socialist regimes had been officially atheist – the Czech Republic, Estonia, Latvia, Hungary; France, for reasons mentioned above; and some NWE and Nordic countries where Protestantism had traditionally been dominant (the Netherlands, Sweden, Norway, the United Kingdom, Germany). In general, the Orthodox churches have resisted secularization more successfully than the western ones, and (with the exception of Belgium) Catholicism

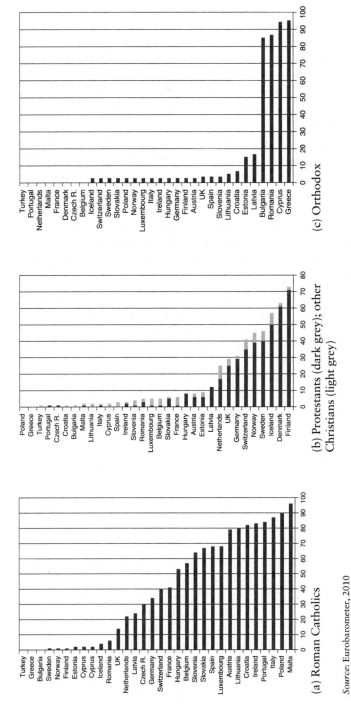

(a) Roman Catholics

(b) Protestants (dark grey); other Christians (light grey)

(c) Orthodox

Source: Eurobarometer, 2010

FIGURE 3.1 *Proportions of (a) Roman Catholics, (b) Protestants and 'other' Christians, (c) Orthodox Christians in adult population, European countries, c. 2010.*

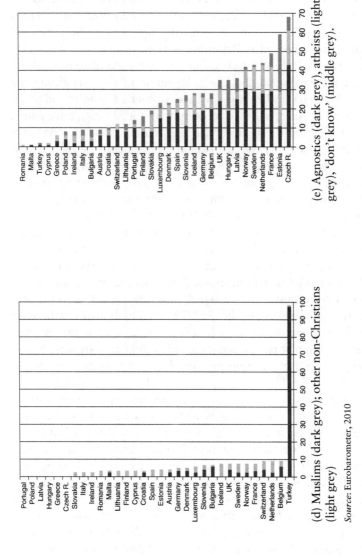

(d) Muslims (dark grey); other non-Christians (light grey)

(e) Agnostics (dark grey), atheists (light grey), 'don't know' (middle grey).

Source: Eurobarometer, 2010

FIGURE 3.1 *Proportions of (d) Muslims and 'other' non-Christian religions, (e) Agnostics, atheists and those not knowing if they have a religion, European countries, c. 2010.*

more successfully than Protestantism. Were we able to take a slightly longer perspective, we should note some rapid recent changes: religion had been very strong in both Belgium (Catholic) and the Netherlands (Catholic and Calvinist Protestant) until the past 30 years or so.

It is striking that whether or not countries experienced state socialism seems to have little effect by itself on longer-term differences in durability among the main forms of Christianity: Bulgaria and Romania have remained as Orthodox as Greece; and Poland as Catholic as Portugal, Italy and Ireland. But there are exceptions. Catholicism is a lot weaker in the Czech Republic than in neighbouring Slovakia, Hungary and Poland – all also formerly Catholic and in the Soviet bloc – or Austria. The Czechs, but not the Slovaks, have a long history of resisting the Catholic Church, dating from an important early, but rapidly suppressed, Protestant movement (the Hussites) in the early 15th century; does this medieval legacy explain more than four decades of state socialism? It is particularly interesting to compare the current state of religion in the two parts of Germany. The western *Länder* of what had from 1949 until 1991 been the Federal Republic of Germany had historically been more strongly Catholic, and today register 42 per cent Catholics against 33 per cent Protestants and 16 per cent agnostic, atheist or unsure. The eastern *Länder*, until 1991 the German Democratic Republic and within the Soviet bloc, had a Protestant majority, which today means about 16 per cent Protestant, 7 per cent Catholic, and 79 per cent agnostic, atheist or unsure. There therefore seems to be a far stronger secularization effect in the ex-communist part, which would if still a separate state be the least religious country in Europe, ahead in that respect of its neighbour the Czech Republic.

Given the complexity of German religious history from the 15th to the present century, it is instructive to take a closer look at its current geographical dispersion. This is shown for the year 2011 in Table 3.1. The data have a different source from the Eurobarometer survey, being based on German tax returns, and therefore are not easily compared with it. (If German citizens profess a religious faith and want to use its resources for marriages, burials and other ceremonies, they can choose to pay a small tax, collected with their usual income tax but additional to it.) The statistics in Table 3.1 are based on these returns, with the country divided into its different *Länder*. The longer-term post-Reformation religious history that I have indicated in the second column is very broad and ignores various exceptions, but it enables us to see how enduring these patterns have been, despite considerable

TABLE 3.1   *Religious adherence, German* Länder, *c. 2011.*

Land	History		Per cent indicating affiliation			
	Pre-20th century	Pre-1990	Cath.	Prot.	Muslim	None (or other)
Baden-Württemberg	Mixed	BRD	37	33	6	24
Bayern	Catholic	BRD	55	21	4	20
Berlin	Protestant	Part BRD; part DDR	9	19	8	63
Bremen	Protestant	BRD	12	41	10	36
Hamburg	Protestant	BRD	10	30	8	52
Hessen	Mixed	BRD	25	40	7	29
Mecklenburg-Vorpommern	Protestant	DDR	3	18		79
Niedersachsen	Protestant	BRD	18	50	3	30
Nordrhein-Westfalen	Mixed	BRD	42	28	8	23
Rheinland-Pfalz	Catholic	BRD	45	31	4	20
Saarland	Catholic	BRD	63	19	3	14
Sachsen	Protestant	DDR	4	21		75
Sachsen-Anhalt	Protestant	DDR	4	14		81
Schleswig-Holstein	Protestant	BRD	6	53	3	38
Thüringen	Protestant	DDR	8	24		68

Source: Statistisches Bundesamt, 2013

Notes: Federal Republic of Germany (Bundesrepublik Deutschland) (BRD) German Democratic Republic (Deutsche Demokratische Republik) (DDR)

social change and also geographical mobility: areas that became Protestant at some point after the Reformation have remained that way, and similarly for Catholics. The third column indicates whether a *Land* was part of West (BRD) or East (DDR) Germany from 1949 to 1990. It is clear that the citizens of the former state socialist parts of Germany (where religion taxes did not exist) did not use unification in 1990 as a chance to affiliate to a church. It is also notable that in the small, urban, mainly Protestant city states (Berlin, Bremen and Hamburg) and in Protestant Schleswig-Holstein on the border with Denmark, the Muslim population is now almost as large as the Catholic.

The United Kingdom also has a very varied religious geography. The distinctive form of Protestantism embodied in the Church of England is the main faith in England, and has the status of a state church, in that the monarch is its head in England, Wales and Northern Ireland, and its bishops sit in the upper house of parliament (the House of Lords). In addition to a currently growing Roman Catholic minority, there have since the late 18th century been various Methodist, Baptist and other minority forms of Protestantism, with roots in areas remote from London and often in the industrial towns of the 19th century. This is particularly the case beyond England, in Wales, where a distinct national identity also produced alienation from London-dominated England. In Scotland the situation is different. Here the state church, the Church of Scotland, belongs to the Calvinist confession otherwise found in the Netherlands and Switzerland. This means that in theory the monarch adopts different beliefs when moving between England and Scotland. Protestantism is vulnerable to fragmentation, and in Scotland this has led to a mass of small church groupings outside the framework of the Church of Scotland, as well as there being the Church of England in Scotland and the Catholic Church (strong on the west coast). Divisions of a similar kind are found in Northern Ireland, where a mass of small Calvinist churches confronts a large Catholic minority. As already noted, this has had profound political significance, as Catholic allegiance in Northern Ireland usually indicates a preference for the province to be reunited with the neighbouring Republic of Ireland, which is very strongly Catholic. Religious as well as political issues lay behind the violence between groups in Protestant and Catholic communities that lasted from the late 1960s until the late 1990s, constituting the last of the violent struggles between Catholics and Protestants in Europe that had been unleashed by the Reformation.

These brief descriptions of religion in modern Germany and the United Kingdom indicate the complex set of identities that lie behind the apparently straightforward question of what religion, if any, people believe in.

It is not easy to compare data for countries that were not part of the Eurobarometer survey, as questions will often be asked in different ways. However, statistics from the national censuses for the United States, Russia and Japan give us some basic ideas. Those for the United States for 2008 (the latest for which data are available) suggest a distinctive pattern. Protestants and 'other' (i.e. non-Catholic) Christians (it is difficult to separate these two categories) dominate, accounting for over 53 per cent of the adult population, a figure resembling that of the Scandinavian countries or the United Kingdom. About 25 per cent are Catholic, slightly higher than the Netherlands and Latvia, while Orthodox represent less than 0.5 per cent. Muslims account for fewer than 1 per cent, less than in most western European countries, though the proportion of Jews is over that figure and therefore higher than anywhere in Europe. This last is a continuing consequence of the exodus of Jews from Nazi-occupied Europe before and during World War II. Other religions account for less than 4 per cent, similar to several European cases. The proportion declaring themselves to be agnostic, atheist, humanist or of no religion account for about 15 per cent. This is low by the standards of European countries, except for those with large Catholic and Orthodox populations. The United States therefore differs from anywhere in Europe in being a mainly Protestant country that has only a small number of non-believers.

Russia fits the profile of European Orthodox-dominant countries, though with only 75 per cent Orthodox it has a larger number of people from minority religions (5 per cent Muslims, 1 per cent each of Catholics, Protestants, other Christians and Jews) and of people without a faith (15 per cent). While this last percentage is high for an Orthodox country, it is interesting to reflect that, after 70 years of official state atheism, the proportion of non-believers in Russia is not much higher than that of the United States. The diversity reflects the great cultural diversity of the vast land mass covered by the Russian state.

Japan has a completely different religious structure, with 84 per cent being Buddhist or Shinto or both (they are not mutually incompatible), 0.7 per cent Christian and 16 per cent for various others. No separate account is given of non-believers.

We cannot take for granted that particular attitudes and behaviours follow from particular identities of any kind – though in the case of religions we can take more note of respondents' stated identities than we shall find in a later chapter with social classes, as their names are in general less ambiguous. We can gain a further insight by examining the extent to which people attend the religious services that are a fundamental aspect of religious identity. Figure 3.2 displays the proportions of the adult population who say that they 'never' attend religious services except for weddings and funerals, plotted against the proportions saying that they are atheists, agnostics or uncertain about their beliefs. The relationship between the two variables is very strong ($r^2 = 0.7487$), which suggests that people's statements of their religious beliefs (or non-beliefs) are rather accurate. There are three real outliers (i.e. their actual level of religious attendance is higher or lower by more than one standard deviation from what one would expect on the basis of their proportion of non-believers). One is Estonia, where people report a higher level of attendance than we would expect from their high level of non-believers. However, Estonia was notable for the high number of 'don't knows' rather than actual agnostics and atheists. Another outlier, Turkey, is an Islamic country, which until very recently had a state that was distinctly secular and rather hostile to religion, rather as republican France has been at certain periods. Spain is more remarkable, with considerably lower attendance than the small number of non-believers would lead us to suggest; this might imply that the high level of religious belief in Spain is about to decline. Several countries showed higher than expected levels of religious attendance in the sense of having levels higher by more than 0.5 of one standard deviation from what one would expect on the basis of their proportion of non-believers: Greece, Latvia, Poland, Iceland and Sweden. With lower levels are Belgium, France, Switzerland and the United Kingdom. Overall, it continues to be Orthodoxy that produces the highest proportions of believers and church attenders, followed by Catholic southern Europe except for Spain. There are considerable differences across central Europe, seen particularly in the extraordinary contrast between the Czech and Slovak Republics, which had been joined as Czechoslovakia from 1918 to 1991.

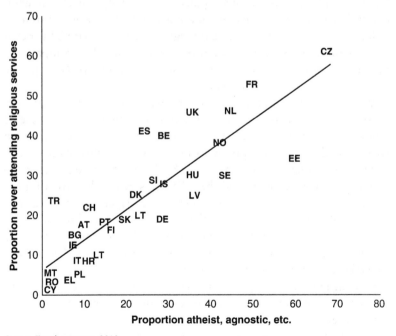

Source: Eurobarometer, 2010

FIGURE 3.2   *Proportions of those never attending religious services by non-believers, European countries, 2010.*

Ethnicity, immigration and cultural diversity

The internal religious diversity of those European countries that are not dominated by a single religion has five main sources: the wars between Catholics and Protestants of the 16th and 17th centuries; secularist movements that started with the French Revolution in the late 18th century and continued throughout the 19th and 20th, with France remaining the most prominent example; divisions within Protestantism, mainly during the 19th century; the even stronger secularizing tendency associated with the imposition of official atheism on countries in the sphere of influence of the Soviet Union; and waves of immigration over several centuries, bringing with them the distinctive religions of the various immigrant groups. Once immigrants have settled and have produced new generations, we can no longer talk of immigrants but of settled communities with distinctive cultures. The descendants of immigrants often merge into the culture of the surrounding society, perhaps marrying into it and producing a new, mixed population. To the extent that at least some descendants of immigrants retain some separation across generations, we often refer to them as 'ethnicities', though this is a complex term.

Ethnic identity is not easily defined for modern societies. For most of human history, and especially before the development of modern transport systems, people living in particular locations developed distinctive ways of life, cultures and religions, and married and produced children within narrow circles of neighbours and acquaintances. Human populations therefore produced distinctive cultures, based on a geography of settlement and a limited level of biological mixing through reproduction. From this comes the idea that people from particular parts of the world have physical, attitudinal and social characteristics that distinguish them from others, and thence the concept of ethnicity. But it is not a concept rooted in biology; it is not possible to use natural science to define different types of human being. Most of what are commonly understood to be separate ethnicities are cultural and social constructions, and their identity is flexible. Even in the remote past when travel was difficult, there were often important disruptions to patterns of settlement that had given people distinctive characteristics. Wars, famines and natural disasters drove whole populations to move and find new areas in which to live. The predominant movements across Europe have been westwards, as when peoples known as Huns, Goths and Visigoths moved into the area of the Roman Empire, eventually provoking its collapse, in the 4th and 5th centuries. These movements were often accompanied by violence, rejection or conquest, but eventually there was usually a settling down, mutual borrowing from cultures, languages and religions, and the formation of sexual unions and therefore children of mixed descent. Nearly all these diverse groups became Christian, which facilitated their integration, intermarriage and in many cases a gradual loss of a separate identity as they merged with the rest of the population. There were some exceptions: as already noted, groups of Jews settled across the European land mass; until the end of World War I Muslims mainly remained within the parts of Europe ruled over by the Ottomans; gypsies maintained their nomadic way of life, mainly in the south east; and Sami people inhabited the far northern parts of Finland, Norway and Sweden.

From the 16th century, when something that was coming to be seen as 'the nation' was beginning to be the main focus of many people's identity, these ethnic identities began to weaken, though there have continued to be exceptions. Where members of an ethnic group had settled into a particular geographical area, they sometimes sustained an ethnically defined nation state, as in the case of the Huns in Hungary. Elsewhere maintenance of a separate language enabled a group to maintain an ethnic identity even if governed by an external power: the Finns under the domination of Sweden and later Russia; the Welsh under the English; Highland Scots under first Lowland Scots and then the English; the Irish under the English; Basques and Catalans under Spain; Poles under both Germany and Russia; and most of the rest of central Europe under Austria-Hungary. Even then, none of these groups retained enough separation from those around them to maintain a purely biological identity. There have always been cases of children of mixed parentage. It is better to talk of cultural rather than ethnic identities, partly because it is impossible to support the implication of historical biological separateness that the idea of ethnicity seems to imply. There are certainly far more cultural differences and identities than we can account for with the idea of biological ethnicity.

Movements of populations across wide territories have continued and even intensified in the 20th and early 21st centuries, as outlined in the previous chapter. The diversity of geographical origins of people in those contemporary European societies that have attracted large numbers of immigrants has produced even more variety than does religion, with which of course it overlaps.

Gathering evidence on a remotely comparative basis that would enable us to estimate the degree of this cultural diversity is impossible for a number of reasons. The size of an immigrant population does not indicate the size of an ethnic sub-culture. In countries where immigration has been in progress for a lengthy time, these sub-cultures include the children and grandchildren of immigrants. In some cases these later generations disappear from view, becoming fully integrated into the main national culture, if there is such a thing. This is most likely to happen where barriers between host and immigrant cultures are low. The most important point here is the likelihood of marriage or other forms of enduring sexual partnership across the boundary, as once this occurs a new generation is born that inherits something from both cultures. Since marriage is often signified in a religious service, the children and grandchildren of immigrants are more likely to become an indistinguishable part of the host society where both practise the same religion. Thus, the children of many Italian and Portuguese immigrants into France in the late 19th century formed no distinctive communities, a Catholic culture being present in all countries concerned. On the other hand, Jews have retained a separate identity in many different countries for two millennia.

As most parts of Europe have become secular, earlier tensions between the religion of the host society and that of immigrants have sometimes been replaced by one between secularism and religion. Important examples of this can be seen in current confrontations between Islamic minorities and the secularism of French and Scandinavian societies. Islam is a religion, not an ethnicity, though in Europe one associated with a number of different distinctive immigrant minorities. The size of Islamic minorities can therefore be calculated using the data discussed above for religions (Figure 3.1d). It is far more difficult to estimate the size of ethnic groups not associated with a distinctive religion, as few countries seek such data. The United Kingdom is an exception to the extent that its official censuses ask people about their skin colour and certain other distinctive attributes in a confusing mix of criteria, though this is in itself only a crude measure of the existence of sub-cultural communities.

We therefore have to rely for the most part on statistics on the size of first-generation immigrant populations, which is inadequate for our purposes, but which requires only a question about country of birth or citizenship. Given that migrants tend to come to countries, and to cities within countries, to which other people from their culture have already moved, we can speculate that where there is an immigrant population there is also likely to be a larger ethnic community. However, this depends on the timing of immigration. The pattern of movement in post-war Europe has changed. Many of the grandchildren of those 1950s and 1960s immigrants from former colonies into France, the

Netherlands and the United Kingdom, and from Turkey and southern Europe into Germany, have completely entered the host society. Some others retain some indicators of separate identity: religion, distinctive food and pastimes, sometimes clothing and other aspects of personal style, and maybe a preference to keep friendship circles and in particular marriage within the original group. Often it is members of the host society who defend their own identity by erecting informal barriers against immigrants and their descendants, excluding them from their social circles, and in particular discouraging marriage with them. More recent waves of immigration, mainly those from central and eastern Europe to western, from various disaster areas around the world into Europe or from former Portuguese and Spanish colonies into those two countries as these grew in prosperity, have only very recently, if yet, begun to produce a second generation.

Another change has been in the gender pattern of immigration. During the 1950s and 1960s western European countries were rebuilding and expanding their manufacturing industries in the wake of World War II. The first waves of immigration were often invited or directly recruited by governments and firms worried about growing labour shortages. The vacancies were primarily for men of working age. They might be followed later by wives and other women. Today employment expansion is mainly in the services sectors, with particular recruitment difficulties in the relatively lowly paid personal services and care sectors. As we shall see in the next chapter, these are jobs more likely to attract women. The new waves of immigration from eastern into western Europe are therefore either gender-balanced or dominated by women. A different logic applies to people escaping as refugees and asylum seekers from disaster-torn parts of the world. These may come in balanced numbers of men and women, unless women are escaping from wars in which many men have been killed.

A further problem with collecting data on immigrants is that the main collated comparative source for Europe, Eurostat, picks out the main countries of origin, lumping rather large remainders of mainly small countries together as 'other'.

Finally, and very importantly, we cannot tell from mere statistics about countries of origin whether a group of immigrants constitutes a social 'issue' of any kind. For example, a group of French people living in a French-speaking part of Belgium is unlikely to attract any attention at all, and apart perhaps from a tendency to form friendships within the group, is not likely to have a particularly strong identity – no stronger perhaps than people drawn together by a preference for certain kinds of music or support for a football team, and perhaps rather less strong than that last. A group of asylum seekers from North Africa in Belgium is likely to be far more noticeable. They will have very distinctive social customs and dark skin, are probably Muslims and will in general be poorer than the native population. All these characteristics potentially, though not necessarily, create barriers between them and the host society.

In trying to estimate the importance of ethnic identity in different parts of Europe through the interpretation of immigration statistics we have to bear all these difficulties in mind. The overall size of immigrant or 'foreign-born' populations in EU member states and our key extra-European comparators is shown in Figure 3.3. Since this is a variable that we might expect to be related to national income, the statistics for foreign-born people are shown against this other variable. Luxembourg has been excluded, as a country with a very small population, a very high mean national income and a foreign-born population of 50 per cent. If Luxembourg had been included, the two variables would have correlated strongly at $r^2 = 0.4875$; excluding it reduces the correlation to $r^2 = 0.2871$. This shows that high national income is certainly a factor in attracting immigrants, but one that is offset by other

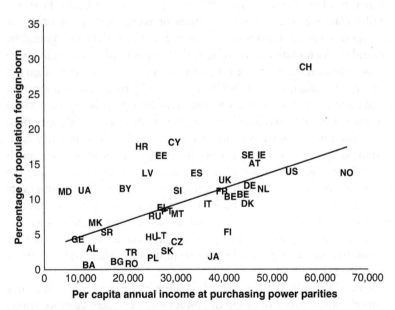

Source: United Nations, 2013

FIGURE 3.3 *Foreign-born populations by national per capita income (US$) at purchasing power parities, European countries and key comparators, 2013.*

important elements. Not surprisingly, some other very small countries, such as Cyprus, have particularly high proportions of immigrants. But also with considerably more than would be expected on the basis of national income (i.e. with values more than one standard deviation more than the predicted value) are three poor eastern European countries: Croatia, Estonia and Latvia. All three are countries that have broken off from larger units within the past quarter century: Croatia from ex-Yugoslavia, and Estonia and Latvia from the ex-Soviet Union. In both cases people who had previously made a move within an existing state now count as foreign-born. This indicates the variety of different notions that can be included within the general idea of 'immigration'. Japan has a far smaller immigrant population than countries of similar wealth in Europe or than the United States. Although the United States has historically been seen distinctively as a country of immigration, today similar or higher levels of foreign-born populations are found in several western European countries, and the United States does not appear at all as a country attracting particularly high numbers of new immigrants.

To gain a more detailed picture we need data on individual countries or groups of similar countries. We shall proceed as follows. First, we shall collate statistics on the countries or world regions of origin of immigrants for all European countries for which data are available. Second we formulate the hypothesis that issues of identity are likely to be more important the more different the country of origin is from the country of destination. We shall estimate this by regarding immigration from countries in the same broad region of Europe as being from 'similar' countries and therefore less likely to create issues of identity than those from either other regions of Europe or elsewhere in the world. This assumption may be false. Certainly in earlier decades, when much of the United Kingdom was clearly Protestant Christian and when the United Kingdom was wealthier than Ireland, Catholic Irish immigrants in England felt very distinctive. To take another example, it is doubtful whether a US immigrant into Ireland or the United Kingdom is seen as quite as 'different' as a French one, if only because of language. Our central hypothesis is plausible but certainly vulnerable, and this needs to be borne in mind.

Appendix Table A.3 is constructed in line with these criteria. It shows countries and regions of origin of immigrants expressed as proportions of the host populations, as matters stood at the end of 2014. In the final column, indicated X, will be found the proportion of the total immigrant population, *minus* those coming from the same region of

Europe. This is a potential estimate of the total population that might, with the several reservations indicated, be defined as constituting distinctive ethnic minorities. 'Regions' for this purpose have been defined as follows:

- Nordic and North-West Europe (NNWE): The countries of continental Europe north of the Alps and Pyrenees and west of the former 'iron curtain', the Nordic countries, the United Kingdom and Ireland;
- South-West Europe (SWE): Greece, Italy, Portugal, Spain and the smaller islands in that region;
- Central and Further Eastern Europe (CFEE): Former Soviet bloc countries now in membership of the EU; this distinction replaces that between CEE and FEE used elsewhere in this book, because the free market in labour within the EU marks a difference for immigration purposes between all its member states and others;
- The countries of ex-Yugoslavia: While two of these (Croatia and Slovenia) are now EU member states and are being treated in the rest of this book as parts of CEE, immigration from this region is most likely to have been a consequence of the civil wars that devastated it in the early 1990s and therefore to have a distinctive character;
- Countries of the former Soviet Union: These are mainly Russia, Ukraine and Moldova. The Baltic states that had been part of the Soviet Union but which are now EU member states have not been included here but instead as CFEE;
- 'Distressed' countries (other than those of ex-Yugoslavia): These are countries that have been affected by natural disasters, famine, war and civil conflict. Foremost among them have been Iran, Iraq, Afghanistan and Somalia. (The flood of refugees from war in Syria began to arrive in large numbers after these data were collected in 2012, and therefore cannot be included here. It will have important consequences for the size and structure of the immigrant population, especially in Austria, Germany and Sweden.);
- Ex-colonies: countries which had once been part of the extra-European empires of European countries, and which retained certain ties with the colonial power. European countries of the former Austro-Hungarian Empire are not included here, but feature instead within central and eastern Europe and ex-Yugoslavia; and
- Turkey and Morocco, two Islamic countries, appear in the list as particularly important among the many other countries from which immigrants into Europe have come. They stand out partly because

of their size, and partly because they are among the few neighbours of Europe that did not become part of European empires, though France exercised considerable influence over Morocco from the mid 19th to the mid 20th centuries.

Unfortunately no data are available for France (a particularly important country of immigration), Germany, Greece or Portugal, and those for Austria and Poland relate to 2012 not 2014. Germany and Portugal do provide statistics for their inhabitants who possess foreign citizenship. This is by no means the same as numbers of immigrants; these statistics have been given in Appendix Table A3, but listed separately.

It is notable that while NNWE countries are the main recipients of immigrants, they also account for large numbers of emigrants – Germans and British in particular being prominent among residents of other countries. Switzerland is a special case, with nearly a quarter of its population having been born outside the country. Many of these come from the three large countries sharing borders and languages with Switzerland (Germany, France and Italy) or from the rest of north-west Europe. The figure in Column X of Appendix Table A.3 is therefore considerably smaller than that for the total (Italy has been included as a country in the same region for Switzerland only, as some parts of Switzerland are Italian-speaking). Nevertheless, even after these deductions Switzerland remains the country with the highest number of people from potentially different cultural identities. The large number for 'Other' indicates the diversity of origins of Swiss immigrants, many of whom work in the large number of international organizations based there. Without more detailed knowledge of these it is not possible to say much about the nature of this diversity, except for the fairly high proportion of Turks (nearly 1 per cent).

Belgium (where similar points about international organizations apply as to Switzerland), Austria, Ireland and Sweden all have immigration levels above 15 per cent of total population. In the case of Ireland many of these come from the United Kingdom and elsewhere in NNWE rather than from more remote cultures. A notably high number of Austrian and Swedish immigrants have come from troubled parts of the world: from neighbouring ex-Yugoslavia in the case of Austria and from such places as Iran, Iraq and Somalia as well as ex-Yugoslavia for Sweden. This has been asylum immigration. Austria, Belgium and Ireland have also experienced considerable economic migration from Turkey, Morocco and CFEE – this last being particularly important for Ireland.

A mixed group of countries has immigration levels of between 10 and 14.9 per cent of the total population: Estonia, Latvia, Norway, Spain, the United Kingdom, Iceland, Slovenia, the Netherlands and Denmark. Some of these fit the stereotype already set by the preceding countries of being wealthy NNWE lands attracting immigrants and (as in the case of Austria and Sweden) refugees from poorer parts of Europe and the rest of the world. The Netherlands and the United Kingdom have immigration dominated by former colonies, also from CFEE in the United Kingdom, and from Morocco and Turkey in the Dutch case. Norway and Iceland have attracted large numbers of immigrants from CFEE. But there are four exceptions within this group: Estonia, Latvia, Slovenia and Spain.

Estonia and Latvia are special cases, as discussed above. Russians and the citizens of other former Soviet bloc countries account for around 12 per cent of their total populations. This does not mean that the movement of Russians into Estonia and Latvia constituted 'neighbourly' movement: the Russian and other Soviet population lived there as part of what many ethnic Estonians and Latvians saw as an imperial occupation. After independence the ex-Soviet population was subjected to various restrictions; it had been much larger, but there was considerable emigration back to Russia and elsewhere.

Slovenia is a special case of a different kind. Again, the large number of immigrants results from the collapse of a larger entity (in this case Yugoslavia), leaving people from what had been the same country in a 'foreign' one; something similar had occurred with the independence of Ireland from the United Kingdom in the early 20th century. Unlike the Latvian case, there was no group that suddenly moved from being dominant to an excluded minority. Rather, there were various tensions among Catholics, Orthodox, Muslims and those of no religion. These cases serve as a reminder of the complexity of European migration, which is not just a matter of the residents of former colonies or of CFEE moving to NNWE.

Although Spain is not as wealthy as the main immigrant countries of NNWE, and, like Ireland, had been a country of major net emigration, between the 1980s and the crisis of 2010 it experienced considerable inward population movement. Immigrants have come from CFEE, former Spanish colonies in Latin America and from neighbouring Morocco.

Finland and Italy have between 5 and 10 per cent of immigrants, both attracting large numbers of central and eastern Europeans as well as Russians. Finland, like Denmark and Sweden, has taken large numbers of refugees and asylum seekers – a process that was beginning also in Italy by the end of 2014, but not enough to show in the data.

The remaining countries have had low levels of immigration until the current refugee crisis. They are all relatively low-income countries by European standards, and all in CFEE.

The statistics for non-citizens living in Germany suggest a pattern similar to that for other NNWE countries, while Portugal resembles the Netherlands, Spain and the United Kingdom in its large number of people from former colonies.

Conclusion

Religion and country or ethnicity of origin are, alongside nationality, about the most powerful sources of identity to be found among human populations, and they overlap heavily. Between them, they have been major sources of wars and hatreds. Within Europe the historical trend has been for religion and possibly nationality to become gradually less important. Centuries of conflict over these two identities culminated in the two horrifying global conflicts of the 20th century's world wars and the mass murder of Jews and others in the Nazi holocaust. It is as though European people and their governments have ever since been recoiling from the passions implicated in those disastrous events. This can perhaps be seen in the declining statistics of religious observance in most of Europe, especially when compared with the United States. It is more difficult to track changes in national identity, as in this book I am not using data on attitudes to indicate identities, but only indicators of behaviour. The only behavioural evidence we have of what might have been happening to national identity is the willingness of large numbers of Europeans to accept and welcome their countries' membership of the EU, and its gradual adoption of functions which during the 19th century were associated with states. Western and eastern Europeans share this historical experience, but it was differentiated between 1947 and 1990 by the division of most of the continent between countries allied with the United States and those that formed part of the Soviet bloc. As we have seen, patterns of secularization are today similar across Europe, and the majority of countries in CEE and several in FEE have chosen to seek admission to the EU. We have also seen major exceptions to this retreat from passionate religious and national identities in ex-Yugoslavia, Ukraine and other parts of central and further eastern Europe, and in the many examples throughout Europe of the strength of national feeling.

It should therefore not be taken for granted that deep hostilities based on religious and national identities are disappearing within Europe, but many of them seem to have done so, such as those between Catholics and Protestants in most areas, or between French and Germans. New tensions have, however, arisen in the wake of the migrations discussed above, in particular between parts of native populations and some groups of Muslims, but also in resentments against immigrants from CEE moving into the west. In some respects these new animosities continue familiar historical patterns, such as the treatment of Jews and gypsies in many countries for centuries. But these 'old' minorities had been settled in their lands for many years. The new encounters concern groups who had not had much to do with each other in previous centuries. Often accommodation and integration take place very easily and members of the minorities are absorbed into the host society, contributing something to it of their own cultures as they do so. But occasionally there are opportunities for tension, usually when there appears to be competition for a scarce resource, such as work or physical space. The possibility then always arises that cultural signifiers and identities will be used to interpret that competition as one between different cultures, and outright hostility can result.

The issues we have discussed in this chapter concern deeply rooted and sometimes passionately held beliefs. In the following chapters we move to the more prosaic and typically 'modern' world of the economy and work. However, as we shall see before the end of this book, deeply rooted and powerful identities are often also at stake here.

Chapter 4

Europeans at work

Human work takes a bewildering variety of forms – even if, as here, we concentrate on paid employment only. Two main ways have been developed by social scientists of organizing this variety to enable us to make sense of it. First is to look at different kinds of products or outcomes of work; second is to examine different kinds of work tasks themselves. In this chapter we shall make use of both approaches in order to draw some conclusions about the character of work in contemporary Europe, searching, as throughout this book, for any distinctive characteristics of European societies among advanced societies in general, and for groupings within Europe. Unfortunately the former task is more difficult to achieve in this chapter than in some others, as most other advanced economies have not yet joined European ones in using a shared international classification system devised by the UN and used by the ILO.

Employment sectors organized by type of product

The main means used, for example in newspaper discussions, to describe different kinds of economic activity from the perspective of its products is to distinguish primary (agriculture and mining), secondary (mainly manufacturing and construction) and tertiary (services) sectors. This approach was first developed in the 1930s, when observers noted that the predominant change that had been taking place since the late 18th century of people moving from agriculture to industry was being joined or replaced by moves out of industrial employment into the so-called 'services'. In subsequent decades this idea has become too crude, as services cover very diverse activities, which together now account for the great majority of employment in most European and other advanced countries. The idea behind the original formulation was to mark successive moves away from nature; as societies developed, people moved from wresting means of survival from nature (farming and extracting metals, fuel and other minerals), via fashioning goods out of the materials so wrested (manufacturing and construction), to moving those products around and trading them (services). Attempts by international statistical agencies to update this to take account of the diversity within services have mainly tried to follow the logic of the original scheme. The current UN/ILO scheme, known as ISIC Revision 4 (2008), does this but in an implicit way. Table 4.1 shows how it operates, and how I am here adapting it slightly.

First, agriculture, fisheries and forests are taken as a separate sector (A in the ISIC scheme). This is close to the original idea of a primary sector, extracting usable material for human life from nature, except that the original idea, rather more logically, also included mining, quarrying and other forms of mineral extraction as primary activities (B in the ISIC scheme). I have here kept with the original approach, combining A and B as parts of what I call Sector I: agriculture and extraction.

Next, ISIC lists in order all the sub-sectors that comprised the original secondary sector: by far the largest, manufacturing (C); two very small sub-sectors: gas, electricity and air production (D) and water management (E); and the larger one of building and construction (F). I retain these as in the original scheme as Sector II: material production. This is the sector where materials that have been extracted from nature in Sector I are turned into usable products.

Third, recent analytical approaches bring together trade (shops and other commerce) (G), transport and storage (H), and accommodation and food services (i.e. restaurants and hotels) (I) as a tertiary sector concerned with the movement and sale of goods. The ISIC scheme does not group these explicitly, but lists them consecutively, as it did for the different activities coming together under material production. These are at one stage further removed from nature than Sector II, as they deal with movement and sales rather than manufacture, but are still mainly concerned with physical objects. Some theories separate out restaurants, hotels and similar activities as being more concerned with the provision of a direct service rather than with the sale of material objects, and put that sub-sector with some others in a different personal services sector; I shall follow that approach here. Of course, food is sold in restaurants just as it is in food shops, but the value added provided by the restaurant is the cooking, presentation and service of the food, not in the raw materials. I here therefore keep only G and H together as Sector III: material services.

TABLE 4.1   *Schemes for analysis of employment sectors.*

Activity (as defined in ISIC Rev 4 2008)	Simple sectoral scheme	ISIC Rev 4 2008	Scheme used in this book
Agriculture, forestry and fishing	Primary	A	I (Agriculture and extraction)
Mining and quarrying		B	
Manufacturing	Secondary	C	II (Material production)
Electricity, gas, steam and air conditioning supply		D	
Water supply; sewerage, waste management and remediation activities		E	
Construction		F	
Wholesale and retail trade; repair of motor vehicles and motorcycles		G	III (Material services)
Transport and storage		H	
Accommodation and food service activities		I	Part of VI (NB) (Personal services)
Information and communication	Tertiary	J	IV (Business services)
Financial and insurance activities		K	
Real estate activities		L	
Professional, scientific and technical activities		M	
Administrative and support service activities		N	
Public administration and defence; compulsory social security		O	V (Citizenship services)
Education		P	
Human health and social work activities		Q	
Arts, entertainment and recreation		R	Rest of VI (Personal services)
Other service activities		S	
Activities of households as employers; undifferentiated goods- and services-producing activities of households for own use		T	

Fourth, current theory identifies a set of services that are primarily, though not solely, concerned with provisions for businesses rather than for private individuals. Unlike those in Sector III, these services do not themselves involve material objects, but they are close to businesses, many of which are concerned with producing and handling such objects. It therefore constitutes another step further away from material objects. Included here are information and communication (J), financial and insurance activities (K), real estate (L), various professional, scientific and technical services such as engineering and architecture (M), and the provision of administrative and business support services (N). I group these as Sector IV: business services. Interesting among them is information and communication. Until recent changes to international statistics, these used to be included in ISIC's previous H alongside transport and storage. The reasoning was as follows: material goods were transported; so were written communications (e.g. letters), often by the same postal organizations. It was therefore impossible to separate the transport of goods from the transport of messages. During the 19th century the telegraph and telephone developed as alternatives to letters, usually under the auspices of the same postal organizations. These activities too were therefore seen as related to transport, though they were very remote from the movement of goods. The development of the information technology sector during the past quarter century has finally made the inclusion of all these non-material communication activities alongside transport absurd. They have now been moved into the fourth sector alongside other more abstract services. This example illustrates two points. First, how we conceive of sectors changing with time and technology, as activities start out seeming to be part of something else from which in time they become very different. (In the early 20th century air pilots were counted in British national statistics alongside jugglers and trapeze artists, as most aeroplane activity took the form of circus and similar stunts and entertainments. Flying was not yet part of a transport sector.) The second point that the emergence of the information and communication sub-sector illustrates is the difficulty of comparing statistics on economic sectors over time. Information and communications have been separated from transport in most statistical sources only since 2008.

The four sectors discussed so far have taken us from the idea of the extraction of usable material from nature to the ancillary services that surround the whole process of extraction, manufacture, transport and sales. This is the process of successive abstraction described above.

We are left with activities that are primarily concerned with the provision of services directly to persons rather than to firms and other corporate organizations, a further move away from material objects. These are usually divided into two types. There are those, first, that are commonly described as 'public and community' services or 'services of general interest'; and second, those that are of purely personal interest. The first set, which are grouped together as sectors O, P and Q by ISIC, are usually those that are either used collectively (such as police or public administration (O)) or which, although used individually, are seen to be provided for some kind of public good, such as education (P), health and care (Q). I here group these as Sector V: citizenship services, as they constitute those services that are seen as sufficiently important to one's ability to be an active member of a society to justify special measures being taken to ensure their availability. This does not mean that we include only public services, but purely private activities tend to be small components of them.

Finally come those services that are solely for personal enjoyment: artistic, entertainment and recreational activities (R); domestic services of various kinds (S and T); and, in my view, hotels and restaurants (I). I group these as Sector VI: personal services.

None of the activities we have been discussing fits perfectly into its sector; neither are activities always carried on within their main sector. For example, although the information sector is seen as mainly a business service, included here will also be the production of computer games, which should better be seen as an aspect of recreation. Similarly, 'research' is counted in business services (here Sector IV), while much of it is conducted in universities (education, part of Sector V). Even more troublesome is the fact that activities have to be classified according to the main sector of the organization concerned. For example, if an engineering firm employs its own cleaning staff, they would be counted as part of manufacturing, Sector II. However, if the engineering firm contracts out to a specialized cleaning company, those workers would come under Sector VI, personal services. This is a particularly important point, as during the past 30 years there has been a gradual trend for firms and other organizations to contract out services such as cleaning, some kinds of administrative support and canteens, increasing the numbers of persons who seem to be employed in sectors IV and VI, even where there is no change in the work actually being done. This tendency is found most frequently in the wealthier economies, inflating the impression of a shift to services taking place within them.

Despite these tendencies for organizations to contract out ancillary activities and concentrate on their core business, it is important to remember that the sectors in which people work do not tell us what *kind* of work they do. Just because people work in manufacturing does not mean they are factory workers; or because they work in schools that they are teachers; or in restaurants that they are chefs and waiters. In each case they might be administrative support workers; while someone working for a firm in the administrative support sub-sector might be employed looking after the office gardens – a job we would associate with Sector I.

Underlying the extended scheme is the idea that as wealth increases consumption of the products of the different sectors moves from I to VI, but this is not a simple historical progression, nor is it straightforward. Movement from poverty to wealth can take place synchronically across different social groups: at every point over past centuries the wealthy have consumed more culture and restaurant meals than the poor. Also, we cannot at all assume that increases or declines in employment in a sector reflect changes in their consumption. Productivity tends to rise faster in production sectors (I and II) than in the others, meaning that over time a smaller number of workers is needed to produce a given unit of output. Also, the production sectors are more heavily engaged in international trade than most, though by no means all, services sectors; changes in employment may therefore represent shifts in exports and imports rather than domestic consumption.

For all these reasons we must examine information about employment in economic sectors with great care. Figure 4.1 shows the distribution of total employment across all sectors for EU countries and also for Japan as an international comparator. Unfortunately the United States does not collect data for sectors defined on a comparable basis, while for Russia and non-EU FEE countries we have statistics from an earlier version of ISIC, which are not strictly comparable. We can quickly establish that Japan has an economic structure similar to many European countries: it is towards the upper end for Sector III, while perhaps more striking is the fact that it has a low level of employment in Sector V, coming above only the two poorest European countries, Bulgaria and Romania.

Figure 4.2 tries to approximate statistics for Russia and those parts of FEE for which data are available on the earlier version of ISIC in the following ways.

Mining is included with manufacturing and it is not possible to reallocate it to Sector I; therefore sectors I and II are here marked with

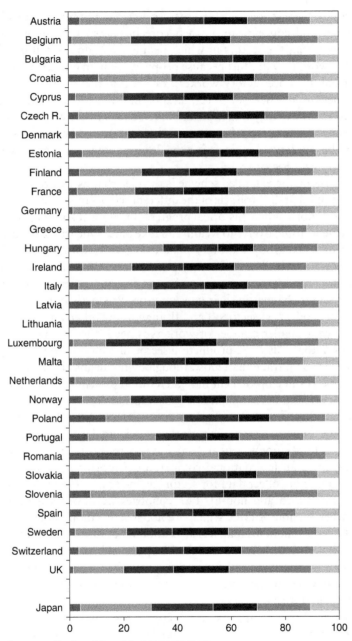

Note: Sectors, reading from left to right: I, II, III, IV, V, VI

Source: Eurostat, 2014

FIGURE 4.1   *Employment by economic sectors, European countries and Japan, 2013.*

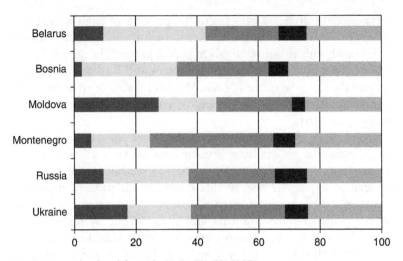

Note: Sectors, reading from left to right: I*, II*, III*, IV*, V–VI*

Source: UNECE, 2013

FIGURE 4.2 *Employment by economic sectors, non-EU eastern European countries and Russia, 2011–13.*

asterisks (*) to differentiate from those sectors in Figure 4.1. Mining is important in Russia and Ukraine, and this leads to an exaggeration of Sector II and an underestimate for Sector I. Information and communications technologies are included with material services, and it is not possible to reallocate them to Sector IV; therefore sectors III and IV are also marked with asterisks. It is likely that these activities are small in these countries, but there may be some exaggeration of Sector III* and an underestimate for IV*. It is not possible to separate hotels and restaurants from Sector III*; and it is not possible to separate personal from citizenship services; therefore sectors V and VI have to be combined and are here marked with asterisks.

The discussion will be simplified by concentrating on ranges for the size of sectors, either across the whole group of countries or across the geographical regions of groups of countries that we identified in Chapter 1, and paying separate attention to the non-comparable group in Figure 4.2. We shall note occasions where countries occupy extreme positions, unless these are only one of the three very small countries (Cyprus, Luxembourg and Malta). Small countries often have economies strongly biased towards particular activities.

Sector I (and I*) (agriculture and extraction) is now very small almost everywhere in Europe; in all but four countries covered in Figure 4.1

it ranges only from 1.2 per cent to 9.0 per cent of employment. The exceptions are all in southern or eastern Europe: Croatia, Poland, Greece and, with an outstandingly high 26.6 per cent, Romania. Among the countries covered in Figure 4.2, Belarus and Russia stand slightly beyond the range of the rest, while Moldova resembles Romania, and Ukraine is also high. Bosnia-Herzegovina and Montenegro fit the main European pattern.

Sector II (and II*) (material production), the emblematic sector of industrial society, now accounts for between 16 per cent and 37 per cent of employment (discounting Luxembourg). All countries covered in Figure 4.2 also fit this range. At the peak of industrialism in mid-20th-century United Kingdom, it was never much above 40 per cent, so some countries still count as highly industrial. In particular it is the two components of former Czechoslovakia, the Czech and Slovak Republics, which now stand as the countries in Europe with the highest levels of industrial employment, at around 36 per cent. It is striking that, in general, employment in manufacturing and related activities is now concentrated in CEE and parts of FEE, with Belarus, Bosnia-Herzegovina and Russia also having high levels. Austria and Germany are the only western European countries to have levels above 25 per cent (followed by Portugal). The fact that, after Luxembourg, the two cases with the lowest proportion of workers in Sector II (16 per cent) are Greece and the Netherlands indicates the complexity of the processes behind these statistics. The Netherlands industrialized in the late 19th and early 20th centuries, and is therefore now 'deindustrializing'. However, it never became as industrial in its economic activities as some of its neighbours, long having (like the United Kingdom) a large financial sector. Greece, on the other hand, industrialized late, in the mid 20th century, and will never go through an extensive industrial period, as it now shares in the deindustrialization affecting all advanced economies.

Sector III (and III*) (material services), the heart of what was originally perceived as the main services sector when this was primarily a matter of the transport, storage and sale of goods produced by the primary and secondary sectors, is a stable one with little variation across countries. Among the countries in Figure 4.1, the range is from 17 per cent to 25 per cent. The highest levels are found in the three Baltic states, some southern European ones (Bulgaria, Cyprus, Greece and Spain), the Netherlands and Japan. With the exception of these last two, this is a concentration among (in European terms) low- and medium-income states. The geographical location of the Netherlands has long given it a specialism in the logistics sub-sector. The countries in Figure 4.2 all have high levels in Sector III*, Montenegro especially so. This is consistent with the finding concerning low-income states, though it must be remembered that two sub-sectors are included for these countries here that are found elsewhere for countries using the latest version of ISIC.

Employment levels in Sector IV (and IV*) range from 7 per cent to 22 per cent, but if the low outlier Romania is ignored it becomes 11 per cent to 22 per cent. The Figure 4.2 countries all fall below the lower value, though for them information technology is included in Sector III* and not IV*. This probably puts Russia above the 11 per cent level, but not the others. It is clear that this is a sector whose share of employment is increasing in nearly all countries – partly but not solely because of the sub-contracting process discussed above. There is a clearer geographical base to diversity among countries here than for the other sectors: in all CEE and FEE countries fewer than 15 per cent of employment is in this sector; in all western European cases (and Japan) apart from Greece and Portugal it is above that level; in a few cases (Sweden, Switzerland, the United Kingdom and the Netherlands) it is above 20 per cent. There is a combination of two elements here. First, this was a sector that was particularly small in the state socialist economies, where there was little role for financial and property services. Second, as the position of Greece and Portugal shows, growth in this sector is associated with national wealth.

Romania is again a very low outlier in Sector V (and part of V*), its share being 13 per cent while the next lowest is neighbouring Bulgaria with 19 per cent. Luxembourg and the Scandinavian countries have the highest levels, with Belgium, the Netherlands and France all with over 30 per cent. As with Sector IV (business services), nearly all western countries have higher levels of this kind of employment than those in CEE. In addition to Greece and Portugal, Austria is an exception here, while Japan is found among the lowest levels. The Figure 4.2 countries fit the general pattern, especially when it is remembered that we have no separate data for them for Sector VI*.

Finally, Sector VI is fairly small in most countries, reaching above 13 per cent in only two cases: Spain (16 per cent) and Cyprus (18 per cent).

In the countries for which we have full data, the two most important sectors of employment today across all 30 European countries and Japan are II and V; Sector II is one of the two largest sources of employment in 21, and Sector V in 26. This places the idea of post-industrialism in some perspective; it has not yet led the majority of advanced economies to a point where manufacturing, construction and other material production have become insignificant. The only countries in which Sector II is not among the two largest are Cyprus, Greece, Ireland and Spain (among those who have never been strongly industrial); and Luxembourg, the Netherlands, Sweden, Switzerland and the United Kingdom among those where the sector has declined from a previous high point. As might be expected from the above discussion, it is mainly in CEE and FEE where Sector II is the single largest: Bulgaria, Croatia, the Czech Republic, Estonia, Hungary, Lithuania, Poland, Slovakia and Slovenia; for those covered by the Figure 4.2 definition of the sector: Belarus and Russia, marginally Bosnia-Herzegovina. The only western cases are Austria, Germany, Italy and Portugal. Japan also falls in this category.

Sector V (citizenship services) is the largest sector primarily in NWE and Nordic (NNWE) countries: Belgium, Denmark, Finland, France, Ireland, Luxembourg, the Netherlands, Norway, Sweden, Switzerland and the United Kingdom, but also Greece, Malta and Spain in the south west.

Two other sectors feature among the leading two in a small number of countries: III, which appears in ten cases and, with a somewhat different definition, Montenegro and Russia; and IV, in four. Only in Moldova is agriculture still the largest sector, and only in Romania the second largest. Sector III (material services) appears as a leading one alongside II in three CEE countries (Bulgaria, Latvia and Lithuania), Japan and (with a slightly different definition) Russia. Given Sector III's ancillary role to industrial activities, these might be considered the cases that are furthest away from post-industrialism. Sector III appears alongside V as one of the two largest in six cases: mainly southern countries (Cyprus, Greece, Spain), but also Ireland, the Netherlands and Norway. In all four cases where Sector IV is the second largest, Sector V is the largest: Luxembourg, Sweden, Switzerland and the United Kingdom. These might be considered the most post-industrial countries.

Sectors below national level

Within individual larger countries the association of high levels of employment in Sector II (material production) with relatively low income is by no means so clearly reproduced. Eurostat data (Eurostat,

2015e) provide statistics on employment in various economic activities for individual regions. For simplicity we shall examine here only employment in manufacturing, the largest sub-sector of Sector II, and for NUTS 1. For several of these larger countries there is a positive relationship between regional employment in manufacturing and household income. This is strongest in France ($r^2 = 0.6092$), where the wealthy wider Paris and south-east regions (containing Grenoble and Lyon) have also the main concentrations of manufacturing. The relationship is only slightly weaker for Italy ($r^2 = 0.5023$), where the main exceptions of wealthy regions with low levels of manufacturing are Lazio (containing the capital, Rome) and Liguria (containing the major port city of Genoa). The relationship is considerably weaker, though still mildly positive ($r^2 = 0.1239$), for Germany. Here the rich regions in the south have considerable manufacturing (Baden-Württemberg and Bavaria), while the small industrial *Länder* (regions) of Bremen and Saarland have only moderately high incomes. Hamburg combines high income with a very low level of manufacturing, while the *Länder* of eastern Germany all have low levels of manufacturing and low incomes. Unfortunately Germany provides no statistics for its capital city, Berlin. It is likely that this has a low level of manufacturing employment, in which case the overall correlation for the country as a whole could turn negative. Spain has a virtually identical correlation to that of Germany ($r^2 = 0.1230$). Here we have a contrast, with the richest region (around the capital, Madrid) having a particularly low level of manufacturing employment and the second richest, the north east (containing Catalonia and its capital Barcelona), having a particularly high level.

In the other two large European countries, the relationship between household income and manufacturing employment is negative. This is especially the case for the United Kingdom, where the inverse correlation is very high indeed ($r^2 = 0.7985$). The capital region, London, is by far the richest region and has considerably less manufacturing than anywhere else in the country, though the negative relationship is strong even without the special position of the capital. For Poland the correlation is negative, but so weak at $r^2 = 0.0739$ it is better to say that there is no relationship at all between regional wealth and the strength of manufacturing. Notably, the two regions with the lowest levels of manufacturing are the richest Centralny region (containing the capital, Warsaw) and the poorest Wschodni (eastern) one.

The economic structure of capital cities emerges as central to understanding the relationship of sectoral specialization to the regional distribution of income within large countries. Capital cities are normally the richest or among the richest locations in European countries; Germany is an exception here, as its present capital, located far to the east of the country overall, was for many years divided between a part that was integrated into the western capitalist economy and another that was incorporated into the eastern state socialist one. Where capitals are located in regions that maintain considerable manufacturing, as in France and Italy, then that sector shares in that wealth. Elsewhere, capitals are becoming the major centres of specialization in financial and other business services that attract the highest incomes in the post-industrial economy.

Sectors and gender

The rise of the post-industrial sectors has been associated with a major increase in women's participation in the paid labour force. During the 20th century manufacturing, construction and the other components of Sector II, and also mining in Sector I, were overwhelmingly male in western Europe; in Russia, eastern Europe and also the United States the female minority was somewhat larger. (The patterns in pre-industrial society had been more varied; where agriculture was characterized by family smallholdings, whole families worked the land; where large-scale employers directly employed workforces, employment was more male.) Very early industrial work in the late 18th and early 19th centuries had been less heavily male, with particularly large concentrations of women in textiles and clothing, one of the key industries of early industrialism. Campaigns for the improvement of working conditions in industry led to a decline in female working – there being concerns about women's exposure to strenuous physical activity and danger, and moral concerns about women working on night shifts and closely with men. These concerns were pressed for different reasons by trade unions and Christian churches. Neither of these forces was so strong in state socialist economies, where both unions and churches had to conform to government preferences, or in the United States, where unions were usually weaker than in western Europe and (at that time, unlike today) religion had little political influence.

By the mid 20th century there was therefore a widespread consensus in western European societies that paid industrial work was a male province, that men had an obligation to be the 'breadwinners' for their wives and children, and that, while girls would enter employment after they left school, they would leave work when they married in order to raise children and keep a home for their menfolk to come back to at the end of the working day. The situation continued to be different in state socialist countries and, to a lesser extent, in the United States.

As noted in Chapter 2, during the 1920s and 1930s women in many European countries had postponed marriage until their late twenties; large numbers of them also remained single, especially in countries that had been combatants in World War I, which had killed so many young men. There were therefore women in the labour force; during World War II their numbers increased again in combatant countries, as they entered employment to replace men who were engaged in the war. In western Europe women left the labour force when men returned from war, while in the east state socialist regimes favoured their continued employment because of the chronic labour shortages suffered in these countries as their elites sought rapidly to industrialize their backward economies, but often with low-productivity production methods. From the mid 1940s onwards women's age at first marriage began to decline and a rising proportion of women married. There was also a general decline in the clothing and textile industries in northern European countries. The initial post-war decades therefore saw a decline in female labour force participation. The situation began to change rather suddenly, starting in some parts of north-western Europe, during the 1970s. It is difficult to disentangle a causal sequence among the factors involved. A major change in women's ideas about their place in society was clearly taking place. Perhaps related to that, the age of marriage started to rise, the birth of children began to be delayed and proportions of women (and men) remaining single started to rise. Separately, the sectors of the economy in which women were most likely to work began to grow in importance. This last point is highly important; when women's (more accurately, mothers') employment began its dramatic rise in western Europe from the 1970s onwards it did not mean the entry of women into sectors that had previously been male preserves, but the growth of those sectors in which women had long been important.

It is a remarkable fact that, particularly in western Europe, women's participation in the paid workforce has mainly involved them in the kinds of task associated with their domestic activities. The manufacturing industries in which women have mainly worked, clothing and textiles, resemble the work of making and mending garments that has long been associated with homemaking. Women are also employed in relatively large numbers in the food industry. As employment in offices grew during the 20th century, large numbers of women found work in ancillary, support activities as secretaries, typists and personal assistants – their support to managers resembling the traditional concept of being a 'helpmeet' to husbands. But it was the expansion of care activities, particularly those in Sector V, that brought large numbers of typically 'maternal' activities into the paid labour force: looking after children, including teaching them; nursing the sick; and the care of the elderly and other dependents.

As a result of these processes, female employment began to grow earliest and most rapidly in those countries where sector V grew the fastest. However, in the 1990s the ending of state socialism temporarily brought the opposite process in some but not all CEE countries: women began to leave the labour force as the old state socialist system of workplace nurseries collapsed, and in some countries (particularly Poland) a renewed Catholic influence on social policy gave mothers incentives to become housewives.

The overall situation today compared with that around 1990 is shown in Figure 4.3, where countries are ranked in order of the female percentages of their employed populations in 2013 (for some countries 2012); the dark-shaded bars show the countries' positions around 1990 (for Bulgaria, the Czech Republic and Slovenia the earliest available figures were for 1993; for Slovakia 1994; for Russia 1992; and for Germany 1991). Statistics are not available for all countries of interest to us. It can be seen that during this period the female proportion of the labour force has increased almost everywhere, and in some countries is now close to 50 per cent. The only cases where it has declined, and then from earlier high levels, are Hungary, Slovenia, Romania, slightly in the Czech Republic and marginally in Sweden. Earlier post-1990 declines in Poland and some other CEE countries have now been reversed. Countries that had very low levels (below 40 per cent) around 1990 have had particularly large rises: Cyprus, the Netherlands, Ireland, Switzerland, Belgium, Spain, Luxembourg and, to a lesser extent, Italy and Greece. As a result, there is now far less diversity among countries than had been the case in 1990, which was itself a way station on the overall rise in female employment, at least in the west. Whereas the range in Europe in 1990 had been from 31.82 per cent in Spain to 48.40 per cent in Hungary, it is now from 40.44 per cent in Greece to 48.93 per cent in Estonia. Outside Europe, the United States fits towards the upper end of the European range,

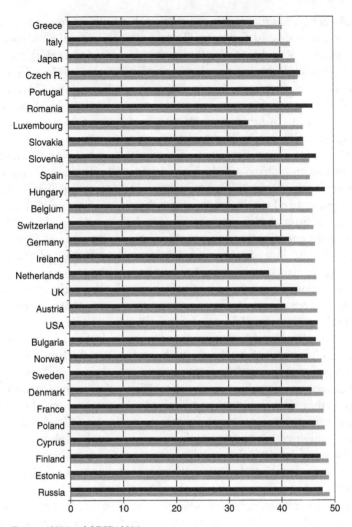

Source: Eurostat, 2014 and OECD, 2014

FIGURE 4.3 *Female percentages of employed population, European countries and main external comparators, c. 1990 (dark shading) and c. 2013 (light shading).*

Japan very much to the lower end of it; but Russia has the highest female proportion of all.

The continuing legacy of the state socialist period can be seen by comparing the female proportion of employment in the two parts of Germany in 1990, the last year in which they existed as separate states:

46.45 per cent in the state socialist DDR, but only 40.06 per cent in the Federal Republic of Germany. Today, all *Länder* of the old German Democratic Republic (including previously divided Berlin) continue to have slightly higher female proportions of the employed population than do all western *Länder* (Statistisches Bundesamt, 2013), with levels of over 48 per cent against a national level of 46.18 per cent. The only western *Land* to have over 47 per cent is Schleswig-Holstein, geographically close to Denmark.

More data are available on a slightly different base for all countries of interest to us from World Bank data on female shares in the total labour force (World Bank, 2015c). This includes women registered as unemployed and seeking work as well those actually in work. Inclusion of the additional FEE countries shows their continuing higher levels of female participation than most western counterparts (Appendix Table A.1, Column E). On the other hand, the inclusion of additional ex-Yugoslavian countries further emphasizes the low level of female participation in much of southern Europe, whether in the east or west. However, female labour force participation since 1990 increased particularly strongly in SWE and also in Ireland and the Benelux (Belgium, the Netherlands and Luxemburg) countries. It declined in several CEE and FEE countries, as well as in Turkey where it was already low.

A key variable in differentiating countries is the size of the sectors in which women are mainly employed, and their relative dominance of certain sectors. This complexity of factors leads to a diversity of patterns. If we concentrate on countries with the highest and lowest levels of female employment (defined as those having overall levels at + or – 0.5 of the standard deviation), and ignore countries for which we do not have up-to-date ISIC data as well as the three smallest economies, we find the pattern shown in Box 4.1.

This leaves a number of countries unaccounted for. Austria, Germany and Ireland have moderately above-average female participation rates, based on a moderately high or low rate across all three sectors. These countries are almost a hybrid between items (1) and (2) in Box 4.1. Belgium and Switzerland resemble these, but with a resulting pattern of female participation somewhat below mean. Overall this means that there are two kinds of economy that feature high levels of female participation: first, those (all in NNWE) with high proportions of women working in large citizen services sectors, even though women's participation in other sectors is low; second, those (all in CEE) with high levels of female participation across a range of sectors, even though the main sector that employs women in most countries, Sector V, is small in these cases.

BOX 4.1   Highest and lowest levels of female employment in
Europe

- *Highest levels*:

  1. The three Baltic states have above-mean manufacturing sectors, below-mean sectors IV and V, but above-mean levels of female participation in each. Similar but with weaker profiles are Bulgaria and Croatia.
  2. Three of the four Nordic countries (excluding Norway) have below-mean manufacturing, above-mean sectors IV and V, but above-mean female participation only in Sector V. Similar but with weaker profiles are the Netherlands, Norway and the United Kingdom.
  3. Portugal has above-mean Sector II and female participation in it, but is low on both variables for sectors IV and V.
  4. France is similar to the Nordics, but with moderately low female participation in Sector II, and moderately high in sectors IV and V.

- *Lowest levels*:

  A. Two southern countries, Greece and Italy, have low female participation in all sectors. Similar but with a weaker profile is Spain.
  B. Certain CEE countries (Czech and Slovak Republics, Hungary, Poland, Slovenia and Romania) have high female participation in Sector II and overall patterns similar to the Baltics, but a relatively low female presence in sectors IV and/or V.

Types of occupation

We now need to examine the kinds of work that people do, before putting those together with the economic sectors. Sociologists and statistical agencies tend to classify occupational types according to a mixture of criteria, reflecting different skill and authority levels and some aspects of the sectoral analysis used above. The current UN standard, the International Standard Classification of Occupations 2008 (ISCO-08), used by the ILO and followed by all European national statistical offices, is based primarily on skill levels, of which the scheme defines four (see Box 4.2).

It should be noted that these skill levels are not defined solely in terms of levels of formal education, as countries differ in their formal

---

BOX 4.2 UN International Standard Classification of Occupations 2008 (ISCO-08)

1. Jobs requiring simple and routine physical or manual tasks, often requiring physical strength but only basic numeracy and literacy. A primary level of education is often all that is necessary, though some jobs in this group may also require basic training.
2. Jobs that usually involve handling, operating or repairing machinery or electronic devices, or the organization and storage of information. A good level of numeracy and literacy is usually required and some social skills. These jobs are usually associated with completion of the first stage of secondary education, and often with further levels of vocational training or qualifications.
3. Jobs involving complex technical, mechanical or organizational skill and interpretive ability, advanced numeracy, literacy and social skills. Some experience of higher education is often a requirement.
4. Jobs involving complex problem-solving and decision-making with extensive knowledge, literacy, numeracy and or social skills. Successful completion of at least first-degree level of university education is often required.

---

requirements for certain jobs even if the content of the work is largely the same. Also, on-the-job experience often counts for at least as much as formal training. This is particularly the case with managerial jobs, managers being primarily defined in terms of their control over the work of others rather than their possession of formally defined professional skills. This concept of 'manager' extends from leading positions in major corporations and governments to managers of small business and organizational units. Despite this wide range, managerial positions account for only between 2 and 11 per cent of jobs in any given national economy. Even so, they cannot be considered to constitute a kind of ruling class; this would constitute a far smaller grouping at the top of the managerial category, and imply political as well as occupational power. This is a topic to which we shall return in later chapters. In general, and with some exception for the managerial group, skill levels suggest differences in income-earning capacity, discretion and control at work, and (particularly to the extent that they reflect different educational backgrounds) in cultural life. It is for this reason that they are of wider sociological interest.

The occupational groups identified by ISCO on this basis are summarized in Box 4.3. It can be seen that the majority of job types in this list – and at least in European countries the majority of the workforce – involve skill level 2. To simplify further discussion, we shall therefore amalgamate several of these. Groups D and E both constitute intermediate levels of non-manual work, so we shall combine them. It has historically been important to distinguish between manual and non-manual work. We shall here therefore provisionally separate D and E from F and G, though we shall inquire into whether this historically important distinction still holds, given that work of many kinds today, whether formerly manual or non-manual, involves using a computer keyboard. We amalgamate F and G, as the distinction between agricultural and largely industrial craft skills is a sectoral rather than a skill division, and we have analysed sectors separately above. There was once also considerable distinction between the kinds of skill involved in groups G and H, but this is diminishing as all come together at skill level 2. Occupations in group I are at a different and lower skill level than all these. This gives us the simple scheme shown in Table 4.2, which can be seen as more or less a vertical one, as positions in it are ranked by a combination of authority, control and skill levels.

Figure 4.4 shows the distributions of employment in European countries across these different types. Data are unfortunately available only for EU member states, Norway and Switzerland. As noted, the managerial category is the smallest in all European countries except a few where it is slightly larger than the 'elementary' worker category: Estonia, Luxembourg, Norway, Sweden, Switzerland and the United Kingdom. The range is from 2 per cent (Denmark and Romania) to 11 per cent (United Kingdom). As the pairing of Denmark and Romania suggests, there are no discernible patterns in these differences. The two 'anglophone' countries (Ireland, 8 per cent, and the United Kingdom) both come high in the scale, but beyond that there is little to distinguish different European regions. One source of variation might be differences in the classification of managerial jobs, some of which might be regarded as professional or some other category. This could be just a meaningless question of different approaches to classification, but it might also tell us something substantive. For example, Denmark is a country in which workers at several levels take on responsibilities that in many other economies are the tasks of a specialized managerial staff (Kristensen, Lotz and Rocha, 2011). In the absence of detailed information of this kind on other countries, we cannot take this discussion further.

BOX 4.3   Occupational groups identified in ISCO-08

A. Managers (typically skill levels 3 and 4) 'plan, direct, coordinate and evaluate the overall activities of enterprises, governments and other organizations, or of organizational units within them, and formulate and review their policies, laws, rules and regulations'.

B. Professionals (typically skill level 4) 'increase the existing stock of knowledge, apply scientific or artistic concepts and theories, teach about the foregoing in a systematic manner, or engage in any combination of these activities'.

C. Technicians and associate professionals (typically skill level 3) 'perform mostly technical and related tasks connected with research and the application of scientific or artistic concepts and operational methods, and government or business regulations'.

D. Clerical support workers (typically skill level 2) 'record, organize, store, compute and retrieve information related, and perform a number of clerical duties in connection with money-handling operations, travel arrangements, requests for information, and appointments'.

E. Service and sales workers (typically skill level 2) 'provide personal and protective services related to travel, housekeeping, catering, personal care, or protection against fire and unlawful acts, or demonstrate and sell goods in wholesale or retail shops, and similar establishments, as well as at stalls and on markets'.

→

TABLE 4.2   *Hierarchy of jobs in advanced economies, ISCO 2008 scheme.*

Managers (3, 4)	Professionals (4)
	Technicians (3)
Clerical support and sales workers (2)	Skilled agricultural and all craft workers (2)
	Plant and machinery operators (2)
Elementary workers (1)	

Note: Numbers in parentheses indicate typical skill levels

A higher proportion of contemporary workforces counts as 'professional', typically the range is between 14 per cent and 24 per cent, with some outliers: Slovakia is at the low end with only 11 per cent; Sweden and Denmark at 26 per cent and 27 per cent respectively, and the small economy of Luxembourg at 33 per cent are the highest. Here there

→

F. Skilled agricultural, forestry and fishery workers (typically skill level 2) 'grow and harvest field or tree and shrub crops, gather wild fruits, breed, tend or hunt animals, produce a variety of animal husbandry products, cultivate, conserve and exploit forests, breed and catch fish and cultivate or gather other forms of aquatic life in order to provide food, shelter and income for themselves and their households'.

G. Craft and related trades workers (typically skill level 2) 'apply specific knowledge and skills in the fields to construct and maintain buildings, form metal, erect metal structures, set machine tools, or make, fit, maintain and repair machinery, equipment or tools, carry out printing work, produce or process foodstuffs, textiles, or wooden, metal and other articles, including handicraft goods'.

H. Plant and machine operators, and assemblers (typically skill level 2) 'operate and monitor industrial and agricultural machinery and equipment on the spot or by remote control, drive and operate trains, motor vehicles and mobile machinery and equipment, or assemble products from component parts according to strict specifications and procedures'. Such tasks are sometimes known as 'semi-skilled' and though this might not properly describe their relationship to those in G, the term is a usefully well-known shorthand.

I. Elementary occupations (typically skill level 1) 'involve the performance of simple and routine tasks which may require the use of hand-held tools and considerable physical effort'.

are some clearer patterns. The anglophone and Nordic economies all have levels in the small high range of 22 per cent to 27 per cent, while the range among southern countries is also small but lower: from 14 per cent to 19 per cent. One might attribute this contrast between regions to differences in national income, and there is a relationship ($r^2 = 0.5564$), but there is then a puzzle. Considerably higher than expected proportions of professionals are found in the Nordic countries (except Norway), Luxembourg, the Netherlands and the United Kingdom; but also in Greece, Estonia, Lithuania and Slovenia. Considerably lower than expected proportions occur in Austria, the Czech Republic, Slovakia and Italy. It is notable that the share of professionals is low in countries with particularly high numbers of employees in Sector II (material production).

The technician group is generally somewhat smaller, ranging widely from 7 per cent to 22 per cent of the workforce. Here the association with national income is still positive, but weaker at $r^2 = 0.3671$. There are no strong patterns, except that employment in this category is

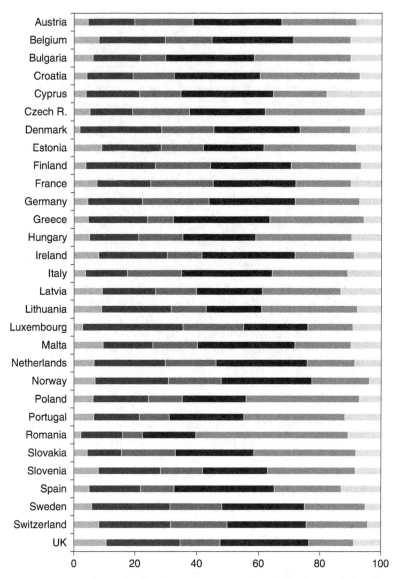

Note: Occupational types, reading from left to right: managerial, professional, technical, clerical and sales, skilled manual, elementary

Source: ILO, 2015

FIGURE 4.4   *Employment by occupational types, European countries, c. 2010.*

particularly low in SWE (except for Italy), the anglophone countries and FEE.

In all western European countries except Portugal clerical and sales workers constitute the largest single category of worker; in Portugal and all CEE countries except Lithuania they are the second largest group (after similarly skilled manual workers). The overall range is extensive, from 17 per cent to 32 per cent. The sharp east–west distinction might suggest an association with growing national income, but there is no statistical association between the variables, and in fact the level is highest in some very poor countries (Bulgaria and Croatia), and (with the exception of Portugal) is higher in SWE than in most of NNWE. On the other hand, the lowest levels are to be found in the remaining FEE countries, while among the highest are the two anglophones.

Skilled manual workers of various kinds are the largest category in all CEE and FEE countries, and the second largest in a diverse group of western cases: Austria, Finland, Germany, Greece, Italy and Malta. Today this kind of employment is negatively related to national income ($r^2 = 0.4433$, or 0.4884 if the two extreme cases of Romania and Luxembourg are disregarded). However, the association is strongly driven by the predominance of manual work in the highly industrial middle-income countries of CEE rather than by the very poorest.

Finally, elementary workers are a minor group in most countries, with a range from 4 per cent to 13 per cent (if one excludes Cyprus at 18 per cent). The level remains under 10 per cent for all except for the majority of SWE (Spain, Italy and Portugal) and two FEE countries (Latvia and Romania).

Although the statistical agencies strive for comparability across countries in the ways that jobs are allocated to the scheme, it is still possible that some variation is caused by different approaches in different countries. We can try partly to overcome this by looking at broader groupings of occupations. This also helps simplify the data and discussions of it. We can amalgamate managerial, professional and technician jobs as constituting a set of what we shall call upper levels in the hierarchy of jobs and skill levels (all at skill levels 3 and 4); clerical, sales and skilled manual occupations as intermediate levels (skill level 2); and elementary employment as lower levels (skill level 1). Figure 4.5 shows the positions of different countries according to this simpler plan. It will be seen that in all cases the greatest number of

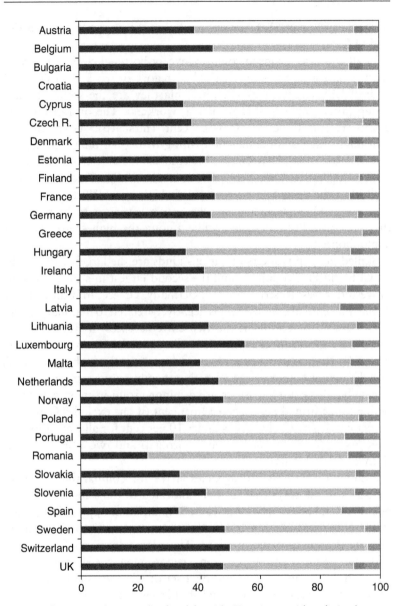

Note: Broad occupational types, reading from left to right: Upper (managerial, professional, technical), Intermediate (clerical and sales, skilled manual), Lower (elementary)

Source: : ILO, 2015

FIGURE 4.5   *Employment by broad occupational types, European countries, c. 2010.*

positions is intermediate (skill level 2), and that there are more upper positions (skill levels 3 and 4) than lower ones (skill level 1), which is a small category almost everywhere.

Clear differences now appear among some groups of countries, though there is very little relationship between any of these occupational types and national income. All NNWE countries have from 39 per cent to 50 per cent of their workforces at the upper levels (if we disregard Luxembourg at 55 per cent). Nearly all members of the SWE group fall below this, with a range of 31 to 35 per cent (if we disregard Malta at 40 per cent), clearly below NNWE. Interestingly, the CEE and FEE countries overlap both groups, CEE ranging from 33 to 42 per cent, and FEE with an exceptionally wide range of 20 to 43 per cent (30 to 43 per cent if the low outlier Romania is ignored). The highest-ranking countries in this group are the three Baltic states.

NNWE countries have distinctly lower levels than the others for intermediate workers, ranging from 30 per cent to 39 per cent. Again, the clearest distinction from this is the SWE group, which ranges from 40 to 48 per cent (ignoring Malta). CEE and FEE can be considered together as one group, with a range from 33 to 46 per cent.

For lower-level occupations, the NNWE and CEE groups are very similar with a shared range of 4 per cent to 10 per cent, and again the extreme contrast is with the SWE group, running from 10 per cent to 13 per cent if the outlier Cyprus is ignored. Again, the FEE countries overlap the others with a range of 7 to 13 per cent.

We can fairly confidently conclude from this that there is a considerable skill gap between the northern and southern parts of western Europe, with the former fulfilling the vision of many observers of an upskilled post-industrial economy, while the southern countries have found a path in primarily lower-skilled activities. It is then interesting to see that several countries in the east, and not only in the relatively wealthier CEE, have similar profiles to NNWE. Particularly strong divisions exist within FEE, with the Baltic states coming closer to both their wealthier CEE neighbours and to NNWE. A north–south division seems to be opening on both sides of the east–west one. This essentially socio-geographical distinction overwhelms any association there might otherwise be between occupational type and national income.

Occupations and gender

Finally, we need to consider the distribution of the genders across the occupational types (Figures 4.6a–f). Overall, around one-third of

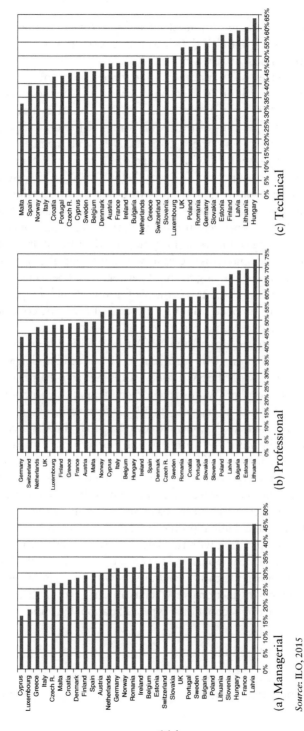

(a) Managerial

(b) Professional

(c) Technical

Source: ILO, 2015

FIGURE 4.6 *Proportions of (a) managerial, (b) professional, (c) technical posts held by women, European countries, c. 2010.*

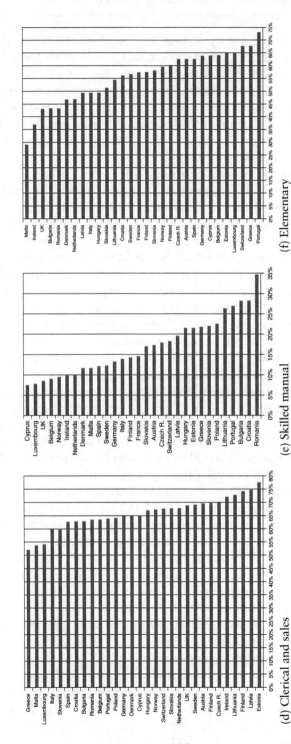

(d) Clerical and sales

(e) Skilled manual

(f) Elementary

Source: ILO, 2015

FIGURE 4.6 *Proportions of (d) clerical and sales, (e) skilled manual, (f) elementary posts held by women, European countries, c. 2010.*

managerial posts are held by women, always a lower level than their participation in the labour force as a whole, which as we have seen ranges from around 45 per cent to 50 per cent (Figure 4.6a). The overall range is from 23 to 39 per cent, if we ignore particularly low scores in two small countries, Cyprus and Luxembourg, and a particularly high one in Latvia. The range in SWE is slightly lower than in the other regions (23 per cent to 33 per cent), but it is notable that there are no notable differences among the others.

The proportion of women in professional positions is considerably higher, and exceeds the proportional level of overall female participation in the labour force in all countries except Germany, and very marginally in Finland, the Netherlands and Switzerland (Figure 4.6b). The overall range is from 43 per cent to 72 per cent. In most countries the female share of professional jobs is over 50 per cent, the exceptions being Austria, Finland, France, Germany, Greece, Luxembourg, Malta, the Netherlands and the United Kingdom – though this list does include the three most populous countries in Europe. If men continue today to dominate managerial positions, the other upper-level posts are now gradually coming to be at least equally shared by women. We can easily relate this to the above discussion of sectors: women tended to occupy a majority of posts in citizenship services, and that is the sector where the highest proportion of professional posts is concentrated, mainly in education and in health and care. There are interesting regional differences here. The highest shares of women in professional posts are clearly in FEE countries, with a range from 57 per cent to 72 per cent, with high levels also in the wealthier CEE cases (53–61 per cent). SWE resembles the Nordic countries (both groups at 47–57 per cent) and the two anglophones (47 per cent and 55 per cent) in interim positions, with the lowest ranges in the rest of NWE (43 per cent to 53 per cent). Several cross-cutting factors produce this unusual combination. First, where economies are not highly advanced there are not many professionals engaged in the material production sector of the economy, leaving citizenship services as by far the main employer of professionals. Professionals in the productive sector are more likely to be men; those in citizenship services, women. This produces the predominance of female professionals in FEE and to a lesser extent in CEE and SWE. Meanwhile, citizenship services employ a greater proportion of the workforce in the Nordic countries than in NWE, which leads to a greater number of female professionals in the former countries.

There is a slightly wider diversity in the employment of women in technical jobs, from 39 per cent to 63 per cent (Figure 4.6c). The figure exceeds that for overall female participation in the three Baltic states, Finland, Germany, Hungary, Ireland, Luxembourg, Netherlands, Poland, Romania, Slovakia, Slovenia, Switzerland and the United Kingdom. There are no particular patterns across regional groupings for this diverse set of positions, which are found in a variety of sectors. A notable point is the high share of women in technical, and indeed professional, jobs in the Baltics – the only countries to date where women constitute a slight majority of the workforce.

Clerical and sales workers are predominantly female, women being above 50 per cent of the workforce in all countries and at 60 per cent or above in all but three (Figure 4.6d). The main geographical feature is again the high proportion of women in the Baltic countries and the low proportion in southern Europe, both west and east.

As one might expect given the dominance of manual work in the heavily male-dominated industrial and to a lesser extent agricultural sectors, the female share of skilled manual employment is low or very low, from 7 per cent to 35 per cent overall (Figure 4.6e). There are clear regional divides here, with all parts of NNWE having particularly low shares (9 per cent to 18 per cent), distinctly higher ones in CEE (15 per cent to 22 per cent) and even more so FEE (19 per cent to 27 per cent). SWE falls between the two, with a range from 10 per cent to 25 per cent (or 21 per cent if one regards Portugal as an outlier). There are indications here that the wealthier the country overall, the fewer women are engaged in manual work. There is in addition probably a continuation of the pattern, discussed earlier in connection with sectors, of women in the former state socialist countries having been more engaged in the workforce, including in manufacturing, than their western counterparts. This may apply particularly to the Baltic states, which had been part of the Soviet Union itself, where this pattern was most dominant. This will also help explain the female dominance of technician jobs in those countries, much technician employment being in manufacturing and allied sectors.

The widest range of female employment is in low-skilled, elementary occupations, overall from 28 per cent to 72 per cent (Figure 4.6f). Three anglophone countries (here including Malta) have a lower level of this employment than any of the others, but apart from that there is little to distinguish the regional groups.

Finally, we can repeat the above exercise of combining these groups of occupations at three main levels. Women occupy between 43 per cent and 62 per cent of positions in the three upper-level forms of employment (managerial, professional and technical), that is a share either just below or considerably above their overall workforce share. It is in fact below the overall share only in Austria, Cyprus, France, Ireland, the Netherlands, Norway, Switzerland and the United Kingdom. The highest levels are found in CEE and FEE, prominently in the Baltic countries; there is interestingly little difference among the different geographical groups of NNWE countries. There is much less diversity in the intermediate group, which brings together the most highly and contrastingly gendered forms of work: clerical and sales against skilled manual – a range from 36 per cent to 48 per cent. Here the NNWE economies tend to have the highest levels, the SWE and CEE cases the lowest, with FEE countries coming in between. Only in the United Kingdom is the level of women's intermediate employment higher than their overall rate. Lower-level employment follows the patterns already outlined above.

Conclusion

Some of the international differences in these proportions of different kinds of worker result from different sectoral balances within countries, as clearly different sectors have differently structured workforces. For example, skilled and semi-skilled manual workers make up between 49 per cent and 66 per cent of the workforce of the material production sector, but everywhere less than 8 per cent of business services and even lower in the citizenship services. Therefore a country like the Czech Republic, with a large industrial sector, is likely to have a higher proportion of skilled manual workers than one such as the United Kingdom, where that sector is small. However, there remains considerable diversity in different national workforces within sectors. To remain with the example already considered, skilled manual workers in the material production sector, these proportions are highest in some CEE and FEE (Romania, Slovakia, Hungary and Estonia) and SWE cases (Greece and Portugal), and lowest in some NNWE ones (France, the Netherlands, Germany, the United Kingdom and Denmark). There are, however, exceptions, with relatively high levels in Sweden and Norway, and a low one in Croatia. This is partly because in the wealthier countries higher proportions of the industrial workforce hold technician status, the range for all NNWE cases being from 11 per cent to 19 per cent, with France an outlier at 24 per cent, while in all except three CEE countries (Croatia, Czech Republic and

Slovakia) it is below 9 per cent. The SWE countries have a wide range, with Greece among the lowest but Italy at 17 per cent.

In two sectors of the economy, IV and V, professionals constitute the biggest single group in the workforce. In Sector IV their share ranges from 23 per cent to 42 per cent (disregarding Luxembourg at 48 per cent). There is no recognizable pattern at all to the differences among countries here. In Sector V the range of professionals is also wide, from 29 per cent to 53 per cent. Again, there are no clear patterns.

The evidence we have considered in this chapter confirms the common-sense perception that much of NNWE has become a post-industrial society, with a high proportion of its workforce in skilled non-manual jobs and with women occupying a high proportion of the posts in key parts of this 'new' economy. Perhaps less widely understood is the role of what we have called here citizenship services, rather than more market-oriented sectors, as the paradigm case of the professionalized and feminized post-industrial economy. Outside this part of Europe these developments are still present, but with more ambiguities. Industrial production remains more important in a central European region that spans the old east–west divide, as it includes Germany and Austria as well as the Czech and Slovak Republics and Hungary. Further east, Belarus and Russia also remain strongly industrial. Countries in the south, both east and west, with the clear exception of Italy, had been slow to leave an agricultural economy, and some FEE countries remain quite rural. These are now passing directly to a post-industrial structure, but, especially in the west, with an emphasis on trading rather than citizenship services.

Since women are far more likely to work in services of most kinds than in manufacturing and construction, the move to economies dominated by services includes a feminization of the paid labour force. Here change is more strongly felt in western than eastern Europe, women having been more economically active in the Soviet system – with its constant labour shortages and lack of religious inhibitions about women in the labour force. Strong differences among countries in the degree of female participation have been remarkably reduced in the past two or three decades, and this reduction takes the form of a convergence towards the Russian and eastern European pattern.

The sectoral and gender characteristics of post-industrial society also have typical implications for the distribution of skill and authority within the workforce. As already noted above, associated with these developments there is a considerable skill gap between the northern and southern parts of western Europe, with the former fulfilling the vision of many observers of an upskilled post-industrial economy, while the southern countries have found a path in primarily lower-skilled activities. Several countries in both CEE and FEE, and not only the wealthier ones, have acquired similar profiles to the NNWE cases. Within FEE the Baltic states are coming closer to both their wealthier CEE neighbours and to Norden and NWE. A north–south division seems to be opening on both sides of the east–west one. These north–south and east–west contrasts are then reflected in gender differences, as variations in the decline of industry and the rise of various services overlap with religious and other earlier factors associated with differences in female labour force participation.

The issues discussed in this chapter are only the beginnings of a consideration of the social implications of work, which shapes so much else of our lives than the jobs that are its primary focus. We shall address more of these in the following chapter.

Chapter 5

From occupations to classes

The different kinds of work that people do have implications for their lives outside the workplace. Work places people in relations to authority that can affect whether they feel among the world's decision-makers (at various levels) or among those who are usually on the receiving end of orders. The kinds of job that we do often reflect the education that we have had, and this will also have shaped our general cultural environment: the kinds of books we read, the music we listen to and the television programmes, films and plays we watch. This will also have been shaped by our parental homes, and this will in turn have been a major determinant of our education. The workplace is often also an important source of friends, partners and associates, where people meet others similar to themselves, reinforcing all these characteristics. The kinds of work we do therefore strongly shape the kinds of person we become.

At least as important as these social and cultural forces is the fact that similar occupations typically bring similar incomes. Their job is the main source of income for the great majority of adults. There are exceptions. Very wealthy people derive an important part of their income from the ownership of property, ranging from real estate to stocks and shares; very poor people, as well as the elderly and the disabled, depend on various welfare-state benefits and pensions. Yet even most of these non-work forms of income are linked to work. Today, more than in past periods, many of the richest people have derived their large wealth from holding senior positions in company management (Piketty, 2013). They join those who have inherited their wealth from earlier generations, and as they pass their own wealth on to their children, these will join the ranks of a new generation of inheritors. The poor are poor because they either are too disabled or sick to work, can only find work that offers very low incomes or can find no work at all, except only occasionally. The incomes of many elderly people are based on pension schemes to which they belonged during their working lives, and which pay a return based on the earnings they derived from that work.

Work and its income therefore do much to determine our lives. We can distinguish between two aspects of this, which (following Max Weber, 1922) sociologists term lifestyle and life chances. Differences of lifestyle can initially be seen just as differences without implications of inequality: some people prefer some sports to others, or some kinds of music to others; or they consistently choose clothes of a certain style. Such cultural differences are not necessarily ranked according to some criterion of social prestige; but they often are. For example, the game of Association football emerged in its modern form in 19th-century England in elite schools and the ancient universities of Oxford and Cambridge. Fairly soon, however, it became popular among young working men and boys, and at some point in the early 20th century became a primarily working-class sport. Elite schools then started to avoid it and instead favoured rugby union football. Whether one played or watched Association or rugby union football became a kind of badge of class identity in England – though not in Wales, where rugby was a mass sport. (A different form of rugby football, known as rugby league, flourishes in northern England as a distinctly working-class sport – mainly because it became professional long before rugby union, enabling working men to earn a living from it.) Today Association football ('soccer') has become a global game attracting support from all classes. Nothing intrinsic to the sport itself has determined its curious social career. In Italy opera is a popular art form; it is not possible to use a love of opera as a means of distinguishing an elite from other social groups – though access to first-class opera houses like La Scala in Milan will certainly be limited by the high price of tickets. In the United Kingdom, in contrast, opera tends to be seen as an art form that people would be able to enjoy only if they come from certain family backgrounds and education. Love of opera can therefore be used as a social distinction; and dislike of opera can be used to demonstrate rejection of that kind of social distinction. All this can go on without any serious reference to whether people actually like or dislike the music.

In contrast with lifestyles, life chances refer *explicitly* to the unequal opportunities that people in different occupations and income levels have of achieving certain generally desirable states. For example, if one person comes from a poor family and has had to spend her early life in damp, unhealthy living conditions, whereas another had an affluent childhood in fine houses, then the former is very likely to die younger than the latter. That is pure life chance. Longevity and the chances of incurring various physical and mental illnesses provide some of the main examples of inequality of life chance produced by different occupational and income backgrounds. The occupations performed by those on low incomes are often (though not always) the most dangerous or unhealthy, and this combined with low income means that poorer people usually suffer more from diseases and disablement and die younger than wealthier people in comfortable jobs. Further, higher-earning occupations tend (though not always) to be those requiring higher educational preparation, and the children of well-educated parents grow up in a family culture that makes it easier for them to succeed at education than their contemporaries whose parents have occupations requiring little formal education. This in turn enables culturally advantaged children also to acquire higher-paid jobs. In this way the life chances of one generation are passed on to the next.

Differences of lifestyle are not necessarily involved in unequal life chances, but might be. If one person prefers wine to beer and another prefers beer to wine, that might just be lifestyle. However, if the latter's beer-drinking leads to him being excluded from social circles that can bring important opportunities, then his lifestyle has negatively affected his life chances. The relationship between lifestyle and issues of hierarchy and inequality is therefore complex and even arbitrary, though there is often a kind of rationale involved. Elite groups tend to develop lifestyles that require considerable preparation through family and education as means of distinguishing themselves as superior. This is partly because such preparation can in itself be costly, and partly because ability to have spent time on preparation can be a signal that one is too rich to have to spend much time working. This latter has become less important in modern times, when many large fortunes result from highly paid occupations rather than from inheritance. Cultural distinctiveness today is more likely to emerge through education. Cultural and other lifestyle choices are strongly affected by educational experience, and are therefore likely to be related to types of work. People *can* acquire access to cultural styles different from those in which they were brought up; those who leave school early can in later life discover an interest in lifestyles usually associated with experience of higher education; people with an elite upbringing can enjoy popular culture. But in general there will be strong links of this kind. If lifestyles can successfully be ranked in this way, they become forms of inequality and become implicated in differences in life chances.

The combination of occupation and income is therefore a powerful determinant of inequalities of life chances and differences of lifestyles and therefore of importance far beyond the workplace. Almost every individual occupies a specific place among the myriad different aspects of lifestyle and life chance that affect us, with a mixture of educational background, job, income, cultural preferences, health and other characteristics that makes him or her as unique as an individual snowflake or fingerprint. But it is also the case that these individuals come in clusters. One could see a group of 50 people, 25 of whom are highly paid managers and 25 of whom are poorly paid elementary workers as just 50 human beings, all of whom are different from each other. But that would involve refusing to see that there were far more similarities among individuals within the two sub-groups than between any two individuals chosen across the sub-groups. It is these broad similarities within occupational and income groups that lead sociologists to talk of social classes, and to identify class-related inequalities in health and many other aspects of life. That is at least part of the story of class; there is another equally important aspect concerned with politics and power, which we shall consider in the next chapter. First we must pick up where we left the last chapter, and explore the link between occupations, incomes and class.

Occupations, income and social class

The analysis of occupations in Chapter 4 gave us elements of hierarchy. Within organizations people in managerial jobs are able to give commands to those lower down; and since a capacity to give commands is usually accompanied by higher incomes, we should expect them to earn more than their subordinates too. People in occupations requiring high levels of education are likely to earn more than those with lower levels, as the higher the level of education a job demands, the smaller is the supply of potential candidates. Senior managerial positions are also likely to be held by people who have high levels of education. We should therefore expect the highest incomes to be enjoyed by managers, with professionals coming next, followed by technicians, then by skilled manual and non-manual workers, with the lowest-skilled earning the least. There will be further differences of incomes within each of these groups, reflecting skill, experience and organizational position – especially within the managerial group with its long hierarchies reaching from chief executive officers at the head of global corporations to supervisors of small work groups. Unfortunately only a very few countries – Austria, the Czech Republic, Denmark, Germany, Poland, Switzerland and the United Kingdom – publish data that match the occupational scale used in Chapter 3 with average earnings. However, those that do publish them are located in different parts of Europe, which enables us to explore the expectations in some detail.

Appendix Table A.4 displays mean annual incomes by occupational group for these countries, expressed as a ratio of the group mean to the overall national mean for all incomes, alongside the relative size of the various occupational categories. The only one of our provisional geo-social groups not covered is SWE, Poland being at least as representative of eastern as of central Europe on several dimensions. The German data are calculated on a slightly different classification of occupations and on a sample of those, and are not therefore strictly comparable. The Swiss figures are based on median rather than mean incomes, and those for Denmark and Germany are not divided by gender. Further, the ratios between the incomes of the different groups are not calculated according to the same scale. For example, it seems from the figure that the gap between managers and others is greater in Denmark than elsewhere, whereas the opposite is the case. For example, the ratio of managers' earnings to those of elementary workers in Denmark is 2.30 while that in the United Kingdom is 4.02. These statistics cannot therefore be used to make comparisons among countries, but to gain an idea of the overall structure of income differences within them.

We can make some generalizations, which will probably hold for other advanced economies in Europe and elsewhere:

- Everywhere managers' incomes are, on average, considerably higher than those for all other groups. This is the case even though the category of manager covers a very wide range of posts. At the present time that gap is growing in many countries.
- Professionals come a clear second, and after them technical staff.
- These three groups are in general the only ones whose mean incomes come above the national means for all incomes. Between them they hold the positions identified in the previous chapter as having a combination of workplace power and higher levels of education.
- There is no clear ranking between clerical and skilled or semi-skilled industrial workers; the order among these varies, and they are always close together. In industrial society the division between clerical and skilled manual work had been very important for class structure, with the former comprising, with managers and various professionals and technicians, part of the 'office' against manual workers in the 'factory'. This division survived even as, gradually, the earnings of skilled manual workers rose above those of clerical workers. Today,

as skilled factory work in the advanced economies has fewer of the characteristics of dirt, noise and physical danger associated with earlier industrialism, this distinction becomes of little or no importance. The class analysis of post-industrial societies therefore has almost no need of this formerly fundamental distinction.

- These last two groups, and to some extent the technicians, come relatively close together, though skilled agricultural workers are usually at some distance below the others.
- Sales and service staff and elementary workers are always the lowest paid. In general they have the lowest education levels and are at the base of chains of command.

With the exception of the United Kingdom, managers constitute less than 10 per cent of all persons employed in the countries we are able to study here. Given their high average incomes, they are the elite of the workforce, though as we shall see in the following chapter only a smaller sub-set of senior executives constitutes the real elite of most countries. At the other end of the scale, elementary workers potentially constitute a small socially excluded out-group of the poor and the low skilled. Here will be found what is increasingly becoming known as the 'precariat' (Standing, 1999, 2011), people with highly insecure or temporary jobs, or working on zero-hours contracts. Under a zero-hours contract (mainly found in the United Kingdom) workers have to stand by to be available for work during a certain period but are paid only when the employer offers them actual work. The most difficult forms of such contracts for workers to manage are when they are not permitted to work for other employers during the time when the employer has them available on call.

With the exception of Poland, agricultural workers constitute a similar minority. Although they are classified as skilled, their incomes are usually low. They are the remains of an earlier form of pre-industrial economy. Semi-skilled workers are also a small group. They are partly factory workers with skill levels just below those classified as skilled, and partly people working in transport and logistics. Given that their incomes are usually close to those of skilled manual workers, they are best amalgamated with that group, as we did in Chapter 4. With the exception of Austria and Germany, clerical workers also come below the 10 per cent level. This represents an important social change since classic industrial society, where large numbers of routine office employees paralleled large numbers of factory workers. Automation and the computer have reduced the importance of both.

These data confirm the arguments of many sociologists that what had been seen as the pyramid of industrial (and indeed pre-industrial) society has been replaced by a diamond. That is, in place of a small elite, a moderately sized middle-income group and a large proletarian mass at the base the lowest groups have declined in size while the middle ones have grown. This has happened through the rise of professional and technical occupations and the decline of routine industrial work.

Gender and occupational class

The picture changes in interesting ways if we take account of differences between the genders. There is a difficulty in making this comparison, since women are far more likely than men to work part-time; the annual earnings of part-timers are obviously lower than their full-time counterparts. Also, the proportion of women in the paid labour force who work part-time varies across countries, which has various distorting effects when we make comparisons. For example, in a country where there are few opportunities for part-time work, and therefore where the few women in paid employment are full-timers, their earnings will be closer to their male counterparts than in countries where there are many part-time jobs, therefore more women working, and therefore a bigger gap with male earnings. We could resolve these problems by examining hourly rather than annual earnings, but that would give a misleading view of the actual income that men and women are receiving. In a discussion of social class, we are interested in the link between work and life chances/styles. This means we are interested in actual income levels rather than hourly rates. If women earn less because they work part-time as a result of having to do more household and childcare tasks than men, that constitutes a handicap to their ability to secure high earnings and is therefore relevant to their class position.

Consideration of household tasks reminds us of a further difficulty for class analysis. Many people live in households with more than one earner (typically a man and a woman, but sometimes people of the same sex, or groups of friends, or employed family members of more than one generation); many others live in households with only one earner but more than one adult (with the same variety of combinations as households with more than one earner); other households comprise only one adult, with or without children. These differences will affect life chances and lifestyles; a couple, both members of which work in moderately paid occupations, may earn more than one in which only one member has a highly paid job. These issues are relevant to class position, and are among the reasons why the class analysis of advanced economies is highly complex. It used to be conventional for sociologists to resolve this problem by arguing that, since wives' employment was usually much more lowly paid (mainly through being part-time) and also more likely than husbands' to be interrupted by spells out of the labour force (mainly for childbirth and childcare), their work should be ignored and class analysis confined to men's occupations. Whatever its justification at some points in history, this approach became increasingly implausible as female labour force participation grew in most countries, and as state and other provision for maternity leave and assistance with childcare was increased – albeit at different speeds and to different extents in different countries. Ignoring women's work eventually meant that class analysis was neglecting nearly half of all paid work. Also, as marriage rates declined, it was also ignoring all households where there was no male earner. Further, taking no account of female work meant treating occupations where women dominated (such as some professions, clerical work, and sales and service employment) only in terms of the small proportion of males in them. Here we shall follow normal contemporary practice and examine both genders, together (as above) and separately (as below).

Unfortunately we now lose more countries from our small initial group, as available Danish data do not provide separate information for men and women, and the general comparability problems of the German statistics make it unwise to use them for these finer analyses. The following generalizations seem to hold across the remaining five countries, and we can probably assume that they are also valid for the great majority of other European and advanced economies.

- With a small number of exceptions, women's earnings are always lower than those of men in similar occupations; this is especially the case in the higher-paid groups, where there is typically a wide range of earnings within the group concerned. This gender gap results from a combination of women tending to occupy the more junior positions within a category, their being in part-time work, and (where this is legally possible) from the existence of many women's rates of pay that are lower than men's. In particular, female managers usually have earnings more similar to those of male professionals rather than other male managers; in Austria their earnings are closer to those of male technicians.

TABLE 5.1 *Ratio of occupational group incomes to national means, by gender.*

	Managerial		Elementary	
	All	Male	All	Female
Austria	2.17	3.14	0.56	0.44
Czech Rep.	2.16	2.35	0.56	0.51
Poland	2.07	2.37	0.58	0.53
Switzerland	1.45	1.55	0.66	0.75
United Kingdom	1.93	2.17	0.48	0.32

- The numerical dominance of a particular gender in an occupational type, combined with a wide inter-gender income disparity, means that one gender's earnings are more closely typical or paradigmatic of those in the occupational type concerned. Thus men's earnings as managers and (except in Poland) as skilled and semi-skilled industrial workers are more typical of those occupations; women's earnings are more typical of clerical (again except in Poland) and sales and services jobs.

Some of the main overall effects of these elements are summarized in Table 5.1, which presents mean incomes for the gendered occupational groups at the extremes of earnings (i.e. managers and elementary workers) as ratios to the overall national mean for all occupations and both genders. In each case the ratio of the mean of male managerial earnings to the national mean is higher than that for all managerial earnings, and the lower is that of the mean of women working in elementary occupations.

Income inequality, taxation, transfers and public services

These statistics by themselves tell us only a limited amount about the overall level of inequality in a society. Other factors, apart from the incomes typical of occupational types and the numbers working in them that we have considered so far, affect this, including: sources of income apart from occupational earnings; the combination of all kinds of shared earnings of individuals within households; and the effects of government policies of taxation, income transfers and social policy spending. We also need to get beyond the averages of earnings of occupational groups, which obviously conceal a large amount of internal variation.

Included in sources of income apart from occupational earnings will be incomes from investments of inherited wealth and persons' own savings, and rents from properties that are owned and let to others. Occupational positions tend to be partly inherited, since, as we have seen, parents usually pass on their educational level to their children, and high investment earnings (including rents) are clearly related to the savings opportunities of past and present generations, which are in turn related to occupational earnings. Investment income therefore tends to exacerbate the inequalities that result from occupational earnings, and from inherited social positions; people towards the bottom of the income distribution are likely to have no incomes of these kinds at all. These other forms of income therefore tend to reinforce class inequalities.

The combination of individuals' earnings of all kinds as household earnings is more complex, because class is by no means the only factor determining whether one or more member of a household is in paid employment or whether people live in single-adult, two-adult or multi-adult households. Class effects are, however, reinforced as we move from individuals to households, because of the tendency to assortative mating. People are likely to form relationships with and to marry individuals from similar cultural, educational and economic backgrounds to themselves, if only because their social circles tend to reflect these similarities. Overall therefore there will be a relationship between individuals' occupational class position and the level of living of the household in which they live, and therefore between individuals' class positions and inequality among households, though this relationship will not be as direct as that between individuals' income and their non-occupational earnings.

These trends are being strongly affected by the rise in women's participation in higher education. When men dominated it, the majority of men necessarily married women of a lower educational level than themselves. This has gradually changed until in many countries and for younger generations more women than men have attended universities and similar institutions. Given the increase in female labour force participation, there are far more likely today to be families where each partner has a graduate-level job, and therefore also where neither has such a job. This is very likely to lead to an increase in overall inequality (Blossfeld, 2009).

According to research by Van Bavel (2012), before 1970 the ratio of men to women having education at higher level was over 2:1 in several countries, mainly in NWE: Belgium, Germany, Spain, Austria and Switzerland. It was slightly below that in Hungary, the United States, Greece, Czechoslovakia, Russia, France, Denmark, the United Kingdom and Italy. In some further countries, however, there was already rough parity between men and women: Romania, Finland, Ireland, the Ukraine and the Netherlands; while in others again, mainly in northern and eastern Europe, women already outnumbered men: Norway, Slovenia, the three Baltic states, Poland, Portugal, Bulgaria, Sweden and also Canada. By the 1980s or 1990s women had become the majority in higher education in most countries covered in the above lists. Belgium, Germany and the Czech Republic crossed the line by 2000; Austria by 2010. Only Switzerland remains with a slight male majority. The United Kingdom had been an early case of female dominance (by 1980), but female participation then slipped back, not overtaking men again until around 2010.

There is, however, no clear relationship between this potentially major force for increased household inequality and the overall state of inequality in individual countries. These overall levels will be discussed in detail below, but we can now note that among those with until recently a strong male dominance are some highly inegalitarian countries (e.g. Spain, United States and Greece) and some egalitarian ones (Hungary, the Czech and Slovak Republics). Among those with a long-standing gender balance or slight female dominance are some relatively equal countries (all the Nordics), as well as some with high levels of inequality (the Baltic states and Canada).

The actions of government policies on inequality tend to reduce the inequalities stemming from family background and the market. Many, though by no means all, forms of taxation take more from those on higher incomes. Income tax, for example, is usually 'progressive', in that higher rates are imposed on higher earnings. However, in recent years some international organizations have been encouraging governments to move towards 'flat taxes', which tax people at all income levels at the same rates. (This was based on a belief that increasing inequality would improve economic growth. More recently, however, some of these same organizations, such as the OECD, have changed their view on this, and have concluded that in some countries inequality is reaching levels where it inhibits consumption by the mass of the population and might therefore be damaging growth.) Within Europe, governments of the Baltic states and some others in central and eastern

Europe have adopted flat taxes. These undermine the reduction of income inequalities usually achieved by income taxation, especially in favour of the very rich, unless high-income thresholds are set before people start paying income tax at all. Property taxes and taxes on investment incomes and capital gains tend also to reduce inequalities, though there have been general trends in recent years for these income forms to be taxed less heavily than earnings from work. Taxes on sales, such as value added taxes, are regressive, in that they hit people irrespective of their income and therefore take more tax as a proportion of income from the poor than from the rich. However, since wealthier people tend to buy more goods and services they contribute more overall to revenues from these taxes. Meanwhile, some people find legal (and illegal) ways of avoiding paying tax. To do this often involves paying for expensive legal and accountancy advice and having means of changing the national jurisdiction under which one is taxed. It is only wealthy people and large corporations who can do this. The overall impact of taxation systems is therefore complex, though in the end it can be reduced to some simple aggregate effects, as we shall see below.

Governments also affect the income distribution by using tax revenue to allocate money to certain categories of person. The elderly, chronically sick and disabled typically receive state pensions because they are considered unable to work. People unable to find work, or having and caring for small children, or temporarily too sick to work, will often be entitled to various benefits to provide them with some income as they have none from an occupation. Others in jobs that provide insufficient income to achieve a reasonable level of subsistence might receive state support towards certain costs (such as housing) or pay negative rates of income tax (usually known as tax credits). Many of these redistributions reduce overall inequalities, as they are mainly directed to people without other forms of income, though many pension schemes favour people formerly on high earnings. Finally, governments often provide various services, mainly education, health, other forms of care, policing, the maintenance and subsidization of transport networks and cultural and natural resources. If these are provided free or at low cost at the point of use, being financed by tax revenues, they will tend to offset income inequalities, because access to them is independent of ability to pay. For example, if children are educated without fees being charged directly to their parents, then the effect of income inequality on education will be less than if parents had to find the costs from their earnings – though the cultural and other factors affecting educational inequality discussed above will still apply.

Overall therefore governments' taxing and spending activities are likely to reduce the effect of inequalities of occupational class on living standards. It is difficult to assess, country by country, the effects of all these factors on the initial inequalities of occupational income. Even if we could do so, it would be impossible to relate them in detail to the different occupational classes that we have considered, as no country produces data on that basis. We can, however, attempt a more limited task. We know broadly the inequalities that exist between different occupational types, and we have seen how other forms of income (apart from government transfers and services) are likely to reinforce these. If we can then find summary data on the overall state of inequality of incomes before considering government taxation and spending, we can safely assume that these bear a close relationship to the differences in earnings among occupational types that we have observed.

The main statistic that is used to measure overall income inequality is the Gini coefficient, named after the Italian statistician, Corrado Gini, who developed it in the early 20th century. The Gini coefficient sums all incomes within a given unit (in our case and in most other studies a country) and expresses them as a statistic where, if all income were concentrated in the hands of one individual or household, the score would be one, and if there was perfect equality it would be zero. Thus, a country with a Gini coefficient of 0.25 has a considerably lower level of inequality than one with a score of 0.50. Nowadays these numbers are calculated by international organizations on a more or less comparable basis, though one must always be aware that such measures are only as good as the quality of the statistical services of the governments contributing to them. Where this quality is poor, or where there is considerable dishonesty in reporting incomes, the resulting statistics will be unreliable. It must also be remembered that Gini data are usually based on households, and necessarily assume equality of access by a household's members to its earnings. Any systematic inequality of treatment within households, as may happen if a single (usually male) earner controls all income, will not be registered.

The Gini coefficient takes account of all incomes within a society, which for many purposes is what we want to know. However, because the majority of incomes are bunched around the mid-point of a given distribution, it is not so good at dealing with inequality at the extremes: the existence of a very small number of extremely rich people, or of poor groups whose level of living falls way below that of the great majority of people, will not be picked up by the Gini statistic. To gain a richer overall indication of levels of inequality it is therefore also necessary to consider other data concerning the extremes of the distribution. Some attempt has also been made by international organizations to collect relevant data here, though with the same warnings about the quality and comparability of data.

Figure 5.1 displays the Gini coefficients for pre-tax income inequality by household for all countries in our study in membership of the OECD and for Russia. It is not possible to relate differences among these countries to differences in occupational class structure. For example, Switzerland and the United Kingdom appeared in our earlier discussion as having similar structures, but Switzerland is the most egalitarian country in Figure 5.1 after Iceland, while the United Kingdom is the fourth most unequal.

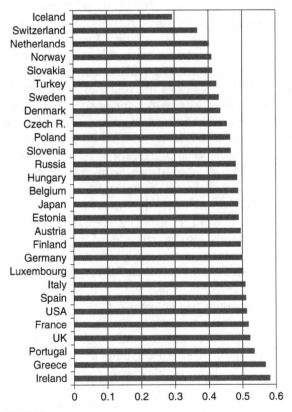

Source: OECD, 2015a

FIGURE 5.1   *Gini coefficients before taking account of taxes and state transfers, certain OECD member states (2012) and Russia (2009).*

There is no statistical relationship at all between national income and pre-tax inequality ($r^2 = 0.00121$), but we can make considerably more sense of the data if we consider some regional groups alongside national income. The Scandinavian and CEE countries (one wealthy group, one poor) tend to have lower levels of inequality than their national incomes might lead us to expect, while the anglophones and SWE countries as well as Turkey (one wealthy group, one relatively poor) have higher. NWE countries are mixed, and we have insufficient data for cases in FEE.

The situation after we have taken account of taxes and money transfers (such as pensions and unemployment pay), leaving households with what is known as 'disposable' income, is shown in Figure 5.2. The overall level of inequality is reduced everywhere, as expected.

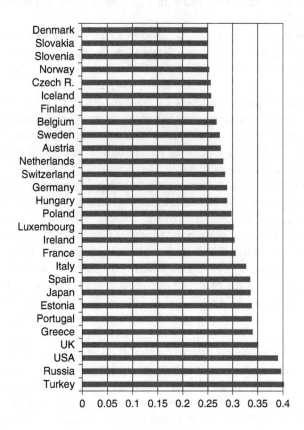

Source: OECD, 2015a

FIGURE 5.2 *Gini coefficients after taking account of taxes and state transfers, certain OECD member states (2012) and Russia (2009).*

Again, there is no overall statistical relationship between national income and post-tax inequality ($r^2 = 0.0670$), but when we set regional groups in relation to income interesting patterns again appear. Nordic and CEE countries continue to have levels of inequality lower than expected, and anglophone ones and those in SWE to have higher levels – though Ireland has now become more egalitarian, reducing the anglophone group to just the United Kingdom and United States. We can now also see something of a contrast between the majority of Europe and the external comparators. Both the United States and Russia have extreme levels of post-tax inequality. Japan is less extreme, but has a similar level to Spain, Portugal, Greece and the United Kingdom. In other words, if we exclude most of SWE and the United Kingdom, Europe appears as a relatively egalitarian world region. The CEE countries, but not necessarily those in FEE, share fully in this European model.

The relationship between pre- and post-tax and transfer inequality varies widely among countries. Several carry out extensive redistribution even though their initial distributions of income were already relatively egalitarian, especially Norway, Denmark, and the Czech and Slovak Republics. Others become relatively egalitarian following state action despite having had more unequal initial distributions, while Russia, Turkey and the United States arrive as the most unequal countries of all because of weak redistributive policies on the basis of existing unequal distributions.

We have used OECD data in order to compare pre- and post-tax and transfer situations, but if we are interested in post-tax and -transfer income alone, data are available for a wider range of countries from Eurostat and the International Monetary Fund (IMF), enabling us to add some information for the missing eastern European countries. The basis of calculation may not be strictly comparable and the numbers must be treated with care, but for most cases their implications are clear: Bulgaria 0.384; Latvia 0.370; Lithuania 0.417; Romania 0.277. With the exception of Romania, these are towards the high end of the overall range, higher even than Estonia, so far the country in all eastern Europe with the highest level of inequality. Romania would seem to be among the more egalitarian countries, but its data are for only 2005. In general FEE as opposed to CEE emerges as a region of high post-tax inequality, similar to but not as extreme as neighbouring Russia.

Finally, for OECD member states alone we can also examine the effect of public services. It is important to include these in our calculations of inequality if possible. There is likely to be less inequality in a society where the public has access free at the point of receipt to education and health than in one with the same level and inequality of disposable income but where this income has to pay for these basic services. Making such calculations is difficult, however. One can fairly safely assume that, where there is compulsory schooling up to a certain age, each child has equal access to that schooling. Tertiary education, on the other hand, is more likely to be enjoyed by children from wealthier families, or from families where the parents' occupations have themselves required higher education. Public spending on tertiary education is therefore likely to be skewed towards the wealthy. More complex calculations are involved in working out which income groups are likely to benefit from elderly care, family services, subsidized public transport or the police. The OECD (2011) has tried to factor all these components into calculations of overall inequality. The results are shown in Figure 5.3. Unfortunately there are no data for

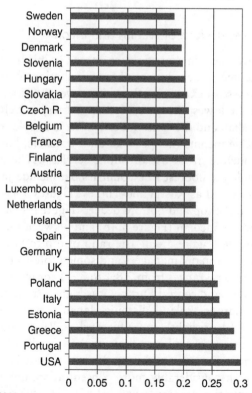

Source: OECD, 2011

FIGURE 5.3 *Gini coefficients after taking account of taxes, state transfers and imputed use of public services, certain OECD member states, 2007.*

Japan and Russia. These data cannot be compared directly with those for taxes and transfers only, as they relate to 2007 and not 2011, and a good deal happened to income inequalities during those few years. However, they again show that most Nordic countries have been the most egalitarian, followed by CEE, while Estonia and Poland are (with SWE and the United States) among the most inegalitarian. NWE countries (including Ireland and now also the United Kingdom) fall between these various extreme groups.

Gini coefficients after taxes and transfers and after taking account of imputed services are very closely related to each other indeed, with $r^2 = 0.9615$, which means partly that services do not have anything like the same impact on inequality as taxes and transfer payments, and partly that countries behave rather similarly on the two aspects – i.e. countries with high levels of redistributive taxation and transfer payments also have redistributive services.

Extreme concentrations of wealth and income

As noted above, the Gini statistic does not tell us much about concentrations of income at the extremes of the distribution. We gain a better indication of these by examining the ratio between top incomes, middle incomes and the lowest incomes, represented respectively by the top decile, the median and the bottom decile. The available statistics here cover disposable income (i.e. post-tax and -transfers, but not including imputed income from use of public services). These are OECD data, so exclude the poorest FEE countries but include Japan and the United States as well as Russia and Turkey. Figures 5.4a–c shows the ratios: between the top and bottom deciles (Figure 5.4a), between the top decile and the median (Figure 5.4b) and between the median and the bottom decile (Figure 5.4c). The ratio of top to bottom incomes (in general, that of many managers and some professionals to that of elementary workers) ranges from 2.8:1 to 3.6:1 for most of Continental north-western and central Europe; it is higher, from 4.2:1 to 4.9:1 for southern Europe, Poland, Estonia, Japan and the United Kingdom, and at 6.0:1 or slightly more for Turkey, Russia and the United States. This pattern is similar to that for the Gini distribution of disposable incomes. The ratio of the top decile to the median is of course far smaller, with considerably more concentration among countries. Nearly all fit into the ratio range of 1.6:1 to 2.0:1, with a few at higher levels (Portugal, the United Kingdom, Estonia, Italy, the United States, Turkey and Russia). Overall the patterns of countries are similar across these figures and similar to what we found from the Gini coefficients.

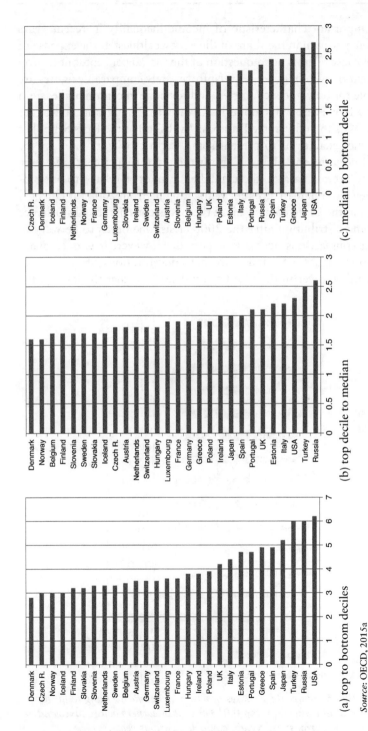

(a) top to bottom deciles

(b) top decile to median

(c) median to bottom decile

Source: OECD, 2015a

FIGURE 5.4 *Ratio of (a) top to bottom deciles, (b) top decile to median, (c) median to bottom decile of income distribution after taxes and transfers, certain OECD member states (2012) and Russia (2009).*

An important characteristic of income inequality in recent years has been a growth in the share of the very wealthiest at the expense of everyone else. This is not a question of the top 10 per cent, but the top 1 per cent or even 0.01 per cent. Unfortunately comparable figures are available for only a few countries, and for none in central and eastern Europe. However, work done by Alvaredo, Piketty and colleagues (World Wealth and Income Database (website)) at the Paris School of Economics enables us to present some statistics (Figure 5.5a for the top 1.0 per cent and Figure 5.5b for the top 0.01 per cent). We here return to pre-tax data, so these numbers cannot be related to our others. They also relate to different years, ranging from 2005 for Portugal to 2014 in the United States. Since there was considerable disturbance to income distribution after the 2008 crisis, one needs to be wary in making comparisons across that period. However, it is once again clear from Figure 5.5a and 5.5b that concentrations of income are considerably lower in the Nordic countries, and that the level in the

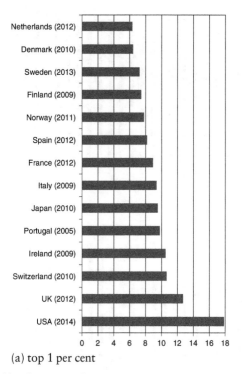

(a) top 1 per cent

Source: World Wealth and Income Database, 2015

FIGURE 5.5   *Percentage shares of national income accruing to (a) top 1 per cent of earners, (b) top 0.01 per cent of earners before taxes and transfers, certain countries, various years.*

United States is higher than anywhere in Europe for where we have records (or Japan).

A growing concentration of incomes at the very top has been in progress for over 30 years in the United States, setting in somewhat later in Europe. The immediate impact of the financial crisis was to reduce these very high incomes, but they then recovered quickly and in the most recent years have advanced considerably faster than those of the rest of the population. An OECD staff paper (Förster, Llena-Nozal and Nafilyan, 2014) considered this phenomenon in detail, presenting data on the share of overall income *growth* captured by the top 1.0 per cent of the population from 1975 and 2007 (i.e. just before the crisis). The results are shown in Figure 5.6. Unfortunately again numbers were available for only a few countries, and none in CEE. Diversity among Continental European countries cannot easily be related to our earlier categorization, and there are too few cases on which to base generalizations, though it does seem that once again the Nordic countries were

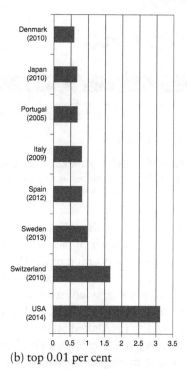

(b) top 0.01 per cent

FIGURE 5.5 *Continued*

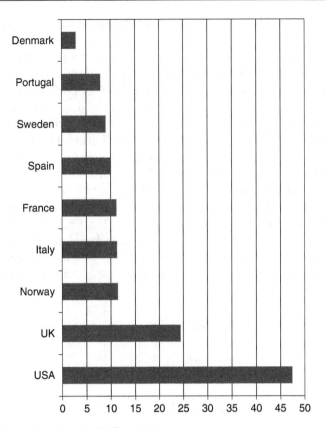

Source: Förster, Llena-Nozal and Nafilyan, 2014

FIGURE 5.6   *Share of growth of national income accruing to top 1.0 per cent of earners before taxes and transfers, certain countries, 1975–2007.*

more egalitarian than most others, though southern countries have not shown the heavy increase in the share of the very wealthy that we might have expected. The inegalitarian position of the United States, and to a lesser extent the United Kingdom, is again extraordinary.

Thomas Piketty (2013) has examined trends in earnings and wealth over a far longer period, back to the late 18th century for France, slightly later for England and the United States, and from the late 19th century for Germany, Italy and some others. Problems of the availability of data for such a long time span prevented anything more extensive. He argues that there is a long-term trend towards an ever greater concentration of wealth among the most wealthy, because in general interest rates have historically given a higher return than growth in the economy as represented by the joint effect of increases in productivity and in population size. This trend was interrupted when two world wars had wreaked havoc on the traditional, rentier wealth-holding that had sustained extreme inequalities for many decades and perhaps for centuries. This reduction in inequality was accompanied by three decades of rapidly rising productivity and, for a while, of population. Then, during the 1970s several factors started to come together to restore the historically more 'normal' process of extreme and increasing inequality. For various reasons, economic growth in the advanced countries started to slow down and population growth stalled, as we saw in Chapter 2. Gradually also the globalization of the economy shifted the balance of economic power in favour of capital and against labour: capital can move quickly around the world to take advantage of varying profit opportunities, while labour is (with the exception of the difficult process of emigration) largely fixed in its place. A mobile factor of production has major competitive advantages over a largely static one.

There is, however, no simple return to the pre-World War I pattern. Until the wars, when inflation and other disruptive forces of the mid-20th-century period started to damage inheritances, the typical wealth-holder was a rentier who did no work. Today it is more likely to be an extremely highly paid executive, the top end of the managerial occupational category, who uses his (occasionally her) very high income to lay up a store of inheritable capital for his family. The executive's primary income comes from employment, even if this often takes the form of stock options. Today therefore the division of national income into a capital and a labour share is only an accounting distinction, not one that identifies a capitalist and a working class. But the key to growing inequality is the conversion of resources, whatever their original source, into investment capital. Piketty shows that it was a decline in capital, not income, inequality that produced the equalizing trends that endured until the late 1970s, though he does not consider the redistributive fiscal processes that we have discussed above. He also demonstrates how extremely high wealth-holdings achieve a higher rate of growth than even slightly smaller ones. Then inheritance intensifies the inequality even further, as we have already discussed above; and the process seems set to spiral out for years to come.

A further difference that Piketty observes affects comparisons between western Europe and the United States. His evidence suggests that wealth was far less unequally distributed in late-19th- and early-20th-century United States than in those European countries for which we have data. Today that picture is completely reversed. The image of the historical United States as a land of openness and opportunities is confirmed; but it no longer reflects today's reality.

The picture in central and eastern Europe is different again, and it is unfortunate that we have so few data on the earnings of the very rich in those countries. The state socialist system adopted in Russia (which included the Baltic states, Belarus, Moldova and Ukraine) after 1917, and spread to central and eastern Europe by the Soviet Army (and by national partisan forces in then-Yugoslavia) after 1945, destroyed or took into state ownership nearly all private wealth. Almost everyone except peasants in a few countries (especially Poland) became an employee, and there were no earnings from investments. There were salary inequalities, but not on the scale that was normal in the west and not reinforced by inequalities in the ownership of and income from property. Following the collapse of the state socialist system after 1989, these countries joined the global capitalist economy with far lower levels of inequality than in the west. Capitalist development then took two different forms. Some countries (in particular the more industrialized ones of CEE, the Czech and Slovak Republics, Hungary and Slovenia) opened to investment from multinational firms, who provided the majority of both shareholders and senior managers. Economic growth in these countries may well therefore have contributed to inequality in the distribution of wealth and income among the United States, Japanese and western European populations, but internally they have not generated a clearly defined wealthy elite. Where we have data for them, these countries therefore now appear among the most egalitarian of all. In FEE, including Poland, it has been different. Elites in these countries have taken very different approaches towards Russia: remaining close to it in Belarus and Moldova, hostile in the Baltic states, Poland and Romania, divided in Bulgaria and (bitterly) in Ukraine. Nevertheless all except Romania have followed Russia in rapidly developing (with the United States) some of the highest levels of inequality in the advanced world.

The OECD (2011; Förster, Llena-Nozal and Nafilyan, 2014) has probed some reasons for overall changes in inequalities in western countries. It appears that large increases in incomes have been concentrated among senior managers and some professionals, particularly in the financial sector. Many of these exceptionally highly paid people have their income source divided between salaries and investment earnings to a far greater extent than is the case of the rest of the workforce. The 'bottom' 90 per cent have between 70 and 85 per cent of their incomes in the form of wages and salaries; the top 0.01 per cent in contrast have only 40 per cent in this form, especially in the anglophone countries. In most countries, government taxation policies have changed to favour the income sources of the rich. Between 1981 and 2010 taxation rates on the highest incomes across the OECD area declined from 66 to 42 per cent; corporate as opposed to individual income tax has dropped from 47 to 25 per cent; taxes on dividends from 75 to 42 per cent. These numbers relate to taxation rates, and do not take account of any increases that might have taken place in the ability of wealthy people to avoid tax, though the deregulation of global finance that took place during the period has made legal tax avoidance easier.

In central Europe industrial production has remained more important to the economy, as we saw in Chapter 3. This has typically delivered lower levels of inequality than either pre-industrial agriculture or the financial and related services that power contemporary advanced economies. Further east and in Russia higher proportions of the population work in agriculture, and in some countries small groups and individuals have been able to take control of an important, monopolistic energy sector, producing a super-rich class comparable to that produced by the financial and energy sectors in the United States and finance in certain western European countries, especially the United Kingdom.

Conclusion

On the basis of the above discussion we can draw certain conclusions about the state of class in European and other advanced societies, as that term is conventionally understood. In the next chapter we shall unpick that conventional understanding and suggest an alternative approach. But to do that we need to see how far the old approach can take us.

First, we can identify a very small group, an elite, of extremely rich individuals and households, accounting for 0.1 per cent or possibly 0.01 per cent of the population who are set apart from everyone else by the diversity of their sources of wealth and by their ability to take a growing share of increases in national income. Included in this group are certainly some traditional, even aristocratic, wealthy families, but the group as a whole is increasingly characterized as holding senior positions in corporate management, particularly though not solely in the financial and energy sectors, with some legal and accounting professionals specializing in related fields. The extent to which this group is separate from the rest of the population varies from country to country. It is least prominent in Continental north-western and central Europe; particularly dominant in the United States and slightly less clearly the United Kingdom; and, to the extent that we have relevant data, also prominent in Russia and countries that once formed part of the old Soviet Union. Southern Europe also has an elite of this kind, but there it is more associated with traditional wealth that has moved into the new corporate opportunities; this may also be partly the British case.

Second, we can identify the great majority of other holders of managerial and professional posts. There is no absolutely clear cut-off point between the highest earners in this category and those in the elite, but overall there is a difference based on sources of income and current rate of growth. Taken as a whole this group, and particularly its male members, have higher incomes than the rest of society, and are defined by holding recognized positions in organizational hierarchies and/or having formal qualifications. We can probably generalize broadly about them across countries, including central and eastern Europe. The only major difference is that in the Nordic and some other countries in north-western and central Europe their income privileges are fewer than elsewhere.

Third come the holders of technical, skilled and semi-skilled industrial, clerical, and some sales and service posts, as well as many women in professional roles. There is no clear cut-off between these and the second group, as managerial hierarchies are very long, with many junior managers and supervisors having lifestyles and incomes close to this third group. As with the second group, these posts occupy similar positions in most countries, with some differences in the position of women.

Finally, elementary workers, the remaining agricultural workers and many sales and service workers (especially female ones) constitute a distinctly poorer group, though again there is overlap between them and the third. They in turn overlap heavily with a marginal group of people in precarious positions, sometimes finding jobs in these lowest-paid categories, but often having no work at all, or having a succession of short-term jobs, with varying patterns of hours and often in illegal or 'shadow' parts of the economy: the 'precariat'. Here will be found that bottom decile of the income distribution, which exists at quite a distance from the median. These too are found across all societies, but their gap from the rest varies considerably. They are not so remote from the majority in Norden, CEE and some parts of NWE as they are in the United States, SWE and FEE.

One could give these groups names, respectively, as an upper (possibly ruling), middle, lower middle or working, and lower class (including the precariat). But does this have significant meaning? What does it imply to label these groups as classes? These are the questions to which we must now turn.

Chapter 6

Delineating the class structures of contemporary Europe

In the last chapter we identified a strong link between income inequality and the occupational groups to which people belong, which we presented as being a structure of social classes. But what does this really mean for the organization of social life? Sociologists mainly see class as an aspect of social stratification, a term which implies a vertical structure by analogy with the geological idea of strata of different types of rock, deposited in vertical layers over long periods of time. This implies inequality – some are on top, others at the bottom – but the relationship between classes and inequality is complex for two reasons that have long been recognized. First, inequality of income places persons in a long, continuous spectrum. In modern societies with complex labour markets and masses of different kinds of occupation there will very rarely be sharp breaks in that continuum. The idea of classes, on the other hand, assumes the existence of discrete groups separate from one another. Therefore income inequality alone cannot determine class position: only if, along with other factors, it forms groups having distinct ways of life. There was evidence in the last chapter that the main occupational categories can form such groups, because of the link between occupation, education, culture, informal association and other components of lifestyle. Second, although classes are usually seen as ranked hierarchically, it is always possible for individuals in a group that overall is ranked above another one to have incomes and standards of living lower than many members of that second group.

Sociologists have long tried to distinguish between these two phenomena – the economic reality of inequality as a constantly shifting continuum and the attempt to impose on it a defined order. Mention was made in Chapter 1 of Max Weber's (1922) seminal approach of calling the former 'class' and the latter 'status'. For Weber and other early sociologists there was here both an analytical and an historical distinction. Put crudely, pre-industrial, post-feudal society was characterized by a legally sanctioned status order; industrial, capitalist

147

society by an economic class structure. A world in which various ranks of aristocracy, an urban bourgeoisie and a peasantry had their status defined by law was being replaced by one in which capitalists, various middle-class groups of non-manual employees and an industrial working class were defined by their role in the factory and by their income. For Weber class and status were analytically different forms of ranking populations and forms that dominated societies at different historical periods. This approach shaped sociological analysis throughout the 20th century.

Analysts clung to this classical account of class as a largely industrial phenomenon after the transition into post-industrial society; a task that they mainly achieved by ignoring women's occupations. It is now widely accepted that this position was deeply flawed. But there were errors right from the start in the Weberian analysis. There has been tension between the continuum of inequality and the attempt to impose categories on it for as long as societies have had systems of law, not just in the industrial period. Pre-industrial societies had highly complicated continua of land ownership, trading wealth and earnings from labour. What appear to have been the clearly demarcated ranks of classes or estates of those societies really represent only attempts by popes, kings and aristocrats to impose an order on the continua, often in order to protect their own position as the formal apex of the system despite the accumulation of superior levels of wealth by some bourgeois. Sometimes rulers might exclude whole categories of persons from certain activities (e.g. Jews from land-holding) and occupations or even from wearing certain garments. But there was a constant tension between the two realities of social differences that resulted from divisions defined by political authority and those that emerged from income from various activities. The former formed broad, fairly clear categories; the latter continua.

Industrial class society was essentially similar to this, except that the categories were defined, not so much by political authority as by factory owners and managers during the course of the 19th century. They designated the hierarchies through which they would organize their businesses, the broad rankings of the factory listed in the previous chapter. What we see as the classes of industrial society were in fact its status groups. There was here a kind of privatization of class definition, though even this was not entirely true. The modern state and army developed before the modern factory as large-scale work organizations, and to some extent furnished models for employers on how to order the hierarchy of a factory. The division between office and factory paralleled that between officers and other ranks in armies. German employers modelled the idea of the trusted manager on the distinctive Prussian state concept of the civil servant (*Beamter*) (Kocka, 1981).

The industrial state took a more active and decisive role in class definition in a paradoxical way: not so much by defining manual workers in terms of an absence of rights, but by defining protective rights for them. This development was linked to the rise not so much of political democracy itself but of pressure for it or the threat of it. Trade unions and radical, sometimes socialist, political parties were capable of disrupting social and economic order and demanding radical limitations to the power of property ownership. Germany again provides the locus classicus, with its early development of a welfare state designed to pacify working-class agitation by reducing the degree of economic uncertainty in workers' lives through limited social insurance schemes (Palier, 2010). These and other initiatives took it for granted that employers were in positions of power over their workers, especially manual workers, and that the lives of the latter were characterized by insecurity and often by poverty. Governments did not wish to change that power relation; indeed they guaranteed it through the laws of property that enabled some people to command the labour of others and to extract profit from the process. They also usually maintained rules for access to the suffrage that defined property and gender rights, marking arbitrary category lines across the continuum of property ownership. But they sought to take some of the sting out of that fundamental inequality through limited legislation for labour rights and social welfare. In many national legal systems it became recognized that the employee was the weaker party in the employment contract, and that therefore that contract was inconsistent with the fundamental principle in contract law that there is equality between the contracting parties. Labour law therefore developed with one of its main aims being the protection of the employee against the more powerful employer (Sinzheimer, 1921; Knegt, 2008).

Starting in France, it became usual by the late 19th century to speak of the *question sociale;* in German, the *soziale Frage.* This referred to the problems of the lives of urban, male industrial workers and their dependent wives and children. These workers were the ones who might threaten social order through their mass status. Rural workers might have worse living conditions, but were rarely successful in organizing protests. Self-employed workers of various kinds might be even less secure, but had virtually no capacity to combine. Some office workers had little chance to provide security against eventual calamities, but usually felt they had more to lose from setting themselves in opposition to the managers with whom they mixed directly and personally within the office. Some or all of these groups were usually excluded from early policy measures adopted to address the *question sociale* among manual industrial workers. These policies became known as *politique sociale,* or *Sozialpolitik,* a term with a somewhat broader meaning than its obvious English equivalent of 'social policy', as it included measures for the rights of workers and trade unions. In these various ways a 'working class' became defined by state policy as a class that needed various kinds of protection.

As the 20th century progressed, and especially its second half, the sharp contours of class society softened, though differently in western and eastern European societies. In the west, and with the exception of Portugal and Spain, which continued to be dictatorships until the 1970s, and Greece, which experienced a period of dictatorship in the 1960s and 1970s, propertyless workers (initially men only) had gained admission to the electorate in systems of universal adult suffrage, reducing the importance of what had been the most pointed political definition of class boundaries. In most societies protective legislation originally limited to manual workers in industry was extended to rural workers, the self-employed and non-manual employees, eventually becoming citizenship rights rather than measures to compensate for subordination and chronic insecurity. With the rise of the various services sectors and decline in industrial employment, the factory paradigm of class structure lost relevance.

In the east, dictatorships claiming to rule in the interests of the industrial working class were established wherever the armies of the Soviet Union were the occupying force following the collapse of Nazi Germany – a pattern that was in fact agreed in advance of the event at the Yalta Conference between the United States, the Soviet Union and the United Kingdom in 1945. In Yugoslavia an autonomous communist movement also triumphed. These regimes claimed to have abolished class and its inequalities. They did abolish most private ownership of property and established some important welfare provisions, but the claim that class no longer existed suffered from two major defects. First, as dictatorships that not only faced no free elections but also prevented the formation of free trade unions and other representative groups of civil society, and suppressed any protest movements with violence, ruling communist parties were not responsible to any class other than their own tight ranks. Second, while some countries in the west of the Soviet bloc (Czechoslovakia, East Germany and Hungary) were highly industrialized, both Russia itself and most of the parts of Europe that it dominated remained very backward and pre-industrial rather than at the forefront of economic development as was claimed.

As industrial passed into post-industrial society in the west, this ensemble moved in different directions under the diverse pressures of the spread of political citizenship, the declining socio-cultural presence of class following deindustrialization, but eventually also the new intensification of inequalities of wealth and income. The former two, in their different ways, reduced the importance of class identity and its political salience; the last reinforced its importance but in an invisible way. Meanwhile new groups of highly insecure workers in precarious forms of employment have been forming the potential new class that in the previous chapter was called the 'precariat' (Standing, 1999; 2011). Many, though by no means all, of these insecure workers are immigrants or members of ethnic minorities, who often lack the citizenship that we erroneously call 'universal'. It is during this period of ambiguous change in the west that the countries of eastern Europe joined the world of capitalism and liberal democracy.

We can now see that Weber's distinction between class and status was not well founded. The purely economic never creates clear classes; it has to be supplemented by acts of public or private authority that define groups of persons and ascribes rights or the absence of rights to them. The idea of status groups as identities ordained by an authority of some kind originally captured this perfectly, but the word 'status' has lost its meaning and no longer serves its purpose. The German word that Weber used was *Stand,* which designated the formal division of society into ranks characteristic of pre-industrial societies; the English word 'standing', in the sense of 'social standing', comes very close to it, but the equivalent term actually used in England to denote formal social rank was 'estate', a derivative of the Latin word 'status'. Membership of an estate endowed someone with a particular set of legal and political rights (or lack of them). The modern use of 'status', as in 'status symbol', has entirely lost this formal, legal and political significance. Meanwhile in English, less so for its equivalents in other European languages, the term 'class' is used with much the same informal cultural meaning as the term status. If someone remarks that society today is 'classless', she usually means that occupational positions are not accompanied by clear cultural symbols or lifestyles, not that there is less economic inequality.

Class and citizenship

Before the arrival of universal suffrage, allocation to classes also defined rights to citizenship. Throughout Europe this formal aspect of class fell away, as nearly all adults living in a society either received the vote or were subjected to dictatorships that in effect admitted no one to citizenship. The legacy of the past still exerts an influence in various ways. Some strong class identities, which had previously been associated with either exclusion from or inclusion in limited citizenship, persist. The generally delayed entry of women into universal suffrage still affects their formal and informal rights in many countries. The position of many immigrants remains problematic. In central and eastern Europe the recent past of dictatorship still casts its shadow.

Yet today class mainly affects citizenship rights in an informal way through the greater power that the wealthy have to influence governments, though more cultural factors such as shared educational backgrounds between various kinds of elite also continue to play their part. To the extent that the wealthy represent major business interests, governments dependent on economic success for their own survival necessarily listen to what business leaders say they need. Their statements of their needs will be a mixture of technical requirements for their firms to do well and their personal interests. They are likely to argue, for example, that high incomes should be taxed more lightly. This will be a claim based partly on their perception of what is needed for business success, but partly on their own desire to pay less in taxes.

This brings us to an important point in the discussion of the relationship between citizenship and social class. Citizenship in societies where formal equality of political citizenship has been achieved operates at two levels. There are the formal, classless rules of democracy, which prescribe a very high degree of equality: a billionaire and an unemployed person each have one vote, and governments are formed on the basis of that process alone. Once governments are elected, however, a second, informal level of citizenship begins to operate, as different interests seek to lobby governments to press their particular concerns. In a liberal democracy there is again a formal equality of capacity to try to do this. But exercising informal political influence costs money. There is therefore nothing resembling the formal equality of 'one person, one vote'. In many European countries, and in contrast to the United States, there are various rules that limit the ways in which money can be deployed politically, but it is always a factor. Also, although formal democratic rights can be exercised only in the country of which one is a citizen, lobbying can be carried on across national frontiers. In fact, multinational firms can be particularly powerful lobbyists, as they can threaten to withdraw from a country if it does not provide what they regard as a suitable environment.

The arrival of formal democracy did not therefore bring an end to the class basis of citizenship, but shifted it from formal voting to informal lobbying and other means of exercising influence. The link here with class is to sheer wealth, not to different occupational categories. However, this does not mean that we are here confronted by the continuum of incomes, as the level of wealth needed to play a major role in the informal citizenship of purchased political influence is very high indeed. We saw in the last chapter that in many societies a very small group – the top 0.1 per cent or it may even be the top 0.01 per cent – holds a distinctive position in the income structure. We may here identify a small 'informal ruling class', restoring to class the political meaning that is often disregarded in modern class analysis. That this class is small by no means undermines its importance; the aristocracies of pre-industrial societies and the major factory owners of industrialism similarly constituted a tiny proportion of the population. Further, its informal status does not necessarily weaken its power. In formally democratic, open societies, power of this kind may be wielded more effectively if it is able, if pressed, to maintain that it does not exist.

It is not the case that modern class analysis has ignored the politics of class. Class analysis has always been at the forefront of studies of voting behaviour and political allegiance; what has been ignored is the existence of an informally operating ruling class and the means through which it operates. This might be excusable on the grounds that, while it certainly continued to exist, such a class became less important during the first three decades after the World War II, when modern sociology acquired its current body of theory. We have already seen from Piketty's work (2013) that the middle part of the 20th century was distinctive in terms of the decline of large wealth-holdings, and that today the position of the very rich is returning to an older, more 'normal' historical pattern. His analysis of the changes that have taken place in the character of the wealthy, so that more of them are senior business executives rather than rentiers, fits well with an account of class structure that stresses the distinctive role of management as a class, although of course that wider category extends way beyond that tiny elite. We also considered in the previous chapter evidence that forms of taxation typically imposed on the very highest incomes have declined in recent decades. Whether or not this decline has helped the economy in general or merely awarded privileges to those already privileged, it is evidence of the informal political power of a group who, being so small, would stand no chance of political influence if formal democracy were sovereign.

The nearest that Weberian analysis came to recognizing a political aspect of stratification separate from class and status was Weber's concept of 'party', which was again at once analytical and historical. If status was an instrument that advanced and protected the position of aristocracies, and class one that advanced the bourgeois capital owner, party was a device available to the working class. By 'party' Weber meant the capacity to form mass organizations, something available to those whose social position was weak except for their sheer force of numbers. At the time of Weber's writing, the working class in Germany and many other European countries had produced trade unions and other campaigning organizations that rallied round social democratic political parties seeking to advance the cause of that class. Governments usually tried to make such organizations illegal and employers hampered their activities, but by the late 19th century unions began to find a legal position, and their associated parties were able to compete in political elections, gaining in size as industrialization swelled the ranks of the working class. Weber's choice of the word 'party' to denote this phenomenon was unfortunate. He used it as a blanket term to cover parties in the strict sense and organizations such as unions. Also, parties soon ceased to be the particular preserve of the working class. When Weber was translated into English by two US sociologists they tried to solve the problem by speaking of 'class, status and power' (Bendix and Lipset, 1953), and this approach has dominated the use of Weber's scheme throughout the anglophone world. It has been problematic, as for Weber class and status were both related to power. By making it the third limb of a stratification scheme, Bendix and Lipset unknowingly conspired at the modern misuse of the term 'class' to denote just occupational groups and of 'status' to denote various characteristics that people use to attract prestige. The point about Weber's triad of class, status and 'party' (or organization as we might better term it) is that he saw all three being used by people as power resources in a struggle for superior life chances.

Historically status, class and organization had the implications for different social groups that Weber envisaged – a usage that lies behind Gøsta Esping-Andersen's schematic history of class relations discussed in Chapter 1. But as analytical categories they can be used by groups other than those originally associated with them. Thus, today high status adheres to men and women holding senior business positions in addition to, indeed in most cases instead of, traditional aristocracy. And property-owning and other wealthy classes have made at least as effective political use of organization as manual workers. The character of their organizations is different: Weber had in mind the sheer weight of numbers of the urban industrial masses; but expending large sums of money lobbying politicians and civil servants can be as effective and, once one is adequately rich, considerably easier to wield.

Organization works differently from class and status. These latter can operate both passively and implicitly or actively and explicitly. Simply by holding and practising, say, a skilled manual job an individual experiences both negative and positive consequences of that position: a higher income than most of the less skilled; a lower one than most professionals and managers and some technicians. There need be no deliberate strategy to exploit the advantages of being in a particular class. But the individual might have chosen to acquire the skills concerned explicitly in order to avoid the low incomes associated with jobs with lower skills. One might call this an active, individual class strategy. Organizations that work for the interests of a group, however, always do so actively and deliberately. For example, an organization that represents the interests of farmers knows what it is doing and does not operate passively. The reason why organization is associated in Weberian sociology with the working class is that, being the class that stood in a low position in class and status, it could advance itself *only* by organizing to try to offset its disadvantages – though this limitation never applied fully to skilled workers, who had the market power of the scarcity of their skills.

Classes and power

The previous chapter demonstrated links between certain occupational positions and typical levels of income. These might be seen as the passive advantages and disadvantages of class. As the foregoing discussion suggests, for classes to be social actors rather than mere boxes to which people can be allocated, we need evidence of a capacity for action on their behalf. This is a distinction that Karl Marx drew between classes 'in themselves' and 'for themselves' (*an sich* and *für sich* in the original German). For a class to be acting for itself it was not necessary that every member of a class be aware of where that class's interests lay, only that formal or informal organizations existed that could claim to define the interests of groups within a class and, in an open society, attract enough voluntary support from members of those groups to be able to work with some effect for the class's interests. In a complex society we should expect only rarely to see organizations claiming to work for whole classes as such; more likely will be those working for particular occupational groups within particular economic sectors; this becomes a class action rather a sectoral one only if a number of these press for similar outcomes. Also, we should not look only for explicit, formal organizations. As theorists of power have argued (Lukes, 1974; 2005), sometimes the most effective power is wielded purely informally, even implicitly; the most powerful of all forms of power do not even need to be wielded; it is enough that everyone knows that they might be wielded if the interests concerned do not get their own way.

One can set about studying this in two ways. First, one can carry out almost forensic, anthropological work, trying to track down in specific cases why certain outcomes occurred rather than others. For example, we can imagine a project to discover why some governments take tougher stands than others on environmental damage and climate change by examining which interests have the strongest informal contacts and relationships with politicians and senior civil servants, which ones went to visit them, or which spoke to large numbers of parliamentarians before key decisions. There are many good studies of this kind. But for a task such as our present one, looking across a large number of countries, this is not feasible. Instead we have to ask what outcomes we would expect to find if representatives of groups within certain classes rather than others were exercising influence, and examine whether that is what we find in the evidence. There is a problem with such a methodology. Assume we find that legislation to discourage smoking is stricter in some countries than others; can we conclude that lobbies of the tobacco industry are more powerful in those with the weakest legislation? It might be the case, but it might also be that people in the countries with the toughest legislation are those where people are more concerned over health risks, or where there is particular sensitivity to the costs of medical treatments. There are therefore hazards in this approach, but we have little alternative if we are to reach some general conclusions about class power. The important point is to bear in mind the limitations of what we can achieve.

We shall here try to determine to what extent different classes in the societies we are studying are able to exercise political power by looking at the consequences of taxation for inequality, as this is an area where we can find a good deal of relevant and comparable statistical data.

It is often assumed that in their fiscal policies governments are responding primarily to pressure to redistribute from the wealthy to the less well-off. If that is so, we should expect to find the highest tax rates for top incomes among those countries with the highest levels of inequality, as these might see the greatest 'need' for redistribution. We can call this the first, 'technocratic', hypothesis, as it assumes a neutral state trying to work for a perceived general interest by reducing the inequalities that emerge from the distribution of income and wealth. If governments are, on the other hand, mainly responsive to pressures from the very wealthy, we should expect to find the lowest top tax rates in countries with the highest pre-tax inequality levels, as it is in such cases that we should expect lobbying by the wealthy to be most successful. This is the second, 'political', hypothesis, as it assumes that political lobbying helps shape the fiscal system. The other side of the coin of this second hypothesis is that if governments are responding to pressures from the less wealthy, we should expect to find the highest top tax rates in countries with some of the lowest pre-tax inequality levels, because it will probably be in these that the less wealthy have managed to wield most political power.

The OECD report *Divided We Stand* (2011) explored many potential reasons why there might have been an increase in inequality across most countries in the advanced world, including Europe. They found that the main causes were changes in 'institutions and policies' (p. 122), which broadly means actions over which human decision-makers had influence, rather than blind economic forces. For example, changes in trade flows associated with globalization were largely neutral, with some inequality-increasing developments being offset by inequality-reducing ones. Technology tends to increase inequalities, as it abolishes routine jobs at the bottom of the skill ladder, creating a surplus of low-skilled people seeking work, while increasing the demand for high skills and therefore the rewards of skill. On the other hand, this tendency has been completely offset by an overall increase in the educational achievement of populations, leading to a reduction in the supply of low-skilled people and an increase in that of the highly skilled. (The important role of education in class structure will be considered in more detail in the next chapter.) According to the OECD, this left such developments as the declining progressivity of tax systems, especially at the top end, the growing role of the financial sector in the global economy and the decline of trade unions and collective bargaining. Taken with the evidence that it has been senior managers and professionals, particularly in the financial and some other business services sectors, whose incomes have increased most, it is reasonable to conclude that at least part of the growth in inequality is consistent with the political, class power hypothesis, though we cannot claim definitely to have found the causal relationship.

It is difficult to determine whether structural changes in the economy occurred first, advancing the economic position of the very wealthy, who were then able to convert that wealth into political power; or whether a rise in their political power happened first, enabling them then to secure policies that further advanced their position. The important point is that both have occurred and continue in a mutually reinforcing process, as a result of the mutual convertibility of political and economic resources: political influence can be used to secure favourable economic policies and wealth can be converted into political influence. Identifying the process and its self-reinforcing character is more important than deciding on where the first blow was struck. This is why inequality is an important issue, particularly within formally democratic societies: it is not just a question of whether one individual has more cars, houses or yachts than another, but how much power they have to persuade governments to favour their interests.

For western Continental, and later central and eastern, European countries the first step in the mutually reinforcing process does seem to have been exogenous, as the most important initial political events took place in the United States and the United Kingdom from the end of the 1970s, with the elections of Ronald Reagan as president of the United States and Margaret Thatcher as prime minister of the United Kingdom. Both embarked on a set of changes in economic and social policy that would alter the direction in which the western world had been moving since the end of World War II. That earlier trajectory, rooted in elites' determination to avoid any repetition of the crises that had engulfed Europe and the world in the first half of the 20th century, had sought social stability and a compromise among social classes through a mixture of Keynesian demand management and the development of national welfare states, with in most countries redistributive taxation. These measures reduced inequality. Demand management, with governments more or less guaranteeing full employment, made labour scarce and therefore increased wages and the market power of employees. As we have seen, the availability of redistributive taxation, transfer payments and public services through the welfare state further reduced inequality. Alongside these developments the process of 'wealth destruction' through war, as described by Piketty (2013), was also taking place. Different countries were at different stages of industrialization, but all were engaged in that process, with a result-ant shift of workers from agriculture to industry. This had important political implications. Manual workers in industry were more likely than any other members of the workforce to join trade unions, which developed the power to challenge managements and to demand higher wages for their members. Also, the rise in industrial workers meant an increase in votes for political parties – called variously Labour, Socialist, Social Democrat or Communist – that challenged ruling elites. Weber's original 'party' concept was now in full operation, over a quarter of a century after his death. This period, extending broadly from 1945 until 1980, produced the biggest reduction in inequality in recorded history and was based on extensive compromises between the key classes of industrial society: industrial owners and senior managers on the one side and manual industrial workers represented by trade unions on the other. By the 1980s this latter class was declining in size throughout the west, as employment in services replaced that in indus-try. The power of 'party' or organization in Weber's sense now began to decline, as union membership shrank alongside employment in its stronghold.

Trade unions and class power

The rise and decline in union power alongside a decline and rise in inequality is consistent with the above hypothesis that the organization of a class's interests should be positively associated with its power. If that is the case, then we should today expect that the countries with the strongest trade unions should be those with the lowest inequalities, as unions ought to be able to exercise their power over both the ini-tial and post-tax and -transfer distribution of income. Union strength can be seen as a combination of two factors: the membership level of unions and some measure of their capacity to affect outcomes. The main international source for this data on unions and employment relations is the Institutional Characteristics of Trade Unions, Wage Setting, State Intervention and Social Pacts (ICTWSS) survey of the University of Amsterdam (Amsterdam Institute for Advanced Labour Studies, 2015). It covers nearly all countries of interest to us up to 2013 or 2014, except Belarus, Moldova and Ukraine.

The ICTWSS survey followed the conventional practice of assessing union density as a proportion of persons in dependent employment. However, we really need to gauge the strength of trade unions in an economy as a whole. Where self-employment or the shadow economy forms a high proportion of employment, that strength is diminished in its overall impact on the economy. For example, imagine two societies, in both of which 50 per cent of dependent employees in the formal economy are members of unions, but where in one all workers are dependent employees, while in the other 25 per cent of workers are either self-employed or working illegally. The impact of union membership is clearly higher in the former case. To give an impression of the power of unions across the workforce as a whole the ICTWSS should be deflated by the extent of self-employment, and by the size of the shadow economy. Data on the former are provided by the OECD and Eurostat. Estimates of the size of the shadow economy are by their nature always approximate, but Schneider and Buehn (2012) have made calculations for many of the countries we are attempting to cover. In an earlier World Bank paper, Schneider, Buehn and Montenegro (2010) provided data for a wider range of countries from 2000 to 2006. Given that these numbers do not change dramatically from year to year, I have used the 2006 figure for Croatia and Russia. Fuller details of these calculations for an earlier version of the ICTWSS data can be found in Crouch (2015: ch. 3).

The resulting patterns for all countries for which we have data on all variables are shown in Figure 6.1 for the years around 2013. Union membership has been in decline for some time, but we are chiefly concerned here with the contemporary situation only. These statistics must be treated with caution, as the assumptions about the size of the shadow economy on which they are based are very approximate. Particular doubt surrounds the data for Russia, where there is little information about the size of the self-employed sector. We can, however, safely conclude that trade-union membership is strongest in the Nordic lands, Belgium, and to a lesser extent in Ireland, Italy, Austria and some very small countries. It is weakest in several central and eastern European countries, France, the United States and Turkey. The mean membership density across all countries covered here is only 19.10 per cent.

By itself union membership strength does not tell us how that strength can be used. We are interested in unions as an indicator of the extent to which a challenge to propertied interests might be incorporated in political and social structures. We must be clear that this formulation embodies a judgement that employees' influence can be exercised in this way, and that sheer membership strength and a capacity for militancy without incorporation do not constitute effective strength. Marxist theorists would contest this and argue that it is only when

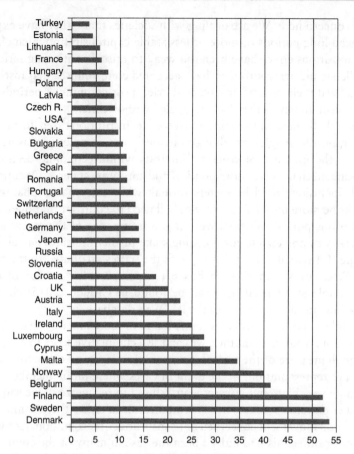

Source: Amsterdam Institute for Advanced Labour Studies, 2015

FIGURE 6.1 *Trade-union membership density as proportion of all gainfully employed population, including self-employed and shadow economy, European countries and key comparators, c. 2013.*

working-class power takes this second form that it is really effective. The Marxist account of power is one that assumes irreconcilable conflict that can be resolved only through major confrontations of forms of society. Its concept of working-class power as embodied in organizational strength is therefore a transitory phenomenon, rising up at the moment of acute conflict before being dissolved into a completely new society. In practice, in the known cases of Marxist revolutions, unions have been dissolved into the apparatus of a party-state and have lost their capacity to represent employee interests. That, however, is not our concern here. We are dealing with societies that either have experienced long periods of more or less stable capitalism (in which class organizations either have been too weak to raise a continuing serious challenge or, being stronger, have accepted compromises that institutionalized their power) or have had brief, post-communist periods of capitalism in which they have struggled with decline.

We shall therefore confine ourselves to institutionalized forms of union power. A relevant, though obviously not complete, measure of this is the presence of workers' interests within economic decision-making mechanisms in both political and corporate spheres. Of course, such inclusion could be merely formal, while informal mechanisms might be more important, and we shall need to confront that question at various points. But first, we can gain some idea of the extent and diversity of any conclusion by using some further indicators available in the ICTWSS database. These, with the scores attributed to them in ICTWSS, are summarized in Box 6.1. Again, a fuller version of the methodology involved here can be found in Crouch (2015: ch. 3), based on an earlier version of the ICTWSS database.

While it is difficult to say whether a unit of score on any one of these indicators is equal to another, we can use a cumulative score to provide a rough measure of the formal inclusion of unions and other forms of worker representation. In the event of cases where union membership became very high, but governments refused to recognize it, we should predict extreme conflict, which would result in either the crushing of the union movement concerned or its institutional recognition. At some point or other this had indeed been the case in many of the countries being considered here, from the early struggles of British unions in the early 19th century to the conflicts around Solidarność in communist Poland in the late 20th. In each case, however, by the time we reach the 21st century these struggles had been resolved into varying levels of incorporation of unions, even if in some cases this is no more than acceptance of their right to exist. In contrast with union membership, which declined, formal incorporation in European countries has been growing slightly.

Figure 6.2 shows the results of matching countries across these two indicators around 2013. There is a modest relationship between them ($r^2 = 0.2639$). The Nordics and Belgium occupy the top right part of the graph, showing relative strength on both dimensions. Austria, Luxembourg, the Netherlands and Germany have high levels of incorporation despite their moderate density levels. It is

> **BOX 6.1   Forms of incorporation of employees' representative bodies in economic governance**
>
> • Existence of a standard (institutionalized) bipartite council of central or major union and employer organizations for purposes of wage-setting, economic forecasting and/or conflict settlement: yes = 1; no = 0.
> • Routine involvement of unions and employers in government decisions on social and economic policy: full concertation, regular and frequent involvement = 2; partial concertation, irregular and infrequent involvement = 1; no concertation, involvement is rare or absent = 0.
> • Existence of works councils: existence and rights of works councils mandated by law or basic agreement = 2; works council is voluntary and/or no sanctions for non-observance of law or agreement = 1; no works council or similar institution = 0.
> • Works council rights: economic and social rights, including codetermination on some issues = 3; economic and social rights, consultation only, with possibility of legal redress = 2; information and consultation rights (without legal redress) = 1; no or only exceptional works councils = 0.
>
> *Source*: AIAS, 2015
>
> The total scores possible on the ICTWSS scale would range from zero to eight points. Since we want to multiply the union density numbers by these scores, we cannot have a zero. We therefore add an additional point to each country's score to indicate the initial step of inclusion, which is a legal right to exist, bringing the range on the ICTWSS scale to one to nine. (If we were to extend our research to countries in which unions had no legal right to exist, their power score would be zero however high membership might be. This would be both mathematically and substantively correct, and in line with the assumption set out above, that we are counting only institutionalized forms as constituting union power.)

notable that the non-European countries, including Turkey, have lower positions on the incorporation index than any European cases (though Japan is similar to Romania), and also have some of the lowest memberships.

We can construct a combined indicator, deflating the membership density figure by the incorporation score. This is a somewhat dubious manoeuvre, as it produces an entirely synthetic measure. In particular,

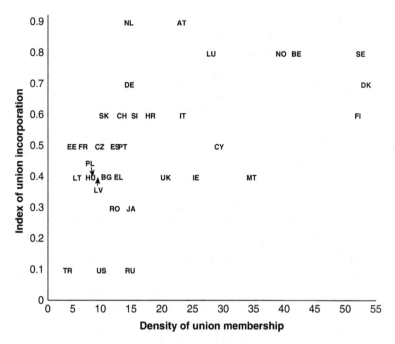

Source: Amsterdam Institute for Advanced Labour Studies, 2015

FIGURE 6.2   *Incorporation of unions by density of union membership, European countries and key comparators, c. 2013.*

it is often argued that French union strength is not appropriately measured by membership, but by various unions' capacity to mobilize strike calls or to attract votes in works council elections. It is also claimed that French unions' institutionalized power is mainly exercised through their role in *cogestion* (or joint management) of pension schemes. It is likely also that the incorporation of Austrian and German unions into the countries' governing institutions is under-estimated by the elements included in the AIAS index. On the other side, it has been argued that unions in many parts of CEE and FEE are unable to use the rights formally accorded to them in the legislative changes that became formally necessary when their countries joined the EU (Meardi, 2012; Ost, 2000). In a comparative study such as that being attempted here, one cannot make allowances for local variations of this kind. We must stick with standard terms and consistent statistics and shall use the term 'class challenge' to refer to this combination of union strength and incorporation. The results are shown in Figure 6.3. The four Nordic countries and Belgium exhibited particularly strong scores,

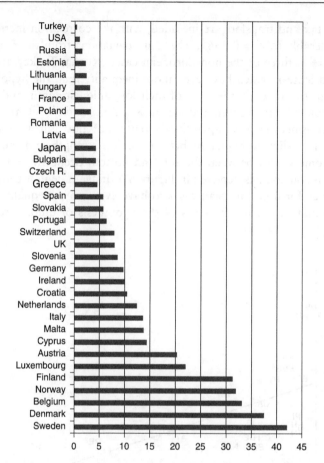

Source: *The author's own calculations, based on* Amsterdam Institute for Advanced Labour Studies, 2015

FIGURE 6.3   *Combined index of trade-union strength (index of class challenge), European countries and key comparators, c. 2013.*

with Luxembourg and Austria shortly behind. With particularly weak scores were all non-European comparators, France, Greece and all eastern (but not all central) European cases.

If increasing inequality of wealth and income is, as the OECD analysis suggests, driven partly by 'institutional' factors, therefore by human agency and therefore by social and political power, we should expect inequalities to be lower in countries where a challenge to class dominance, as defined by trade-union strength, is stronger and vice versa. There is virtually no relationship between union strength and the pre-tax and -transfer Gini score ($r^2 = 0.0544$). There is a remarkable change when tax and transfers are included, with the correlation increasing considerably to $r^2 = 0.3349$. The main deviations from the relationship are in three of the non-European cases (Russia, Turkey and the United States), which have even more inequality than the hypothesis leads us to expect on the basis of their low union strength, and three CEE countries (the Czech and Slovak Republics and Slovenia), which have considerably less. Japan fits the pattern of most European cases. There is a slightly higher fit between union strength and the ratio of income shares between the top and bottom deciles ($r^2 = 0.348$). This last outcome is depicted in Figure 6.4. It again demonstrates the tendency for non-European cases to have even more inequality than we should expect on the basis of the hypothesis of union strength;

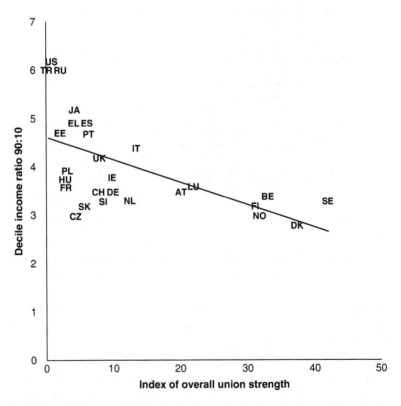

Source: *The author's own calculations, based on* Amsterdam Institute for Advanced Labour Studies, 2015 and OECD, 2011

FIGURE 6.4   *Ratio between incomes of top and bottom decile, by index of union strength, European countries and key comparators, c. 2011–13.*

southern European countries have the same tendency to a lesser extent. Countries in CEE and to a lesser extent NWE have lower inequality levels than we should expect.

These findings suggest a relationship between union strength and inequality operating particularly at the post-tax level and therefore after government intervention, and also some congruence with the geosocial groupings that we have been following. It is notable that Japan, Russia, Turkey and the United States are all found among the weak cases, particularly the last three. Strong union power appears in all these data as a European phenomenon – though not all European countries share in it, especially those in the east and south. There is too much diversity within Europe to enable us to speak of a single 'European social model', but one here sees traces of it.

As with all statistical correlations, we have to be very careful about any causal inferences we try to draw. Is it the case that strong trade unions are able to restrict inequalities, only partly through their bargaining activities but mainly their political work? It might seem surprising that the correlation with union strength is strongest with post-tax incomes, when unions' direct activities are concerned with pre-tax incomes. Are their wider connections with politically strong labour movements more important than their immediate bargaining? If so, this evidence is consistent with that above on the relationship between pre- and post-tax income inequality and the Weberian argument that organization can be used to offset class inequality. On the other hand, might the explanation run the other way round: are unions better able to flourish where the power of the wealthy is reduced? Or are both the level of inequality and the level of union power the results of further contextual factors about the societies concerned, such as the past political power of labour movement parties, or general social values about the acceptability of inequalities of power and income at work? We can probably again draw on the argument developed above that, whatever strictly speaking happened 'first', the two elements involved – here inequality and union power – engage in mutual reinforcement.

Conclusion

The financial and managerial elite fulfils the conditions for being the ruling social class of post-industrial society: it occupies particular occupational positions; typical incomes are associated with these; it is able to convert its economic resources into political power in a self-reinforcing mechanism; and it also has a shared culture and set of ideas. It is a transnational class, rooted mainly in the United States but appearing in many countries or in no particular country. This means that the nation-state form of analysis that we have adopted in this book cannot adequately deal with it: all we can observe is the impact that this class has on individual nation states, not its own global articulation.

Compared with this, the other potential classes of modern post-industrial society have far smaller chances of actualizing themselves. People can use their class position to improve their life chances in two ways. First, simply by preparing for and operating within the scope of the characteristics of their position they obtain certain combinations of advantages and disadvantages. No particular membership of an organization dedicated to advancing the cause of the occupational group concerned is needed for people to be able to use their class position in this way. However, a group that manages to form organizations to do so may gain further. A representative membership organization might seek monopoly control over the labour market of an occupation, as in the case with many professional associations and some trade unions. Or it might develop strategies for improving the group's position, which it seeks to achieve, not through monopoly control but through bargaining with employers, as is the case with most trade unions. Alternatively again, it might lobby governments to improve the group's position, as practised by groups at all levels from the global rich to some, but not many, semi-skilled occupations. Those at the lowest levels typically have no organizational possibilities, just as they lack advantages within the labour market itself. The wealthier that a group is, the less formal its organizations need to be and the easier access they will have to governments and others.

Individuals are not necessarily aware that they are acting to advance their class position, whether they are going through the processes of preparing themselves for and practising an occupation or joining an organization that claims to represent its interests, though it may help them to advance further if they have that awareness. It is when organizations arise to represent the concerns of a group that the issue of awareness of interests arises most clearly, but that may be limited to a relatively small circle of activists and officials, who have the task of developing a detailed understanding of interests representing those who might be less aware of them.

In complex economies class interests, whether in the labour market or in organized expression, are approached only indirectly. Classes are too heterogeneous to be organized as such and appear rather through the aggregation of more limited bodies representing particular groups. For example, lawyers and doctors rarely if ever share labour market positions or organizations; both are united only in as much as through the organizational forms they both use to advance their interests in more or less protected markets. In the late 19th and early 20th centuries organized employees, mainly though not solely male manual workers in manufacturing, in many European countries established political parties to represent their shared class interests, and these have continued ever since to be an important component of democratic countries, known variously as socialist, social democratic or labour parties. But to flourish in mass electorates where male manual workers in manufacturing were never a majority and became a declining minority required these parties to broaden their appeal and reduce their emphasis on class issues. A similar process affected parties that developed to protect the interests of property owners and other very prosperous groups who saw their interests threatened by the rise of manual workers. These too had to broaden their appeal to survive among mass electorates. As a result of these processes the representation of class interests appears blurred in current party competition. The only unambiguous form of organized class representation therefore is that of the very wealthy. Other groups hold the labour market positions that we have considered in this and the previous chapter, but the main form of organized articulation of lower interests remains trade unions.

It might still be argued that these issues of class do not really matter in post-industrial societies, on the grounds that today class is only one among the factors that affect people's lives, and one that is declining in importance. This is an issue that we must explore in the next chapter.

Chapter 7

The wider implications of class

In the previous chapter we treated class primarily in terms of the power that classes are able to wield, differentiating between on the one hand the conscious and deliberate exercise of a class's resources and on the other the fact that merely by operating within one's labour market location one enjoys a certain mix of advantages and disadvantages. Members of a class, it was argued, did not necessarily know precisely what they were doing when they allied themselves with organizational forms of expressing class interests, only that they lent these organizations elements of their strength, perhaps just a regular financial contribution. This discussion, however, begged the question of the extent to which people act, consciously or not, in accordance with what we might expect from them as members of a particular class and how a class identity relates to other identities they hold. In other words, how much does class matter to everyday life?

This goes far beyond discovering that people state in a questionnaire response that they consider themselves to be a member of a certain class, as we do not know what they understand by that class and what implications it has for their lives. Also, popular understandings of class are unlikely to use the terms developed by recent sociological research, but will use a few phrases such as upper, middle and working. A scientific analysis of class needs to go beyond this. There is an analogy here with the natural sciences. If we ask people what is coming out of their taps, they will answer 'water'. A mineralogist will give a more complex answer listing various carbonates, sulphates and other chemicals including pollutants that may well be important for understanding what people are taking into their bodies when they have a glass of what they call water. It is important to know if membership of a class has wider implications for people's attitudes and behaviour, irrespective of whether they define themselves as being a member of that class in precise terms or not – just as the chemical content of tap water might affect a person's health whether they know that content or not.

Education and social mobility

A first aspect of life where class membership is highly important is education. This has the added significance that, as we have seen in Chapter 4, education is one of the defining characteristics of occupational groups and income levels: education reproduces class and class reproduces education. To the extent that parental class influences children's educational achievements, class membership is perpetuated across generations, which in turn strengthens the position of classes as social groups with distinctive cultures and lifestyles.

The intergenerational transmission of class positions has been one of the most closely studied themes of modern sociology, not so much through literal property inheritance as through that of cultural property passed on through family contacts and traditions and also through formal education – what Pierre Bourdieu called 'cultural capital' (Bourdieu and Passeron, 1973). The strength of such mechanisms is seen to consolidate class structures. When they are weak, and there is not much connection between the occupation held by one generation of a family and the next, there is said to be a high rate of 'social mobility'. However, a high rate of general social mobility does not necessarily mean that class structures are weak. The question needs some detailed investigation.

Throughout European history there has been a strong tendency for sons to follow the occupations of their fathers; wives, mothers and daughters were also involved, but less so as women did not so often have occupations, or if they did they had fewer rights to them than men. Rich and powerful men passed on their property and legal rights to their sons, very formally so in the case of inherited positions such as monarchs and aristocrats. Tenant farmers and other small-scale land workers would pass on their land tenure rights and agricultural skills to widows, sons and occasionally daughters. Practitioners of professions such as law, cultural activities such as musicians and urban crafts such as bakers, shoemakers and many others would do the same. The Catholic Church stood partly outside this general hereditary principle because of its rule of celibacy among its priests at all levels, though wealthy and aristocratic families often controlled appointments of bishops and archbishops and awarded these posts to celibate family members. In traditional societies class position was as much a taken for granted attribute of families as of individuals. From this came the strong association of lifestyle and culture with different class positions that are characteristic of class societies.

In these earlier societies the inheritance of social and occupational positions could be heavily disrupted by natural disasters, civil upheavals and wars; the image we often have of traditional societies being static and unchanging neglects the fact that life in them was not very stable. Also, traditional European societies seem always to have presented some possibilities for a small number of individuals and families to rise up the social scale, especially through the Church, the law and other professions (such as they were). It is notable that when Portuguese explorers invaded parts of India in the 15th century they were struck by the apparent rigidity of society there; people seemed to be 'cast' into their occupational positions with no capacity to change. They used the Portuguese word *casta* to describe this, which is the same as the English word 'caste' used to characterize the traditional Indian social order. This suggests that the class order of 15th-century Portugal was itself not entirely rigid.

From the 18th century onwards many European societies experienced new kinds of change. The French Revolution destroyed a large part of the traditional ruling elite and then in turn large numbers of the new elite. For a period there were vacancies for many important occupations, what Napoleon Bonaparte called *la carrière ouverte aux talents* (the career open to talents) – posts that would be filled by people possessing the ability to perform them, not by those born to them. In the first instance this lasted only a short period, as following Napoleon's fall the restored Bourbon monarchy re-established the hereditary principle. But the seed had been sown of the idea that posts, even important ones, should be held by those qualified to do them rather than those families who had traditionally practised them. The two approaches are not entirely at odds with each other; when education and training are largely informal, the best way to learn a skill is probably to be brought up in a family where that skill is practised. Having a ruler/farmer/shoemaker as father may well be the best way to become a skilful practitioner of those various activities. Even when education and training are formal, those whose backgrounds have enabled them to know and understand particular activities will have advantages in learning about them.

The other, probably more significant, source of change in systems of occupational inheritance came with the vast transformations of occupations themselves ushered in by the Industrial Revolution. Existing wealthy families were often the only people with the resources to become industrial capitalists; and many of the first industrial skills derived from pre-industrial urban crafts – for example, metal-working developed from the work of blacksmiths. But much was entirely new. New rich families emerged, especially where there were cultural obstacles to landed aristocrats 'dirtying' themselves by becoming involved with trade. An immense number of new occupations appeared in factories and, later, in offices. The skills needed for these could not be inherited from families, as no one had possessed them in the past. Education and training had to become more formal and schools and colleges of many types emerged as countries entered industrialization. Therefore there was necessarily far more social mobility; the occupations pursued by previous, mainly rural, generations were simply no longer available. People had to move. In more recent decades, as we have passed from industrial to post-industrial occupations, this process has intensified. Old industries have declined or collapsed, and even when they have survived their skills and occupations have changed. Mobility from industrial to other kinds of occupation necessarily follows, no matter how strong the hold on privilege maintained by traditional elites.

Increasingly societies make use of formal qualifications acquired through education and training in order to determine whether people should be able to pursue a particular occupation. On the other hand, the pace of technological change sometimes means that the formal skill provision system has not caught up with new types of economic activity. This was notably the case with the early years of the rise of information technology and domestic computers. The early pioneers tended to be self-taught; they were inventing new products and activities, so there was little that could be taught to them through formal means. From this derived the semi-mythical image of computer entrepreneurs teaching themselves in their parents' garages. Eventually the knowledge started to be codified and today's IT entrepreneurs acquire their core skills in universities and colleges.

The overall level of mobility is therefore very high in today's advanced societies. But what does this tell us about the class structure? Much of the movement takes place horizontally within what we have identified as the broad class structure of these societies. The daughter of a skilled manual worker in manufacturing who becomes a social care worker has certainly moved from the occupational world of her parental family into a different one. But we would not necessarily say she has moved up or down. If she becomes a solicitor we would probably say she has experienced not just social mobility but upward mobility; if she becomes an office cleaner we should probably say she had undergone downward mobility. In other words, if we are interested in the implications of mobility for class structure, we need to distinguish between horizontal mobility (movement between jobs at similar levels of income, etc.) and vertical (upward and downward) mobility. This does not mean that horizontal mobility is of no importance to class structure. We have noted that one of the distinctive characteristics of classes is that they generate distinctive cultures around their life chances, lifestyles and educational backgrounds. The lower the rate of change in occupational structures, the more classes are likely to develop these strong characteristics; when change is rapid, clusters of occupations may have no time to develop characteristics at all before they undergo radical transformation. This explains one of the main puzzles of contemporary societies: inequality is increasing, but there are also claims that society is becoming 'classless'. Such a thing can happen because positions within the hierarchy of inequality do not have, or have not yet had, time to establish themselves with distinctive cultures.

Even if we learn that a society has a high level of upward mobility, we still do not know whether that means that there is increasing equality of opportunity. We have seen that in many European societies the number of low-skilled jobs is declining and those that require some training and preparation are increasing. This necessarily means that there will be more upward mobility, as there are more skilled jobs in the economy in which people are finding jobs than in the one in which their parents' generation found jobs. It might, however, still be the case that people from existing privileged backgrounds stand a better chance of entering the more desirable occupations. To know whether class structures are really losing their grip, we need to know to what extent this is happening. Sociologists use the term 'social fluidity' to describe that part of overall vertical social mobility that results from increased openness of access to higher positions rather than just through an increase in the number of such positions.

Popular discussions of social mobility often assume that mobility and even fluidity automatically increase when education plays a major role in allocating people to jobs. Establishing formal qualifications for entry into what are seen as the more desirable occupations and then expanding educational opportunities are therefore seen as key steps in reducing the role of class. However, this assumes that occupying a superior class position does not help a parental generation to secure a superior education for its children. This is clearly false. At the simplest level, money can buy many aspects of education, from ability to pay school and university tuition fees to parents' ability to provide their children with domestic space and materials with which to study. More subtly, the existence of a strong educational culture in a family helps the next generation to access that same culture. It cannot therefore be assumed that expanding education automatically increases class fluidity.

An interesting recent study illuminates some of the complexity. In a comparison of education reforms in three western European societies (Germany, Sweden and the United Kingdom), Marcus Busemeyer (2015) argues that, the less cross-class cooperation there is over education policy, the weaker will be systems of vocational education and training (VET) and apprenticeship. This produced a fascinating contrast between the approaches of secular conservatives (who have dominated change in the United Kingdom) and Christian Democrats (who have prevailed in Germany). The former are hostile to the involvement of trade unions and to some extent organized employers in education policy but willing to see an expansion in educational opportunities (particularly if privately funded). As a result one finds in the United Kingdom (and some other countries that resemble it) a reliance on an expansion of general higher education and the relegation of specific VET to an inferior and neglected status. The more organic approach of Christian Democrats makes them the mirror image of secular conservatives on these two variables: they are happy to include unions and employer associations, but reluctant to see educational expansion of a kind that disturbs the class structure. There has been far less expansion of higher education in Germany than in the United Kingdom, but VET is strong. One perhaps surprising consequence of this is that income inequalities are higher in countries that concentrate on expanding the general education route rather than having a segregated VET system alongside a more exclusive university system. One might also note, though it goes slightly beyond Busemeyer's time frame, that income inequalities have risen sharply in Germany since the development of a more 'anglophone' low-skilled sector of insecure jobs.

The dominance of social democrats in Sweden led to a third set of outcomes: a strong state-dominated VET system in which unions have taken a major interest, but from which employers gradually became disengaged. The result is even less wage inequality than in Germany, but the marginalization of employers from VET seems to be associated with higher youth employment, because the transition from the completion of training to entry into paid work is less smooth. In all three policy regimes it is important to note that a country's dominant partisan constitution affects policy-making, not only through the ideological preferences of the parties involved for educational approaches as such but also through their different attitudes to labour market organizations.

It is less easy to measure social mobility and fluidity than the level of incomes or many of the other issues we have been examining. The necessary data are not generated automatically through tax returns or registers of births and deaths; we depend on sociologists carrying out extensive research projects in which they probe people's backgrounds and occupations. Such surveys are usually conducted on a national basis. To gain knowledge across a number of countries, as we need here, requires surveys that have been carried out on a comparable basis. There is no such research covering all or even most of the countries of interest to us here and nothing very recent. However, Richard Breen and Ruud Luijkx brought together some national studies carried out at the turn of the present century for 11 European countries together with Israel (Breen and Luijkx, 2004). These cover cases from all our putative regions except for FEE: from NWE there are France, Germany and the Netherlands; from Scandinavia, Norway and Sweden; from SWE, Italy and Spain; from CEE, Hungary and Poland; and the two anglophone countries, Ireland and the United Kingdom. Most studies covered the period from 1970 to 2000.

Not surprisingly given the socio-economic changes affecting all these countries, and especially Hungary and Poland, during those three decades, the authors found considerable evidence of overall mobility. Across all countries studied, two-thirds of men were in different class positions from those of their fathers; about half this mobility was vertical, two-thirds of which was upward. This reflects what we would expect given the high level of change in occupations, the decline of elementary jobs, and the net rise in higher-level posts. More surprisingly, in most countries they did not find much change in the levels of upward mobility over time; that is, the level in the 1990s was not very different from that in the 1970s. The only exceptions were Hungary, Ireland, Italy (and outside our range Israel), where the rate did increase. Since these had been countries with relatively low rates in the earlier period, the authors reported some convergence across countries. More women than men experienced mobility, which is again not surprising, since (particularly in western Europe) they have been entering the paid labour force in larger numbers during these decades than in the past. Women have experienced most vertical mobility in Poland and Israel; elsewhere the situation was similar to that for men, with far more upward movement than downward, especially in Hungary, Poland,

Sweden and Israel. There was also more convergence among women than among men, countries having been more distinct from each other in 1970 than at the end of the century.

However, there was less change and less convergence in social fluidity, which was considerably lower than overall mobility. Among men and women alike it changed very little at all over the three decades in the United Kingdom; increased very slightly in Germany; somewhat more in Ireland, Hungary and Poland; and considerably more in France, the Netherlands and Sweden. (Data were not available for other countries on this item.) The net effects include the following. Sweden has remained throughout the period the country with the highest fluidity; Hungary had particularly high fluidity in the 1980s but less since the fall of communism; Ireland experienced high fluidity in the 1990s; France and the Netherlands have moved from having among the lowest levels to being among the highest; Poland has also seen high fluidity; and in Germany and the United Kingdom fluidity has been low.

Assessing the impact of education on occupational mobility involves researchers examining steps between three positions: respondents' class of origin (given by their parents', usually their fathers', occupational class); the educational level they reach themselves; and their class of destination (i.e. their occupational class at the time of the survey). Movements between class of origin and level of education attained measure the extent to which class influences educational level; comparing movement from origin to destination with that from education to destination makes it possible to assess how important education has been to any mobility that takes place. The biggest reductions in inequality in the move from origins to education occurred in France, the Netherlands and Sweden. Inequality also declined in the move from education to occupational destination in these countries and also in Ireland and the United Kingdom – though in these latter countries education itself did not play a role in reducing inequalities. Education played the biggest role in reducing inequality in Sweden; the smallest in the United Kingdom.

It is difficult to draw strong conclusions from this research, particularly when we lack data on so many countries. In the light of other data we have studied, however, it is perhaps not surprising that egalitarian Sweden and the unequal United Kingdom occupy the opposite positions that they do; perhaps more surprising is the absence of stark differences between the two former state socialist countries, Poland and Hungary, and those of western Europe.

Health and life expectancy

Virtually all the demographic issues we discussed in Chapter 2 are affected by class, perhaps the most important being longevity. Eurostat has tried to collect data of this kind, but so far only for a limited number of countries, mainly the Nordics, central eastern Europe and some southern European countries, and no more recently than 2010 (Eurostat, 2012). As an indicator of socio-economic status Eurostat took educational level as the most useful on which they had data, though it by no means corresponds exactly. Taking the statistics for life expectancy at age 30 as being the age for which data are provided that offer the best reflection of current living conditions, and comparing the extremes of educational levels for which they are available, provides the findings as presented in Figures 7.1a and 7.1b. The table presents,

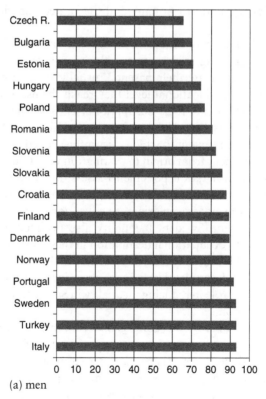

(a) men

Source: OECD 2013

FIGURE 7.1 *Life expectancy (at age 30) of (a) men, (b) women, with only lower secondary education as a percentage of that of same gender with some tertiary education, certain European countries and Turkey, 2008.*

separately for men and women, life expectancy of people who have completed no more than lower secondary education as a percentage of the life expectancy of those who have completed some tertiary education. A figure of 90 per cent means that a person with the lowest level of education has a life expectancy 90 per cent of that of a person with the highest level; a figure of 60 per cent means that a person with the lowest level of education has a life expectancy only 60 per cent of that of a person with the highest level. The male statistics show the biggest differences, which is not surprising as men's working lives are more contrasted by class and educational level than are women's: more men than women work in the paid labour force and more men work in factory environments than do women.

It is notable that, although we saw in Chapter 6 that income inequality was particularly low in the Czech Republic, that country has

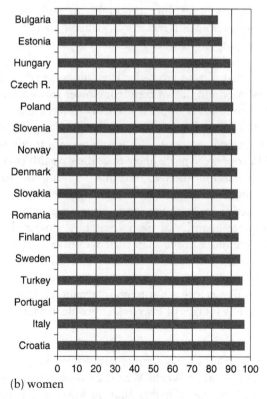

(b) women

FIGURE 7.1 *Continued*

particularly poor male longevity. It will be recalled from Chapter 4 that this country has a particularly high level of employment in manufacturing, industrial work often being unhealthy and dangerous. This does not, however, explain the less extreme position for male longevity of Slovakia, which also has a high level of industrial employment. Overall the male longevity gap between classes is greater for CEE than for SWE or Norden. The Nordic countries have low levels of income inequality, while rich and poor alike benefit from the Mediterranean diet of southern Europe. For women the only large education gaps in longevity are in the FEE cases, Bulgaria and Estonia.

There are no up-to-date, comparative surveys of general European health and mortality patterns, but in 2006 the UK presidency of the European Commission sponsored a survey of the overall state of knowledge about health inequalities in EU member states (Mackenbach, 2006). This confirmed the basic patterns shown in Figure 7.1 for a wider range of countries. Infant mortality as well as that for adults showed socio-economic differences everywhere. There were also interesting geographical and gender patterns. People with lower incomes and/or educational levels were more likely than those higher up the scale to die from stroke and to suffer from illness in general, including mental illness. Men but not women from lower socio-economic backgrounds were more likely to die from many cancers and from injuries and suicide. But other diseases had a more complex pattern. Men and women in lower educational and occupational groups in northern and central Europe were more likely than their wealthier counterparts to die of cardiovascular diseases; but this did not apply to SWE. The researchers argue that the Mediterranean diet played a major role. Outside the Mediterranean zone lower-class people are most likely to eat an inadequate quantity of fresh vegetables. Lower-class men and women alike are more prone than their wealthier counterparts to be overweight in nearly all parts of Europe – though this does not apply to men in SWE or Ireland. There is, however, recent evidence that the Mediterranean diet is losing out to an international fast-food culture, so these health advantages of lower-class people in that region may be declining.

Most of these health differences can be related to class-related lifestyles, but in complex and sometimes paradoxical ways. For example, in the first decades after World War II cardiovascular diseases were bigger killers of people in higher than in lower social groups. This was mainly because poorer people could not afford the 'bad' lifestyles causing these diseases: smoking, drinking alcohol and eating unhealthy foods. Over time people in the higher groups, often defined by having a higher education, learned to make lifestyle changes and live more healthily, while those lower down started to be able to afford the unhealthy things that the wealthier were starting to give up. This has now led to a complete reversal of the earlier relationship. Overall we can conclude from these admittedly limited data that being in a lower socio-economic group is bad for one's physical health, but that this is mitigated by diet for southern Europeans, especially men, though perhaps not for younger generations replacing pasta and tomatoes with hamburgers and fries.

Class and political identity

A further area of research where the influence of class on behaviour has been important is voting behaviour. Politics as such is beyond the scope of this book, but a few basic points can be established. In western Europe there were long traditions of male manual workers in mining and manufacturing voting predominantly for parties variously called social democratic, socialist, labour or communist – parties defining themselves specifically in relation to the concerns of such workers and developing strong links with trade unions. Other groups, including to some extent women in the families of industrial workers, were more likely to vote for parties variously called conservative, Christian or, less often, liberal. In countries with large Catholic populations, the Church organized its own unions and working-class organizations to combat the hostility to organized religion of the socialist and communist labour movement and this attracted many manual workers to Christian parties. Rural workers were also divided between Christian and socialist parties.

Generalizing very broadly, the two fundamental and overlapping identities for the organization of politics for much of the 20th century were therefore class, understood in over-simple terms of engagement in manual or in non-manual work (with differences between industry and agriculture), and religion. Gender was expressed through the greater tendency for women to vote for Christian parties. Protestant churches, especially the Lutherans, were less successful than the Catholic Church at organizing political movements, with the exception of Calvinist churches in the Netherlands and Switzerland.

These combined class and religious patterns were important constituents of the social geography of mid-20th-century Europe. Where the Lutheran Church held a monopoly position and industrialization produced a large manual working class, socialist parties played a major political role and therefore shaped many aspects of social life. This applied only to the Nordic countries. Where other forms of Protestantism dominated (as in England, the Netherlands and Switzerland) or both Catholicism and Protestantism were strong (Germany, also the Netherlands and Switzerland again) this role was weaker; socialist parties were still strong, but conservative and Christian parties captured many workers' votes and tended to dominate. Most countries that were mainly Catholic were also those that industrialized more slowly. For Ireland, where political cleavages remained tied to divisions among different Church-linked movements in the civil war that followed the country's independence from the United Kingdom in 1922, socialist forces were able to organize only a small party. In Italy there was a very divided society. After the lengthy period of dictatorship from 1924 to 1944, Christian democracy dominated heavily while a large part of the working class and many intellectuals identified with the Communist Party. In the two other cases in this category, Portugal and Spain, dictators closely linked to the Church resisted democracy until the mid 1970s, when these countries rapidly acquired a division between working-class based socialist and multi-class Catholic parties. Orthodox Greece had a similar experience to Portugal and Spain. Where strong Catholicism combined with strong industrialism (Austria, Belgium and Luxembourg), political camps were more evenly matched. Germany, divided between Lutheran and Catholic forms of Christianity, showed a more complex pattern. The United Kingdom was also complex, as the extensive empire seemed to lead many manual workers to identify with fellow white English and Scottish members of the ruling class against the black and brown peoples of most of the empire. As neighbouring Ireland became a particular flashpoint within that empire, the Catholic character of its inhabitants similarly united rich and poor British Protestants in Britain and especially in Northern Ireland within the Conservative Party. We can see in these different patterns potential explanations for some of the inter-regional differences that we have observed throughout this book.

France remains a partial exception within these trends. In some respects it seems to resemble Austria or Belgium, a Catholic country with an industrial economy and therefore with deep and balanced divisions between right and left. But the French Revolution of 1789 had anticipated the secularization of the rest of Europe by well over a century. Through a series of revolutionary upheavals and regime changes throughout the 19th century, France was divided into a Catholic, partly upper-class, partly peasant world, and a secular, anti-clerical, urban, partly bourgeois, partly proletarian component. These manifold cross-currents by the second half of the 20th century produced a quadripartite grouping of a nationalist, largely Catholic right, an economically liberal right, a communist left based in the working class and a liberal, more bourgeois left voting for the socialist party and other small republican parties. The communists, as in Italy, were excluded from sharing in government.

As we saw in Chapter 3, the move to post-industrial society in western Europe was (in great contrast to the United States) accompanied by a decline in the social power of the churches. The consequences of both developments for political allegiances have been complex. The linked decline in religion and rural life hurt conservative and Christian parties, forcing them to reshape their appeal. The decline of industrial employment and trade unions did the same for socialist parties, as did the overall rise in high-skilled, and decline in low-skilled, employment. The growth of female employment in the new services sectors produced generations of women who did not define themselves primarily in terms of the domestic life to which churches, and especially the Catholic Church, had tended not just to confine them but also to celebrate. Particularly as symbolized in the role of Mary the mother of God in Catholicism, motherhood was accorded a privileged place in Christianity and with it responsibility for the treasured institution of the family. As women entered the post-industrial paid labour force, the appeal of this symbolism weakened in a context of the already weakening hold of Christianity. These new women are often more likely to vote for leftist parties than their mothers, just as men moving into various non-manual jobs were less likely to vote left than their working-class fathers. A major aspect of the rise of services sectors was the growth of the welfare state and employment in its distinctive sectors: education, health, care and overall public administration. In many countries public employees had historically voted mainly for conservative parties, as they were often given privileged employment conditions by right-of-centre governments anxious to build a popular support base. However, as their numbers increased, their working conditions took on a mass form and they joined unions, often in larger numbers than manual workers – though their unions were often not highly political. This trend provided left-of-centre parties with new constituencies, a process strengthened as rising public spending led many right-of-centre parties to oppose welfare-state growth. The fact that eventually a majority of public employees were women reinforced existing changes in gender voting, until by the late 20th century the earlier position of mainly left-wing men and right-wing women was becoming completely reversed.

The established parties of democratic industrial societies were acquiring more complex patterns of support; historical processes of this kind do not happen quickly, as existing generations usually remain with the allegiances and practices of their own youth, leaving it to the young to represent the new forces at work. Therefore, for example, leftist parties acquired female voters working in public services alongside their older male manual workers. Right-of-centre parties attracted upwardly mobile employees alongside representatives of the old classes. In several polities existing parties proved unable to cope with the strain of these cross-currents and new ones emerged, representing various forms of liberalism and environmentalism.

Behind these trends all parties were affected by something deeper still: a general loosening of ties between parties and voters, until it begins to seem inappropriate to include a discussion of voting behaviour within the framework of a discussion of identities. Does voting for a party, even repeated voting for it, necessarily imply an 'identity' with it any more than frequent purchase of a brand of soap implies an identity with the firm making the soap? If so, what implications might this have for the way in which democracy is practised? This has now become a serious issue for debate. Certainly many election campaigns resemble advertising campaigns for products, suggesting that parties do indeed consider that they no longer bond with voters as they might have done in the past. The economic and social changes discussed here go some way to explaining why such a change might have occurred: allegiances take time to develop, and possibly we have not yet seen the new stable political identities that post-industrialism might produce. But there are grounds for suspecting that something more fundamental is at stake. Religion and class became such powerful forgers of political identity because in the late 19th and early 20th centuries they had been at the centre of struggles over social inclusion and exclusion. Members of minority religions and economically weak social classes were often formally excluded from citizenship rights. Those who benefited from this exclusion would support politicians promising to continue it, as they would derive advantage from the lack of competition for social position that this implied. Those excluded would support parties advocating their inclusion. The identities conferred by these processes went considerably further than voting rights and defined access to jobs and social positions of various kinds. Just as class identity itself is defined and conferred by authorities who erect barriers around various groups, so the political correlations of class identity have historically been associated with the imposition of a further set of defining and identifying barriers. It was from their position in struggles over inclusion and exclusion that people came to define themselves and to draw a deep sense of general social identity from their occupational and sometimes religious identities.

By the end of World War II all adults in western Europe (apart from the continuing southern dictatorships) had gained political citizenship – though women lacked the vote in Switzerland until 1970. Although there was still considerable economic inequality, formal political equality had been achieved; there were no longer excluded persons among adults possessing a nationality entitlement. Any new allegiances being generated through the rise of services sectors, changes in gender employment patterns and the decline of religion did not have the deep implications for identity that such characteristics had in the age of struggle over citizenship and inclusion. These new identities are therefore likely to be far weaker than those inherited from the struggles of industrializing, democratizing society. Political allegiance increasingly becomes mere 'voting behaviour'. Gender may be a partial exception to this, as in many societies women still face various finds of exclusion, but so far this has rarely had major implications for political party organization.

One important area of exception to this has remained or rather emerged. As the societies of western Europe attracted immigrants from other parts of the world, so new issues of inclusion and exclusion have appeared. Immigrant groups are likely to support left-of-centre parties, because these have a tradition of advocating the causes of the excluded. But more important than the political allegiances of these small groups has been a wave of consciousness of national identity among existing native citizens in opposition to the newcomers. It is a further example of mobilization of the included against the excluded. In almost every European country, west and east, north and south, there has been a rise of new xenophobic parties and of similar tendencies within existing ones, aimed at reducing the numbers and/or rights of immigrants. These parties are changing the landscape of European politics. Many different processes are at work here: fears of competition for jobs between native workers and immigrants; hostility to the EU, which is seen as the power 'imposing' immigrants from eastern Europe on the west; anxieties about large numbers of refugees escaping from wars, oppressive regimes and disasters in the Middle East and North Africa;

fears of terrorism from among Islamic minorities; and general discomfort at being confronted with different lifestyles and cultures. If these new political forces seem to have more energy in contemporary democracies than the older parties, it is likely to be because the former address senses of identity that used to be, but increasingly are not, involved in the links of older parties to their supporters.

Some people in the countries of central and eastern Europe are sharing fully in this rise of xenophobia, but their overall legacy of political identities from the 20th century has been very different from that in the west. There were no free elections under state socialism. Citizens were required to vote, but there was no choice of candidates. Everyone was deemed to be politically included, but in practice everyone apart from a small Communist Party elite was excluded. Classes were in theory abolished. The manual working class was deemed to be the class that carried the socialist project and its members received certain privileges, but these did not extend to the right to be able to take part freely in political life. Routine non-manual workers ranked below skilled manual ones in income and prestige (though that was not really different from the situation in contemporary western Europe). These factors have produced societies with distinctive political legacies.

When the southern European dictatorships collapsed, enabling Greece, Portugal and Spain to enter the democratic world, they quickly acquired party systems like those found in the north; the class patterns of capitalist dictatorships had been similar to those of capitalist democracies. This was not what happened after 1990 in the east. The class norms of state socialist countries having been so different, there was no similar process when they began to develop parties. Also, it must be remembered, they were entering democratic Europe at the moment when its own party identities were undergoing the severe decline that we have discussed above. Although some parties with similar names to those in the west have emerged, their links with groups in the wider society representing the corresponding identities have not been strong, their existence has not been stable and they compete with a number of other parties based on wealthy or prominent individuals – as indeed happened in Italy after the collapse of its party system, also in the early 1990s. To date there are few comparative studies of political allegiances across central, eastern and western Europe, but those we have confirm the above account of a particularly weak role for class. Furthermore, turnout at elections in CEE is shrinking more rapidly than in the west – an indication that strong allegiances are not being formed, despite the pleasure with which the populations of those countries initially greeted their ability to participate in free elections.

Class and political identity in post-industrial Europe

The concepts of class on which most research into political and other identities has been based have not fully used the evidence discussed in Chapter 4 that the distinction between manual and non-manual work has far less importance in post-industrial than in industrial societies. The most important contribution to date in the analysis of post-industrial class structures that has tried to confront this is that of the Swiss sociologist, Daniel Oesch (2006a, 2006b; Oesch and Rodríguez Menés, 2011). He takes full account of the fact that the division between manual and non-manual is not fundamental in such societies, that routine workers in various services sectors are at the foot of today's income hierarchies and that women's occupations must be fully incorporated into analysis. He follows the same broad hierarchical division of occupational groups that we used in Chapters 4 and 5, also fitting self-employed persons, whether employers, independent professionals or workers on their own account, into the scheme. Oesch's crucial original step is then further to add important observations on horizontal divisions into three kinds of work task that run right across the vertical structures, distinguishing among those oriented to:

- Technical tasks, producing a hierarchy of technical experts, technicians, skilled craft workers, and routine industrial and agricultural workers.
- Organizational tasks, producing a hierarchy of higher-grade managers, associate managers, skilled office workers and routine office workers.
- Interpersonal tasks, producing a hierarchy of socio-cultural professional workers, socio-cultural semi-professional workers, skilled service workers and routine service workers.

Oesch has applied his analysis to changing occupational structures in Germany, Sweden, Switzerland and the United Kingdom (Oesch, 2006a, 2006b) and to Germany, Spain, Switzerland and the United Kingdom (Oesch and Rodríguez Menés, 2011). His main concern is to consider what has been happening to skills during this process of change and also to offer an adequate account of the gendered character of different work roles – for example, women are most likely to be found in 'interpersonal' occupations. He also found interesting differences among the countries he studied. Because of the dominance within it of business services, the United Kingdom had developed a particularly large number of jobs in the 'organizational' stream; Germany's continuing role as an industrial producer had given it a predominance of technical jobs; while Sweden's strongly developed public services have produced a particularly large number of interpersonal jobs. (Notably, the interpersonal hierarchy has professional rather than managerial leadership. This follows what we found in Chapter 4 to be the distinctive occupational structure of Denmark, a country similar to Sweden.) Switzerland tended to have more people in the independent, self-employed stream. Through analysis of this kind it is possible to identify societal differences that were concealed in the simpler analysis of occupational structure that we conducted in Chapters 4 and 5.

Most importantly, Oesch sees in these different occupational task orientations implications for the self-perception of people occupying them. He argues that important to class analysis has always been a distinction between what Scott (1994) has called class locations – the objective positions that people hold – and the implications that these have for various attitudes and beliefs. Classes may in this sense be 'latent'. For Oesch different kinds of task orientation have this latent capacity. Here might be a key to class identity in post-industrial societies. The analysis leads us to expect different self-perceptions from people in similar hierarchical positions but different task orientations. This would not be unprecedented. During the course of industrialization it was common for manual workers in manufacturing to support radical and socialist movements while those in agriculture were conservative. Analogous processes seem to be at work today. Oesch finds that professionals in interpersonal tasks tend to vote for parties of the political left (especially new and environmentalist parties rather than classic social democratic ones), while managers and professionals in the other task types vote for the right. This is a difference that extends to interpersonal professionals working in the private sector, so it is not just a distinction between public and private sectors. It also applies to men and women alike, even though the two genders are found in different proportions in the different orientations. Patterns of trade union membership see the highest levels among interpersonal professionals and semi-professionals and then technical manual workers, with very little among all levels of workers with an organizational task orientation.

Kitschelt and Rehm (2014) have used Oesch's analysis to address more specifically political questions across a wider range of western European countries: Belgium, Denmark, Finland, France, Germany, Greece, Ireland, the Netherlands, Norway, Portugal, Spain, Sweden, Switzerland and the United Kingdom. They derive three dimensions on which political attitudes in advanced societies might be measured, which they summarize with somewhat forced alliteration as Greed (are people in favour of the redistribution of income?), Grid (do people hold liberal or authoritarian attitudes on social behaviour?) and Group (do people hold more or less inclusive attitudes on citizenship and immigration?). Looking first at the vertical dimension of organizational hierarchy across all task orientations, they found that the higher up the hierarchy they stand, the less likely were respondents to favour redistribution, but the more liberal and inclusionary they were on other dimensions. People low in the hierarchy showed the opposite characteristics, favouring redistribution but being more authoritarian and exclusionary. Particularly among managerial and professional staff there were, however, differences when task orientation was taken into account. The socio-cultural professionals were the least hostile to redistribution; organizational managers the most. These findings seemed to hold across all 14 countries considered and – surprisingly – even after controlling for income, education, gender and sector (public or private). It was not possible for the authors to check the direction of any causality – that is, did working in a particular type of occupation lead people to adopt certain attitudes or did different personality types self-select themselves for certain kinds of work? But that is less important than the finding that such associations exist, as it is these that determine the kinds of values and approaches that people working in different parts of the economy promote.

Conclusion

When we combine this knowledge about perceived interests and values within the post-industrial workforce as a whole with that discussed in Chapter 6 identifying a putative 'ruling class', we begin to have a clearer picture of the structure of classes and their interests. For many years class analysis has concentrated on a decreasingly important division between manual and non-manual work, has ignored the very wealthy and until recently ignored the growing importance of women's employment. We can now move forward from this, but still await more national studies so that we can consider whether various national differences can be explained by differences in economic structure. At the level of full subjective awareness, class may seem to be declining in importance as a guide to people's behaviour, but at a more implicit level it may be working as importantly in post-industrial society as it did in industrial.

Chapter 8

How many Europes?

Each of the preceding chapters has made us aware of the internal diversity of Europe and we have often used a shorthand of socio-geographical groups of countries in order to go beyond a discussion of individual cases. The groupings we have used have been based on the customary usages of the existing literature, but we have now collected enough data on different issues to reconsider those and assess their adequacy for identifying sub-sets of countries within Europe. Before tackling this, we should dispose of the further question whether there are any similarities that unite all or most of the countries of Europe against their principal external comparators: Japan, Russia, the United States and, as at least partly extra-European, Turkey.

For many issues national wealth has seemed to be a more important source of similarity and difference than being in Europe or not. The countries of western and in some cases central Europe resemble Japan and the United States for many vital statistics and for the organization of economic sectors more closely than they do those further east within Europe. This is unsurprising, and it is of more interest to indicate those few points where the majority of European countries do seem to share characteristics against these external comparators. Two important candidates are social inequality and religion. For several measures of inequality the United States, Turkey and Russia appear together as highly inegalitarian outliers compared with most European countries, with the exception of some countries in the east and south west of Europe. But we can identify Norden, NWE and the most industrialized countries in CEE as constituting a distinctive, relatively egalitarian zone. Japan fits towards the less egalitarian end of the European range, but is not an extreme outlier like Russia and the United States.

Where religion is concerned, on the other hand, Japan and Turkey are clear exceptions in not being part of the Christian tradition. Russia is close to European countries from the two Orthodox traditions. The most interesting contrasts are between western and especially Protestant Europe and the United States. In Europe the more Protestant regions have become the most secular, whereas in the largely

190

Protestant United States religion is very vibrant. This European generalization includes the United Kingdom, so often seen as resembling the
United States more than it does other European countries; in fact, the
United Kingdom and in particular England is arguably the most secularized country of all. Given that religious observance tends to be high
in Latin America, and in primarily Islamic countries and poor parts of
the world in general, it is Europe, and in particular its north-western
part, that is distinctive at a global level in its secularism.

The United States clearly resembles the countries of NWE and Norden in having a highly advanced economy. Although strictly comparable statistics are not available, we know that it shares with them
a rapidly declining industrial sector, growing business services and
professional and managerial employment, and a high level of female
employment. Outside that economic core however there are puzzles,
as the United States departs from NWE in a number of respects. Given
its very high overall wealth, it has relatively poor life expectancy, a low
age of first marriage for women, a low level of trade union membership and very high inequality. On these issues it more closely resembles
further eastern Europe and, in the case of inequality, the south west.

Russia, less surprisingly, resembles the further east of which it is
geographically, historically and culturally a part. It shares with those
countries poor life expectancy, a low first age of marriage and a very
high level of inequality – most of these being shared with the Baltic states too. It also shares their pattern of highly uneven economic
development.

One might have expected Japan to have differed more clearly from
all parts of Europe than either the United States or Russia, which have
stronger historical, religious and cultural connections to parts of it.
However, this is not the case. On most issues Japan comes where one
would expect it to do given its level of national income: with the richer
parts of SWE (i.e. northern Italy and northern Spain). It belongs with
those countries for exceptional longevity, for relatively high inequality
and for a relatively high level of industrial employment.

Turkey resembles its neighbours in eastern Europe (Bulgaria and
Romania) in low life expectancy, high death rate and early marriage,
characteristics that differentiate it from the countries of SWE.

We now return to the task of trying to identify the sub-regions of
Europe. The putative sub-regions that were developed in Chapter 1 on
the basis of existing literature were:

- The Nordic countries, with universalist welfare states: Denmark,
  Finland, Norway, Sweden and possibly Iceland.

- The anglophone countries, with residual welfare states: Ireland and the United Kingdom, which many observers would expect to find having important similarities with the United States (and also with Australia, Canada and New Zealand).
- North-West Europe (NWE), with Bismarckian, occupationally based welfare states: Austria, Belgium, Germany, Luxembourg, the Netherlands and Switzerland, with a question over the allocation of France.
- South-West Europe (SWE), with Bismarckian, family-based welfare states: Cyprus, Greece, Italy, Malta, Portugal and Spain.
- Central East Europe (CEE), the ex-state socialist successor states of the Austro-Hungarian Empire: Croatia, Czech Republic, Hungary, Poland, Slovakia and Slovenia, with a question over the allocation of Poland, which had a shared German/Russian and only partly Austro-Hungarian legacy.
- (Highly provisional) Further Eastern Europe (FEE), the previously Russian dominated states: Belarus, Bulgaria, Estonia, Latvia, Lithuania, Georgia, Moldova, Romania, Ukraine and possibly Poland.
- All of ex-Yugoslavia (ex-Y) apart from Slovenia and Croatia (Serbia, Montenegro, Macedonia, the Kosovo enclave and possibly Albania).

The viability of these can now be considered in the light of the previous chapters. It seems immediately that making a separate category of ex-Yugoslavia is not viable. Discussion is hampered by the absence of reliable data on all these new states apart from Slovenia and to a lesser extent Croatia. From the information we do have, it is clear that these are among the poorest countries in Europe, having been torn apart by war and the collapse of the state structures of Yugoslavia. It is remarkable that, while Slovenia on the one hand has an annual per capita income higher than that of Greece and Portugal, on the other hand Macedonia, Bosnia-Herzegovina and Kosovo have among the very lowest incomes in Europe and come only slightly above India. And yet until 1990 they were all regions of the same supra-national state. Apart from Croatia and Slovenia, these former parts of Yugoslavia have a general longer-term history similar to that of Bulgaria and Romania: historically part of the Orthodox world, they came under Islamic Ottoman domination for several centuries. The case for making a separate group of most of ex-Yugoslavia was that these countries had a different trajectory after the end of World War II, having their own distinctive form of state socialism rather than the Russia-dominated form. But this does not seem enough to have distinguished them from what we have called here Further Eastern Europe – though geographically they do not lie in the east.

In order to consider whether a particular set of countries really does constitute a sub-section of Europe, we shall proceed as follows. We shall first assume, as has been discussed throughout the book, that differences between countries result mainly from differences in their national incomes. Where countries have a score on a particular variable that seems out of line with this hypothesis, we count it as an exception needing special explanation. (The means of determining whether a country is an exception are set out in the Methodological Note in Box 1.1 in Chapter 1.) Where countries forming exceptions of a similar kind (i.e. either high above or below the mean) come from the same geosocial group as listed above, we take that as evidence that the group concerned constitutes a sub-section of Europe *for the variable concerned.* If the same group appears as an exception across several variables, we shall regard it as a sub-section in general. If some countries in a group share an exceptional position while remaining countries also come the same side of the mean as these, the group will be regarded as constituting a whole; where the other cases fall the other side of the mean, attention will be drawn to the fact. Where some countries from different sub-sections appear together on a number of variables, we shall consider the possibility that a non-geographical sub-section exists.

We shall discuss the geosocial groups, not in the order listed above, but according to the ease with which the identities of the groups seem to be confirmed in the light of our evidence. We shall start with those where the above scheme seems to fit quite closely, ending with those where the reality of the identity is highly questionable.

Norden

The Nordic countries share many characteristics and have appeared together in many of our discussions. They have long shared a common history, ruling over each other at various times, and with the exception of the Finns have mutually comprehensible languages. This is also the only region of the democratic world to have experienced very lengthy periods of centre-left government. All countries have a highly secularized, fully Protestant tradition, a pattern not shared with any other countries. Very recently there have been high waves of immigration (except Finland).

There are nevertheless important differences among them. Finland had been ruled over by Sweden from the early 16th century until 1809 and then experienced a century of Russian rule. It achieved independence during the revolutionary upheavals in Russia between 1906 and 1917, but there followed a complex economic and political relationship with the Soviet Union that lasted until the latter's collapse in 1990. Iceland was ruled by Denmark until the 1940s and sits at the very edge of Europe with a very small population. It has not been possible to include many data from Iceland in this book. Denmark joined the EU in 1973, with Ireland and the United Kingdom, 20 years earlier than Finland and Sweden, while Norway and Iceland remain outside full membership. Finland alone has joined the Eurozone. Both Finland and Sweden have been neutral nations, while Denmark and Norway are members of NATO. Norway is today further distinguished by its very large natural gas sector, which gives it greater wealth than any other European country apart from Luxembourg. Denmark is the only Nordic country, indeed the only north-western European country, with a large proportion of small firms. Finland remained poor and more agricultural than the others until the 1960s.

Following our proposed statistical approach to identifying groups, the Nordic countries share exceptional positions on the following variables. (It should be noted that data for Iceland are missing for several items.)

- A late age of women's first marriage (Norway less than the others). This position is shared with Italy and Spain.
- Low household size (Norway less than the others). This position is shared with France, Germany, the Netherlands and the Baltic states.
- A high level of female employment (Norway less than the others); shared with France, Cyprus, Portugal, the Baltic states and Romania.
- A low level of employment in manufacturing, etc. (mainly Denmark and Sweden); shared with Ireland, the United Kingdom, France, the Netherlands, Cyprus, Greece, Malta and Latvia.
- A high level of public employment (mainly Denmark and Sweden); shared with Belgium, France and Malta.
- A predominance of workers at higher skill levels; shared with nearly all countries in NWE, including the United Kingdom and Ireland.
- A high level of trade union membership; shared with Belgium.
- A very low level of income inequality; shared with Belgium, the Czech and Slovak Republics and Slovenia.

This constitutes strong evidence that the Nordic countries can be considered to be a distinctive sub-section of European society, though

Norway is an exception on some of the group's distinguishing characteristics. No other country has all these characteristics, but there are overlaps on some issues with NWE countries, especially France, but not enough to allocate France to the same sub-section. There are also some similarities with the Baltic states, but strong contrasts on other variables; it is not possible to identify a general northern or Baltic group.

For much of the 20th century the Nordic countries pursued a distinctive path, much of which can be explained by the dominance of Lutheranism, followed by the not unrelated rise of powerful labour movements and in the 20th century a strong commitment to modernism. From this combination emerged the distinctly non-traditional family forms, sophisticated economies and strongly egalitarian politics that lie behind the exceptional characteristics listed above.

Today the basis for much of this distinctiveness is fading. The rest of Europe (though not the United States) has joined the Nordics' long-term secularizing trend. Alongside the growth of advanced post-industrial economies comes a decline in the proportion of manual workers, leading to an end to social democratic hegemony. In fact the region now supports some of the most successful extreme right-wing parties in Europe. Against these trends, the powerful role for women in the economy (itself a consequence of the 'modern' family) has produced a new support base for the highly developed welfare state in which many women are employed. This factor helps explain the continuity of several distinctive features of Nordic society despite the erosion of much of their original political base.

South-West Europe

The SWE countries are not as homogeneous as the Nordic group, a major contrast being the division between Catholic (Italy, Portugal, Malta and Spain) and Orthodox (Cyprus and Greece) religions. These differences reflect the important historical patterns described in Chapters 1 and 3. Italy, Portugal and Spain (along with the former Habsburg Empire) have historically been the most important champions of Roman Catholicism in the world and this is reflected today in the strength of that religion in those countries. Greece and Cyprus, though dominated by the Islamic Ottoman Empire from the mid 15th century until World War I, continued, however, to adhere to the Orthodox Christian faith, which therefore became a major symbol of national identity.

These countries share exceptional positions on the following variables.

- High life expectancy and low death rates. The exceptionally low death rate is shared with France.
- A low level of public employment (mainly Italy, Spain and Cyprus). Malta is an exception. This position is shared with Austria, Germany, Ireland, Luxembourg, Switzerland, the Czech Republic and Slovenia.
- A low level of professional and managerial employment; shared with Norway, Ireland, Austria, Luxembourg, Slovakia and Romania.
- A high level of income inequality (shared with parts of FEE and the United Kingdom).

On some other variables positions are highly ambiguous:

- Italy and Spain alone have a late age of women's first marriage. This is not typical of the region, but these are its two biggest states. This is a characteristic shared with the Nordics.
- In the majority of the population of the area, especially Greece, Italy and Malta, female employment is particularly low; but in Cyprus and Portugal it is very high. Low female participation is also found in the CEE countries.
- A low level of employment in Sector II (manufacturing, etc.) is found in Greece, Cyprus and Malta, but emphatically not Portugal or, to a lesser extent, Italy.
- Large household size is found in two very small countries – Cyprus and Malta – and marginally in Spain.

Despite considerable differences in religious and political histories, the countries of the south-west are united in having not just the healthy Mediterranean diet, but also long periods of domination by political and religious elites that were hostile or indifferent to social and economic change. The Catholic Church, unlike the Lutheran, has had a strong capacity to mobilize public opinion and action. It has done this to confirm allegiance to traditional family patterns, including in the past the subordinate role of women, and to organize its own labour movement, leading to major political and trade union divisions. The secular labour movement developed a strong hostility to the Church and as a result large parts of it allied to communist political parties. Social compromise was very difficult. In Portugal and Spain authoritarian Catholic regimes opposed modernization of the economy for decades, seeing industrialization as a source for undermining traditional authority.

The Greek Orthodox Church has been less actively a mobilizing force, but as the symbol of national identity against Ottoman rule it acquired a strong place in national life in Greece and Cyprus, supporting traditional ways of life and therefore dominant elites who wished to maintain them to avoid disruptive change.

Much of this has changed today. The power of the churches has either declined or changed its political nature. Communist parties are virtually no more. Elites are all determined to modernize their economies. But the legacy of the past remains, as seen in the variables listed above that link most of the countries concerned. These are, however, limited. Were we to dig below national level we should find a greater diversity among the regions of Italy and Spain. In Catalonia in Spain and in many areas of northern and central Italy there are advanced industrial and post-industrial economies; these regions belong more with Europe north of the Alps than with other regions of their own states. Meanwhile, in the south of those countries the forces of traditionalism remain very strong. South-West Europe does constitute a sub-section of Europe, but with a weaker profile and with greater internal diversity than found in the Nordic countries.

Central Eastern Europe

The countries of central and further eastern Europe shared a lengthy history of incorporation into the state socialist system dominated by the Soviet Union. However, this did not impose on them any major similarities of social structure, the region having long been highly varied, ranging from the highly industrialized countries of former Czechoslovakia to areas further east that remain highly rural. We have provisionally divided the region into two parts, based on deeper historical differences: those (CEE) that had been part of the Austro-Hungarian Empire as well as Poland; and the countries further east that had been under some form of Russian hegemony since long before the Russian Revolution or formed part of former Yugoslavia (apart from Slovenia and Croatia). We shall first consider the potential CEE group.

These countries share a Catholic religious heritage from Austro-Hungarian rule, though today only Poland has a strong pattern of religious adherence. It is notable that most of that country was until 1918 dominated by either Orthodox Russia or Protestant Prussia, and the Catholic Church became a symbol of national identity against foreign rule (as it also had in Ireland against Protestant English domination, and as was the case of the Orthodox Church in Greece and Cyprus under Islamic Ottoman rule). Asserting national identity against atheist Soviet Russia for four decades does not seem to have favoured the Church in the rest of the region in the same way as in the more historically embedded Polish case. The countries of CEE today all count as 'middle-income' in the European range, but there is a difference between Slovenia and the two countries of former Czechoslovakia on the one hand and Croatia, Hungary and Poland. These are interesting differences, as they depart from what might have been expected at the time of the collapse of the state socialist regimes around 1990. Then Hungary and Poland had been alongside the Czech and Slovak Republics as the most advanced post-Soviet economies, the so-called Visegrád group, when EU entry was being planned. Croatia and Slovenia were close neighbours within a Yugo-slavia wracked by civil war.

In the chapters of this book CEE has not appeared as a very distinc-tive region on any variables, but the Czech and Slovak Republics and Slovenia have formed a distinctive sub-group as the lands of contem-porary Europe with the largest proportions of their workforces in manufacturing and with relatively small business and other services sectors and (mainly because of that) low levels of female employ-ment. They resemble some of the countries of SWE on these variables more closely than they resemble the rest of CEE and certainly more than they do FEE. They differ significantly from SWE on life expec-tancy and through their particularly low levels of income inequality. They share few distinctive characteristics with Croatia, Hungary and Poland, though we do not yet have enough data on Croatia to make a firm decision about its location in the overall scheme. On the other hand, Slovakia shares large household size with Croatia and Poland; and Poland belongs with this sub-group rather than the countries of FEE in having a relatively low level of female employment.

Further Eastern Europe

The countries of FEE, on some variables including Hungary and Poland, differ from those in CEE mainly on grounds of economic struc-ture and levels of inequality. The group is, however, very varied within itself. All except Bulgaria and Romania had been part of Russia since at least the 18th century until the fall of the Soviet Union in 1990 – Bulgaria and Romania having been governed by the Ottoman Empire.

The Baltic states had enjoyed a brief period of independence between the world wars. Orthodox Christianity has been the dominant religion throughout the region except in Estonia and Latvia, which had become Protestant during the Reformation when they had come under Swedish domination, and Lithuania, which had remained Catholic and part of a joint political structure of varying geography with Poland until the early 18th century. Unfortunately we lack data on Belarus, Moldova and Ukraine except for a very few variables and cannot tell whether they differ significantly from those countries that are now EU member states. They are all the poorest in Europe. Life expectancy is low and death rates high, with in general low ages of women's first marriage. It is likely that the countries of ex-Yugoslavia apart from Slovenia and to a lesser extent Croatia should be considered with this group, though we have insufficient data on them to make a confident decision. From the information we do have, it is clear that these are also among the poorest countries in Europe. These same parts of former Yugoslavia have a general history similar to that of Bulgaria and Romania: for centuries part of the Orthodox Christian world, they came under Ottoman rule following the fall of Constantinople.

If we examine the variables on which FEE countries have distinctive profiles, we become immediately aware that the three small Baltic republics differ completely from the rest, except for their shared very low life expectancy and high death rates, and are also highly distinctive within Europe as a whole. Their small household size ranks them with their Baltic neighbours in Norden and with NWE, all of these countries together forming a clear grouping of 'northern' European small households. Their exceptionally high levels of female employment also rank them alongside Norden and France. Given their overall very low national incomes, they have very high levels of professional and managerial employment and low levels of intermediate occupations. They do not, however, share Nordic equality or trade union strength; very much the reverse. The Baltic states are embarked on their own development path.

Bulgaria and Romania, and probably the other countries of the region, share a large household size that ranks them with SWE. Romania is an extreme case of a low level of professional and managerial employment, a characteristic almost certainly shared with the rest of the region. However, that country also has a high level of female employment; Bulgaria is similar but less strongly so. Female employment, almost the sole legacy among the variables we have considered of Soviet times, alone joins these countries to those of northern Europe.

North-West Europe

The remaining countries of Continental Europe, broadly the north west, south of the Nordic lands, include two very large countries, Germany and France, and several smaller ones (Austria, Belgium, Luxembourg, the Netherlands and Switzerland). There is considerable historical diversity here, as a few very rapid summaries of the histories of today's states will show. France is the longest-standing nation-state in Europe. For long it was a major champion of the Catholic faith, but in the late 18th century it underwent a major secular and modernizing revolution, thereafter becoming divided between Catholic and strongly *laïque* forces.

Austria had been at the centre of the Holy Roman Empire from medieval times until the early 19th century, a fierce defender of the Catholic Church, though from time to time literally at war with the papacy. As such it claimed a kind of suzerainty over the whole of Catholic Europe, but over the centuries this was whittled away until defeat in World War I left Austria as a relatively small country ranging across the Alps and into the Danube Valley around Vienna.

Germany did not become united until the 1860s, as a country with a Protestant majority but large Catholic minority. Following defeat in World War I it lost its Polish conquests, but did not face dismemberment as did Austria-Hungary. Defeat in World War II, however, saw the division of the country into an eastern part dominated by the Soviet Union and a western one that became part of the United States' sphere of influence in Europe and a founding member of the European Economic Community. The new western Federal Republic of Germany, with its capital in Bonn, was majority Catholic. This situation continued until the collapse of the Soviet Union in 1990, when the country regained its pre-1933 borders (that is, renouncing all claims to Polish territory).

Belgium and Luxembourg share a strongly Catholic religious heritage, but the Netherlands and Switzerland, like Germany, are divided between Catholics and Protestants. In the case of these two smaller nations, the stricter Calvinist rather than Lutheran form of Protestantism dominates. Switzerland emerged as a separate political entity from the late 13th century onwards, as valleys and cities in the Alps freed themselves from rule by the Habsburgs, forming the first European republic. The country has tended to go its own way within Europe from that time onwards, though as we have seen in most of its important characteristics it fits within the overall NWE range.

Given all these differences in their historical trajectories, do the states of north-western Europe (outside the Nordic area) today constitute a coherent sub-region? Several countries in the region share the Nordic pattern of small household size and – with the partial exceptions of Germany and Austria – small proportions of the workforce in industry, but large ones in business services. There is considerable diversity around employment in public services, with Belgium and France sharing the Nordic pattern of high employment, but with Austria, Germany and Luxembourg sharing the SWE pattern of a low level. There is a similar mix around the role of professional and managerial employment. NWE differs as a whole from the Nordic countries in having fairly low (in the French case extremely low) levels of union membership – though Belgium and Austria are strong exceptions here. Only France shares the Nordic pattern of a high level of female employment.

Overall there is little evidence here for seeing NWE as a distinct sub-region. The only issues on which there is overall similarity, small household size and a predominance of skilled labour, are shared with the Nordics. On other issues there is always diversity within the group, often involving important differences between the two largest countries, France and Germany.

The anglophones

Much research isolates the anglophone world as having distinctive characteristics, and the provisional classification we have been using so far follows that scheme. But only two of these countries, Ireland and the United Kingdom, are found within Europe. The basis for seeing all the anglophone countries as a group rests fundamentally on their sharing a heritage of common law rather than statute law – though even here matters are complicated by the fact that Scotland maintains an autonomous, Roman law system separate from the rest of the United Kingdom. The common law tradition assumes that law is not primarily made by governments and parliaments but exists as a set of principles that can be agreed to by consensus among an elite of reasonable men. The existence of a legal rule is discovered when judges, using these principles, are asked to resolve a dispute or decide whether and how an action is to be punished. From this builds up a body of case law or precedents, which is then applied to subsequent cases. In contrast, under statute law a legislator – whether a king, a parliament or some other authority – decides through certain procedures that a particular set of rules ought to govern various areas of life and sets this down in formal laws. Outside England most countries in Europe adopted statute law at some point in the Middle Ages, while the English maintained a mixed system, retaining common law for many areas of life while kings and parliaments also made laws as elsewhere.

The key significance of this difference came, mainly from the 17th century onwards, when capitalist merchants and later manufacturers were developing the modern market economy. The common law system enabled English entrepreneurs to develop their activities without much need of state support or state intervention. Since the British developed the largest of all the European overseas empires, this tradition was taken to the parts of the world that they conquered, including North America. In Continental Europe entrepreneurs and merchants were dependent on rulers' willingness to permit them freedoms to trade and to define the scope of those freedoms. This produced the basic difference between the kind of liberal capitalism developed in the anglophone world and the forms that emerged elsewhere, though the Netherlands and Switzerland, where the polities were dominated by banking and merchant rather than aristocratic elites, were not dissimilar from the British. From this flowed a number of further and continuing differences about the role of regulation in the economy in general. Several accounts of contemporary economies still perceive this underlying distinction as implying fundamental differences. For certain aspects of economic and legal regulation they certainly persist, but over the decades the significance of the original distinction has been weakened. Common law has proved inadequate to set the terms of operation of complex modern economies; the United Kingdom, the United States and other 'liberal' political economies have plenty of statute law governing their operation, and since 1973 the United Kingdom has shared in the statutory processes of the EU. On the other side, case law and judicial pronouncements (in German, *Rechtsprechung*) have shaped Continental systems far more than is implied by the stereotype of law made solely by legislatures. Further still, since the 1980s most countries in Europe, and the EU itself, have followed the Anglo-American path of deregulating key parts of the economy, including banking.

There are major differences between the two European members of the anglophone group. Ireland was ruled over by the English from the 12th to the early 20th centuries, but the smaller country remained distinct in many respects. It remained very strongly Catholic after the English Protestant Reformation. Also, it did not share in the British Industrial Revolution, but remained with a very backward agricultural economy, most of the land being owned by English absentee landlords who were not interested in developing it. Even after the successful armed struggle for independence from Britain in the 1920s, the country remained primarily rural. Its staunchly Catholic rulers shared the view, also important to the dictators ruling Portugal and Spain at that time and more or less sociologically accurate, that economic modernization would threaten the traditional social order and way of life. The Church changed its approach to industrialism in the 1950s and by the end of that decade Irish and Spanish, and to a lesser extent Portuguese, governments embarked on modernization, but progress was slow. When it entered the European Economic Community along with the United Kingdom and Denmark in 1973, Ireland was the second poorest country in western Europe after Portugal. A rapid transformation took place, led mainly by inward investment by multinational corporations, until today, even after its particularly difficult experience during the financial crisis of 2008, Ireland ranks as the fourth richest country in Europe after Norway, Luxembourg and Switzerland.

The United Kingdom, but definitely not Ireland, shares the Nordic pattern of small household size, while both share the NWE and Nordic pattern of small proportions of the workforce in industry but large ones in business services and overall high level of labour skill. The United Kingdom shares the Nordic pattern of high employment in public services, but Ireland has a low level. There is a similar mix around the role of professional and managerial employment. Both countries have union membership levels between the Nordic and NWE groups. The United Kingdom, less so Ireland, departs sharply from the Nordic pattern of low income inequality, belonging more with SWE here. Levels of female employment are typical of NWE. There is little evidence for seeing Ireland and the United Kingdom as a group by themselves; overall they fit within the already loose NWE group.

Conclusion

In conclusion, we can correct our initial view of the sub-regions of Europe as follows:

- Europe consists of states that differ considerably among themselves on several key social characteristics.
- Important parts of Europe appear as a relatively egalitarian zone compared with Russia, Turkey, the United States and (to a lesser extent) Japan, but this generalisation excludes southern, anglophone, most of further eastern Europe and the Baltic states.

- Within this overall diversity, clear sub-regional groups can be identified for a few parts of Europe, normally defined by lengthy shared histories: the Nordic states; the Baltic states; to some extent the countries of south-west Europe; the former components of Czechoslovakia, sometimes with Slovenia; and possibly further eastern Europe outside the Baltics.
- These relatively clearly defined groups exist outside what might be regarded as the north-western core of Europe, dominated by the region's three largest states (France, Germany and the United Kingdom). Within this core there is considerable internal diversity that prevents us from seeing it as a sub-region. On several variables most of the countries in this sub-region share important characteristics with Norden.

Our overall conclusion must be that, although there are clear geo-social differences among European countries on familiar axes between north and south, and east and west, most of these can be attributed to differences in level of national income rather than to strong political or cultural distinctions by themselves that define clear sub-regions within the continent. There are a few exceptions to this pattern. Similarly, none of the outside comparators relate in a clear way to either Europe as a whole or to specific sub-regions – except that Russia understandably 'belongs' among the countries of FEE.

We must, however, bear in mind that we have chosen a particular set of themes for this book. A different set might have produced some different results. For example, had we ignored life expectancy, we should not have identified an important characteristic of SWE countries and Japan. Had we been able to include a full discussion of cultural, sporting and leisure pursuits we might have encountered some new groupings. (How important is it, for example, that rugby union football is played in the United Kingdom where it originated, Ireland, certain parts of France and Italy, and Romania, but not much elsewhere in Europe?) However, an informative survey from Eurobarometer (2013) enables us to probe this kind of variable a little closer. Samples of citizens in all EU member states were asked about their attendance at various kinds of cultural activities. In general there was a positive correlation with national income: the richer the country, the more of its inhabitants participated in a given activity, as one might expect. However, for the majority of activities sampled there was a stronger correlation with the proportion of the population in professional employment. This was the case for watching or listening to cultural programmes on radio and television, visiting museums and art galleries, using public libraries and going to the theatre, ballet, dance or opera. A separate Eurobarometer (2014) survey considered active participation in various kinds of sports and exercise in all EU member states except Greece. The main summary measure offered was of those having zero participation. As for zero participation in cultural activities, there was a negative correlation with both per capita national income and proportion of the workforce in professional jobs. Per capita national income was a better predictor than professional occupations of national differences in proportions reading books, going to the cinema or visiting historical monuments and places of interest.

Applying our usual approach to identifying particularly strong or weak countries on particular variables gives the pattern shown in Table 8.1. Only correlations of more than $r^2 = 0.4000$ or more have been used; as in the other cases further issues that we have not explored clearly play a role. (We have too few cases to be able to carry out multi-variable tests.) For each variable we have presented data for whichever was the stronger variable, proportion in professional employment or per capita national income. Given the fragile nature of the statistics, we should pay attention to only the most striking results. Particularly outstanding are the high levels of cultural participation – given those countries' relatively low levels of both professional employment and national income – by two groups of eastern countries – those of former Czechoslovakia and two of the three Baltic states. Also outstandingly high, even for its already high levels on the two independent variables, were several scores for Sweden. In contrast, the two Greek-based cultures, Greece itself and Cyprus, had very low levels, even taking into account their low levels of professional employment and national incomes. The same applies to Portugal.

These statistics, on a set of issues different from those on which we have focused, suggest two things. First, other factors that we have not been able to uncover in this book are clearly involved in differentiating among and grouping different European societies, producing for example important differences between Baltic and ex-Czechoslovak cultures on the one hand and Greek on the other. These need further exploration in a study of a different kind.

Second, the variables on which we have placed importance, however – national income and professional employment – do help to explain these other issues. Professional employment in particular stands as a proxy for educational level and also for social class. We must be careful here of what is known as the 'ecological fallacy'. Just because a country with a high proportion of professionals in its workforce has a high proportion

TABLE 8.1 Participation in various cultural activities, EU member states, c. 2013.

	Correlation with proportion of workforce in professional employment				Correlation with per capita national income		
	High overall participation	No cultural participation*	Museums, art galleries	Public libraries	Read books	Cinema	Visit historical monuments, etc.
Austria		✓	✓			X	
Belgium	X				X	X	X
Bulgaria		XX					
Croatia		X					
Cyprus	XX	✓	XX	XX	X	X	XX
Czech Rep	✓✓	✓	✓	✓	✓		✓
Denmark		✓			✓✓		✓✓
Estonia	✓✓	✓	✓	✓		X	X
Finland		✓		✓✓			
France		✓	✓			X	
Germany				X	X		
Greece	XX	X	XX	XX			XX
Hungary	X	X				X	X
Ireland	X	X					X

Italy			√		XX	X
Latvia			X	√	√√	√√
Lithuania	XX		√	X	X √	√
Malta	X	X			X	
Netherlands	√		√			
Poland	X		X		XX	
Portugal	X		X		XX	XX
Romania			√		√	
Slovakia	√	√√	√	√	X	
Slovenia		√	√	√	√ √	
Spain	√√	√	√√	√√	√	√√
Sweden		√		√		√
UK		X			√	√

Source: Eurobarometer, 2013

Notes: √√ = proportion exceeds 1.0 s.d. from mean of all countries (column marked * proportion is below 1.0 s.d.)
√ = proportion exceeds 0.5 s.d. from mean of all countries (column marked * proportion is below 0.5 s.d.)
X = proportion is below 0.5 s.d. from mean of all countries (column marked * proportion is above 0.5 s.d.)
XX = proportion is below 1.0 s.d. from mean of all countries (column marked * proportion is above 1.0 s.d.)

of its population using, say, public libraries, does not necessarily mean that these are the people using the libraries. To know more about this we need evidence at the level of individuals. The Eurobarometer (2013; 2014) surveys themselves did have this evidence, and report some findings across Europe as a whole, but not distinguishing among states. The report did not find overall age or gender differences, except that the young tended to go to the theatre (and more obviously to participate in sports) more than older people, and women were more likely to read and to go to the theatre while men predominated in other activities. Lack of interest or time tended to explain failure to participate rather than high cost, though the culture report (Eurobarometer, 2013) found some decline in participation since its previous survey in 2007. It attributed this partly to the impact of the recession and partly to the rise in pay TV across Europe, which had made access to cultural programmes more expensive. Overall they shared our finding of an association between professional occupation and a high level of education on the one hand and high cultural and (perhaps less obviously) sporting participation on the other. These class-related variables clearly need to remain at the heart of any sociology of Europe – or probably of any part of the world.

Class structures, as we have seen, not only persist but change their form as types of economy and their associated occupational types come and go. The post-industrial economy has gradually but in the end radically transformed those associated with industrial society from which 19th- and 20th-century sociology developed. On the other hand, the legacies of earlier social forms do not go away, but continue to exercise their influence on the way in which people approach and organize their lives. The division between east and west that characterized Europe from 1945 to 1989 continues to affect differences between western and eastern Europeans. We have also seen the continuing legacy of past history in the persistent influence of religion and mid-20th-century class structures, particularly in accounting for the differences among different regions of Europe and individual countries. There is an analogy here with the natural landscape. Just because a volcano has become extinct – or perhaps only long dormant – does not mean that it does not continue to shape the landscape and even the way people live their lives. Just as we cannot understand the geography of the Bay of Naples without acknowledging the dominance of Vesuvius, so we cannot fully understand the sociology of contemporary Europe without a knowledge of the enormous eruptions of social division that attended the split between Catholicism and Orthodoxy in the 11th century, the Protestant Reformation in the 16th century and the Industrial Revolution of the 19th and 20th centuries.

Statistical Appendix

APPENDIX TABLE A.1   *Background statistics.*

	A			B	
	1990	*2000*	*2015*	*1990–2015*	*2000–2015*
Albania	3,286,500	3,058,497	2,893,000	–11.97	–5.41
Austria	7,644,818	8,002,186	8,584,900	12.3	7.28
Belarus		10,019,480	9,463,840		–5.55
Belgium	9,947,782	10,239,085	11,258,400	13.17	9.96
Bosnia & Herzegovina	4,499,203	3,753,085	3,825,300	–14.98	1.92
Bulgaria	8,767,308	8,190,876	7,202,200	–17.85	–12.07
Croatia	4,772,556	4,497,735	4,225,300	–11.47	–6.06
Cyprus	572,655	690,497	847,000	47.91	22.67
Czech R.	10,362,102	10,278,098	10,538,300	1.7	2.53
Denmark	5,135,409	5,330,020	5,659,700	10.21	6.19
Estonia	1,570,599	1,401,250	1,313,300	–16.38	–6.28
Finland	4,974,383	5,171,302	5,471,800	10	5.81
France	56,577,000	60,545,022	66,352,500	17.28	9.59
Germany	79,112,831	82,163,475	81,174,000	2.61	–1.2
Greece	10,120,892	10,903,757	10,812,500	6.83	–0.84
Hungary	10,374,823	10,221,644	9,849,000	–5.07	–3.65
Iceland	253,785	279,049	329,100	29.68	17.94
Ireland	3,506,970	3,777,565	4,625,900	31.91	22.46
Italy	56,694,360	56,923,524	60,795,600	7.23	6.8
Kosovo*		1,985,000	1,804,900		–9.07
Latvia	2,668,140	2,381,715	1,986,100	–25.56	–16.61
Lithuania	3,693,708	3,512,074	2,921,300	–20.91	–16.82
Luxembourg	379,300	433,600	563,000	48.43	29.84
Macedonia	1,873,109	2,021,578	2,069,200	10.47	2.36
Malta	352,430	380,201	429,300	21.81	12.91
Moldova		3,644,070	3,559,497		–2.32
Montenegro		603,152	622,100		3.14
Netherlands	14,892,574	15,863,950	16,900,700	13.48	6.54
Norway	4,233,116	4,478,497	5,165,800	22.03	15.35
Poland	38,038,403	38,263,303	38,005,600	–0.09	–0.67
Portugal	9,995,995	10,249,022	10,374,800	3.79	1.23
Romania	23,211,395	22,455,485	19,861,400	–14.43	–11.55
Serbia		7,527,952	7,112,000		–5.53
Slovakia	5,287,663	5,398,657	5,421,300	2.53	0.42
Slovenia	1,996,377	1,987,755	2,062,900	3.33	3.78
Spain	38,826,297	40,049,708	46,439,900	19.61	15.96
Sweden	8,527,039	8,861,426	9,747,400	14.31	10
Switzerland	6,673,850	7,164,444	8,236,600	23.42	14.96
Turkey	55,494,711	67,895,581	77,695,900	40.01	14.43
Ukraine		49,114,950	45,372,692		–7.62
UK	57,156,972	58,785,246	64,761,100	13.3	10.17
Japan	126,999,808	126,870,000	126,500,581	–0.39	–0.29
Russia	148,300,000	146,600,000	142,098,141	–4.18	–3.07
US	249,600,000	282,200,000	321,216,397	28.69	13.83

Notes:
* 2000 figure is for 2003
A = Population size. *Source: Eurostat (2015a); for Japan, Russia, USA: national data.*
B = % change in population size.
C = Life expectancy at age 0, 2013. *Source: World Health Organization (2015a).*
D = Net migration per 1,000 initial population. *Source: Eurostat, 2015a.*
E = Female share of total labour force. *Source: World Bank (2015c).*

C			D			E		
Male	*Female*	*M:F ratio*	*2012*	*2013*	*2014*	*1990*	*2014*	*Change 1990–2014*
61	62	0.98				40.6	41.3	0.7
79	84	0.94	5.2	6.5	8.7	40.9	46	5.1
66	78	0.85				48.8	48.7	−0.1
78	83	0.94	4.3	2.3	3	39	45.8	6.8
75	80	0.94				39	38	−1
71	78	0.91	−0.3	−0.2	−0.3	47.9	46.6	−1.3
75	81	0.93	−0.9	−1.1	−2.4	42.5	45.7	3.2
80	84	0.95	−0.7	−14	−17.6	36.2	43.2	7
75	81	0.93	1	−0.1	2.1	44.4	44.1	−0.3
78	82	0.95	3	2	6.5	46	47.7	1.7
72	82	0.88	−2.8	−2	−0.5	49.6	49.1	−0.5
78	84	0.93	3.3	3.3	2.8	47.1	47.7	0.6
79	85	0.93	0.5	0.5	0.5	42.9	47.1	4.2
79	83	0.95	4.9	5.6	7.2	40.6	45.9	5.3
79	84	0.94	−6.8	−6.4	−6.4	36.1	42.8	6.7
71	79	0.90	1.6	0.6	0.5	44.5	45.8	1.3
81	84	0.96	−0.9	5.1	3.4	45.3	47.6	2.3
79	83	0.95	−7.6	−5.5	−3.6	34.2	44.5	10.3
80	85	0.94	6.2	19.7	1.8	36.3	41.8	5.5
69	79	0.87	−7.1	−5.7	−4.3	49.7	49.9	0.2
69	79	0.87	−5.8	−7.1	−4.3	48.1	50.1	2
80	84	0.95	18.9	19	19.9	34.8	44.2	9.4
74	78	0.95	−0.5	−0.2	−0.2	38.9	39.4	0.5
79	82	0.96	7.4	7.6	7.1	26.7	36.6	9.9
66	75	0.88				46.7	48.5	1.8
74	78	0.95	−1.5	−1.5	−1.5	42.4	44	1.6
79	83	0.95	0.8	1.2	2.1	38.9	46.1	7.2
80	84	0.95	9.4	7.7	7.6	44.6	47.1	2.5
73	81	0.9	−0.1	−0.7	−0.3	45.5	45.1	−0.4
78	84	0.93	−3.6	−3.5	−2.9	43	48.4	5.4
71	78	0.91	−1.1	−0.4	−0.8	44.9	45	0.1
72	77	0.94				40.9	43.8	2.9
72	80	0.9	0.6	0.4	0.3	46.9	44.8	−2.1
77	84	0.92	0.3	0.2	−0.2	46.5	46.1	−0.4
80	86	0.93	−3	−5.4	−2.2	34.3	45.6	11.3
80	84	0.95	5.4	6.9	7.9	47.7	47.4	−0.3
81	85	0.95	8.3	10.2	9.4	42.7	46.2	3.5
72	79	0.91		1.7	1	30.8	30.5	−0.3
66	76	0.87				48.9	49	0.1
79	83	0.95	2.6	3.6	3.3	43.3	46	2.7
80	87	0.92	40.8	42.7	1.9	40.8	42.7	1.9
63	75	0.84	48.2	48.8	0.6	48.2	48.8	0.6
76	81	0.94	44.4	45.8	1.4	44.4	45.8	1.4

212   *Statistical Appendix*

APPENDIX TABLE A.2   *Mean household disposable incomes (€) (2012) and life expectancy at age 0 (2013), regions of largest European countries.*

	France			Germany			Italy	
Region	A	B	Land	A	B	Region	A	B
1.	27,800	83.8	1.	27,000	82.2	1.	20,300	82.7
2.	18,500	81.6	2.	25,500	81.5	2.	20,800	83
3.	17,800	81.2	3.	27,900	81.4	3.	19,700	82.5
4.	18,400	80.6	4.	25,400	80.8	4.	23,700	83.5
5.	19,000	81.2	5.	27,200	81.3	5.	24,900	83.9
6.	17,700	82	6.	19,600	81	6.	21,400	83.9
7.	18,300	81.9	7.	23,700	80.7	7.	20,100	82.6
8.	16,700	79.8	8.	22,700	80.7	8.	22,200	83.4
9.	17,000	81.4	9.	24,000	80.5	9.	19,000	83.4
10.	19,300	82.2	10.	17,700	80.9	10.	17,500	83.3
11.	17,800	82.4	11.	19,200	80.4	11.	17,800	83.6
12.	18,500	82.9	12	21,700	80.2	12.	19,600	82.8
13.	18,400	81.6	13.	17,800	80.2	13.	15,700	82.9
14.	17,700	82	14.	22,500	80.2	14.	14,000	82.8
15.	18,700	82.9	15.	17,300	79.9	15.	12,000	81.1
16.	19,000	83.4	16.	17,100	79.4	16.	12,400	83.1
17.	17,400	82				17.	12,300	82.8
18.	20,100	83.5				18.	11,300	82.5
19.	18,100	81.9				19.	11,900	81.9
20.	18,300	82.8				20.	13,300	82.8
21.	16,500	82.5						
22.	19,400	82.9						
23.	17,700	82.5						

Column A: Mean household disposable income. *Source: Eurostat, 2015e.*
Column B: Mean life expectancy at age 0. *Source: Eurostat, 2015f.*

Guide to region names:

France: 1. Île-de-France, 2. Bassin Parisien, 3. Champagne-Ardenne, 4. Picardie, 5. Haute-Normandie, 6. Basse-Normandie, 7. Bourgogne, 8. Nord Pas de Calais, 9. Lorraine, 10. Alsace, 11. Franche-Comté, 12. Pays de la Loire, 13. Bretagne, 14. Poitou-Charentes, 15. Aquitaine, 16. Midi-Pyrénées, 17. Limousin, 18. Rhône-Alpes, 19. Auvergne, 20. Méditerranée, 21. Languedoc-Rousillon, 22. Provence-Alpes-Côte d'Azur, 23. Corse.

Germany: 1. Baden-Wurttemberg, 2. Hessen, 3. Bayern, 4. Rheinland-Pfalz, 5. Hamburg, 6. Berlin, 7. Schleswig-Holstein, 8. Niedersachsen, 9. Nordrhein Westfalen, 10. Sachsen, 11. Brandenburg, 12. Saarland, 13. Thüringen, 14. Bremen, 15. Mecklenburg-Vorpommern, 16. Sachsen-Anhalt.

Italy: 1. Piemonte, 2. Valle d'Aosta, 3. Liguria, 4. Lombardia, 5. Bolzano, 6. Trentino, 7. Friuli-Venezia-Giulia, 8. Emilia-Romagna, 9. Toscana, 10. Umbria, 11. Le Marche, 12. Lazio, 13. Abruzzo, 14. Molise, 15. Campania, 16. Puglia, 17. Basilicata, 18. Calabria, 19. Sicilia, 20. Sardegna.

Poland: 1. Lódzkie, 2. Mazowieckie, 3. Malopolskie, 4. Slaskie, 5. Lubelskie, 6. Podkarpackie, 7. Swietokrzyskie, 8. Podlaskie, 9. Wielkopolskie, 10. Zachodniopomorskie, 11. Lubuskie, 12. Dolnoslaskie, 13. Opolskie, 14. Kujawsko-Pomorskie, 15. Warminsko-Mazurskie, 16. Pomorskie.

Spain: 1. Galicia, 2. Asturias, 3. Madrid, 4. Cantabria, 5. País Vasco, 6. Foral de Navarra, 7. Canarias, 8. La Rioja, 9. Aragón, 10. Castilla y León, 11. Castilla – La Mancha, 12. Extremadura, 13. Cataluña, 14. Valencia, 15. Illes Balears, 16. Andalucia, 17. Murcia.

UK: 1. South East, 2. East, 3. South West, 4. London, 5. East Midlands, 6. West Midlands, 7. Yorkshire and The Humber, 8. Wales, 9. North East, 10. North West, 11. N. Ireland, 12. Scotland.

	Poland			Spain			United Kingdom	
Region	*A*	*B*	*Region*	*A*	*B*	*Region*	*A*	*B*
1.	10,900	75.4	1.	13,300	82.9	1.	21,900	82.2
2.	15,900	77.7	2.	14,100	82.5	2.	19,700	82.2
3.	10,600	78.5	3.	21,400	84.8	3.	17,300	81.9
4.	12,100	76.3	4.	14,300	83.4	4.	27,100	82.3
5.	9,200	77.1	5.	20,100	83.7	5.	16,200	81.2
6.	8,500	78.6	6.	19,600	84	6.	15,100	80.8
7.	9,300	77.1	7.	12,700	82.7	7.	14,900	80.5
8.	9,200	77.7	8.	16,100	84	8.	13,900	80.3
9.	12,000	77.2	9.	16,900	83.4	9.	14,100	80
10.	10,600	76.7	10.	14,700	84	10.	15,100	80
11.	9,800	76.3	11.	12,300	83.5	11.	14,100	80.4
12.	11,700	76.9	12.	10,500	82.2	12.	17,200	79.3
13.	9,700	77.2	13.	18,200	83.4			
14.	9,800	76.9	14.	13,100	82.8			
15.	9,400	76.3	15.	16,100	82.9			
16.	11,200	77.9	16.	11,300	81.8			
			17.	12,200	82.7			

APPENDIX TABLE A.3   Immigrant populations in European countries, by country or region of origin, c. 2012.

| Countries of immigration | Percentages of persons born abroad | | | | | | | | | | | |
| | | | Named countries of emigration | | | | | | | | | |
	NNWE	SE	CFEE	Ex-Y	Russia and other ex-USSR*	'Distressed' countries	Ex-colonies	Turkey	Morocco	Other	Total	X
Austria**	2.42		0.87	4.01				1.87		6.84	16.01	13.59
Belgium	2.74	1.06						0.88	1.82	9.24	15.75	13.00
Bulgaria	0.08	0.10			0.40			0.12		0.82	1.52	1.52
Czech Rep			0.98		1.18	0.44				1.16	3.76	2.78
Denmark	0.98		0.57			0.37		0.57		7.51	10.00	9.02
Estonia					13.20					1.45	14.97	14.97
Finland	0.58		0.72		1.18	0.18				2.78	5.44	4.86
Hungary	0.30		2.23	0.38	0.34					1.29	4.54	2.31
Iceland	2.04		3.10							5.53***	11.27	9.24
Ireland	5.04		2.20							7.01****	16.02	10.98
Italy	0.36		1.65		0.36				0.69	5.66******	9.44	9.44
Latvia					11.65					1.14	13.65	13.65
Lithuania					3.30					0.66	4.15	3.96
Netherlands	0.67		0.20				1.74	1.09		6.47	10.91	10.24
Norway	1.48		2.06						0.94	9.39	13.64	12.16

	1	2	3	4	5	6	7	8	9	10	11	12
*Poland***	*0.22*		*0.14*		*0.92*	*0.01*		*0.03*		*0.06*	*1.35*	*1.21*
Romania		0.24			0.45					0.32	1.06	1.06
Slovakia			2.22		0.18					0.83	3.23	1.01
Slovenia				9.73						1.67	11.40	1.67
Spain	0.68		1.63				1.69			7.49	12.83	12.83
Sweden	1.65		0.80	0.70		2.00				10.55	15.72	14.07
Switzerland	5.95	5.62						0.95		10.82	23.34	11.77
UK	0.47		1.08				2.00		1.53	8.27	12.41	11.94

Percentages of inhabitants with foreign citizenship

	1	2	3	4	5	6	7	8	9	10	11	12
Germany	0.98		0.99		0.40			1.75		4.91	8.64	8.64
Portugal	0.33		0.33				1.49			1.65	3.87	3.87

Source: Eurostat, 2015d
'Other' includes non-specified countries from within the specified regions
'X' signifies size of hypothetical multicultural challenge
* Excluding Baltic states
** Statistics are for 2012
*** Including 0.61% from the United States
**** Including 0.59% from Nigeria
***** Including 0.72% from Albania

APPENDIX TABLE A.4   Incomes of different occupational groups, certain European countries, c. 2011.

	Austria		Czech Republic		Denmark		Germany*		Poland		Switzerland		UK	
	1.	2.	1.	2.	1.	2.	1.	2.	1.	2.	1.	2.	1.	2.
Managers	4.51	2.17	5.11	2.16	1.90	1.68	4.40	1.91	6.23	2.07	7.86	1.45	10.46	1.93
Male	3.14	2.40	3.77	2.35					3.88	2.37	5.15	1.55	6.82	2.17
Female	1.35	1.56	1.34	1.71					2.36	1.71	2.71	1.20	3.57	1.42
Professionals	15.18	1.57	13.82	1.42	26.39	1.15	17.73	1.22	17.97	1.22	22.29	1.34	23.95	1.35
Male	7.72	1.89	6.14	1.67					6.83	1.42	11.88	1.40	12.58	1.59
Female	7.39	1.29	7.68	1.20					11.14	1.12	10.41	1.25	11.22	1.13
Technicians, etc.	18.88	1.22	18.34	1.10	16.79	1.05	21.35	0.84	10.87	1.03	17.52	1.07	12.82	1.21
Male	10.18	1.48	10.39	1.23					5.15	1.17	8.59	1.14	6.04	1.40
Female	8.62	0.94	7.95	0.98					5.72	0.92	8.94	0.99	6.70	0.97
Clerical	10.96	0.86	9.30	0.86	7.90	0.86	12.18	0.82	6.63	0.84	9.02	0.89	9.95	0.69
Male	3.01	1.11	2.03	0.97					2.36	0.85	2.52	0.91	3.03	0.89
Female	7.90	0.77	7.27	0.82					4.27	0.83	6.51	0.88	6.86	0.63
Service and sales	17.70	0.60	15.19	0.63	19.77	0.76	15.43	0.60	13.91	0.59	15.61	0.75	18.68	0.49
Male	5.67	0.76	5.29	0.69					5.05	0.64	5.07	0.86	5.78	0.61
Female	11.95	0.54	9.90	0.60					8.86	0.56	10.54	0.71	12.78	0.45
Skilled agric.	4.89	0.56	1.36	0.73	2.19	0.78			11.39	0.62	3.08	0.81	1.28	
Male	2.80	0.64	0.88	0.76					6.54	0.67	2.22	0.83	1.12	
Female	2.07	0.44	0.49	0.68					4.85	0.52	0.86	0.68	0.15	

Craft workers, etc.	13.87	1.01	17.51	0.84	8.73	0.88	12.92	0.77	15.12	0.78	12.56	0.89	8.38	0.92
Male	12.67	1.03	15.68	0.87					13.33	0.83	10.55	0.90	7.87	0.97
Female	1.13	0.68	1.83	0.64					1.79	0.56	2.01	0.70	0.46	0.57
Plant and machinery operators	5.72	0.97	13.63	0.81	5.45	0.82	6.54	0.68	10.29	0.85	3.67	0.86	4.96	0.84
Male	4.86	1.02	10.30	0.85					8.87	0.88	2.97	0.88	4.35	0.88
Female	0.83	0.64	3.33	0.70					1.42	0.67	0.70	0.69	0.57	0.60
Elementary	8.29	0.56	5.34	0.56	4.73	0.73	7.10	0.58	7.02	0.58	4.11	0.75	8.80	0.48
Male	3.06	0.73	1.98	0.65					2.96	0.67	1.27	0.82	4.89	0.62
Female	5.19	0.44	3.35	0.51					4.06	0.53	2.84	0.66	3.86	0.32

Sources: Austria: Statistik Austria (2012); Czech Republic: CZSO (2012); Denmark: Statistics Denmark (2012); Germany: Statistisches Bundesamt (2013); Poland: Central Statistical Office of Poland (2012); Switzerland: Swiss Central Statistical Office (2012); ONS (2012)

Notes:
1. Number of persons in occupational group as percentage of total employees.
2. Ratio of mean salary of the group to mean income of all employees (for Switzerland data refer to medians).
* Data based on national rather than ISIC definitions.

References

Ahles, L., U. Klammer and M. Wiedemeyer (2012) 'Labour Market Insecurities of Young People and Family Formation. France and Germany Compared', unpublished GUSTO paper, http://www.gusto-project.eu/, date accessed 15 December 2015.

Amsterdam Institute for Advanced Labour Studies (2015) *The ICTWSS Database 5.0 2015* (Amsterdam: AIAS).

Bendix, R. and S. M. Lipset (1953) *Class, Status and Power* (Glencoe, IL: The Free Press).

Blossfeld, H. P. (2009) 'Educational Assortative Mating in Comparative Perspective', *Annual Review of Sociology*, 35, 513–30.

Bohle, D. and Greskovits, B. (2012) *Capitalist Diversity on Europe's Periphery*. Ithaca, NY: Cornell University Press.

Bourdieu, P. and J. C. Passeron (1973) *Reproduction in Education, Society and Culture* (London: Sage).

Breen, R. and R. Luijkx (2004) *Social Mobility in Europe* (Oxford: Oxford University Press).

Busemeyer, M. R. (2015) *Skills and Inequality: Partisan Politics and the Political Economy of Education Reforms in Western Welfare States* (Cambridge: Cambridge University Press).

Central Statistical Office of Poland (2012) *Statistical Yearbook 2012,* Warsaw: Central Statistical Office of Poland.

Crouch, C. (2015) *Governing Social Risks in Post-Crisis Europe* (Cheltenham: Edward Elgar).

Crouch, C. (1993) *Industrial Relations and European State Traditions* (Oxford: Oxford University Press).

Crouch, C. (1996) 'Revised Diversity: From the Neo-Liberal Decade to Beyond Maastricht', in J. J. Van Ruysseveldt and J. Visser (eds) *Industrial Relations in Europe. Traditions and Transitions* (London: Sage).

CZSO (2012) *Statistical Yearbook of the Czech Republic 2012* (Prague: CZSO).

Ebbinghaus, B. and J. Visser (1997) 'Der Wandel der Arbeitsbeziehungen im westearopäischen Vergleich', in S. Hradil and S. Immerfall (eds), *Die westearopäischen Gesellschaften im Vergleich* (Opladen: Leske + Budrich).

Esping-Andersen, G. (1990) *The Three Worlds of Welfare Capitalism* (Cambridge: Polity Press).

Eurobarometer (2010) *Biotechnology*. Special Eurobarometer 341 (Brussels: TNS Opinion and Social).

218

Eurobarometer (2013) *Cultural Access and Participation*. Special Eurobarometer 399 (Brussels: TNS Opinion and Social).

Eurobarometer (2014) *Sport and Physical Activity*. Special Eurobarometer 412 (Brussels: TNS Opinion and Social).

European Commission (2009) *Industrial Relations in Europe* (Luxembourg: Office for Official Publication of the European Communities).

Eurostat (2012) *Health at a Glance* (Luxembourg: Office for Official Publication of the European Communities).

Eurostat (2014) *Statistics in Focus* (Luxembourg: Office for Official Publication of the European Communities).

Eurostat (2015a) 'Population and Population Change Statistics', http://ec.europa.eu/eurostat/statistics-explained/index.php/Population_and_population_change_statistics, date accessed 11 December 2015.

Eurostat (2015b) 'Share of Live Births Outside Marriage', http://ec.europa.eu/eurostat/tgm/table.do?tab=table&language=en&pcode=tps00018, date accessed 15 December 2015.

Eurostat (2015c) 'Marriage and Divorce Statistics', http://ec.europa.eu/eurostat/statistics-explained/index.php/Marriage_and_divorce_statistics, date accessed 15 December 2015.

Eurostat (2015d) 'Migration and Migrant Population Statistics', http://ec.europa.eu/eurostat/statistics-explained/index.php/Migration_and_migrant_population_statistics, date accessed 15 December 2015.

Eurostat (2015e) http://ec.europa.eu/eurostat/tgm/table.do?tab=table&init=1&language=en&pcode=tgs00026&plugin=1, date accessed 17 December 2015.

Eurostat (2015f) http://appsso.eurostat.ec.europa.eu/nui/show.do, date accessed 17 December 2015.

Ferrera, M. (1996) 'The "Southern Model" of Social Europe', *Journal of European Social Policy*, 6(1), 17–37.

Förster, M., A. Llena-Nozal and V. Nafilyan (2014) *Trends in Top Incomes and their Taxation in OECD Countries*. Social, Employment and Migration Working Paper 159 (Paris: OECD).

Giner, S. (1998) *La societat catalana* (Barcelona: Institut d'Estadística de Catalunya).

Glass, C. and É. Fodor (2007) 'From Public to Private Maternalism? Gender and Welfare in Poland and Hungary after 1989', *Social Politics*, 4(3), 323–50.

Hiekel, N., A. C. Liefbroer and A.-R Poortman (2014) 'Understanding Diversity in the Meaning of Cohabitation across Europe', *European Journal of Population*, 30, 391–410.

Ibanez Garzarán, Z. L. (2007) 'Access to Non-Vulnerable Part-time Employment in the Netherlands, Spain and the UK, with Special Reference to the School and Local Government Sectors', unpublished PhD Thesis (Florence: European University Institute).

ILO (2015) 'Employment by Sex and Occupation: Selected ISCO Level 2', http://www.ilo.org/ilostat/faces/help_home/data_by_subject/subject-details/indicator-details-by-subject?indicator=EMP_TEMP_SEX _OCU2_NB&subject=EMP&_afrLoop=14877941918966&datasetCode =YI&collectionCode=YI&_adf.ctrl-state=syvavp3h0_190, date accessed 18 December 2015.

Kalmijn, M. (2007) 'Explaining Cross-national Differences in Marriage, Cohabitation, and Divorce in Europe', *Population Studies – A Journal of Demography*, 61(3), 243–63.

Kiernan, K. E. (2001) 'The Rise of Cohabitation and Childbearing Outside of Marriage in Western Europe', *International Journal of Law, Policy and the Family*, 15(1), 1–21.

Kitschelt, H. and P. Rehm (2014) 'Occupations as a Site of Political Preference Formation', *Comparative Political Studies*, 47(12), 1670–1706.

Klammer, U. (2012) 'Rush Hours of Life – Die Ressource Zeit im Lebensverlauf aus Gender- und Familienperspektive', in A. Knecht and F. C. Schubert (eds) *Ressourcen im Sozialstaat und in der Sozialen Arbeit. Aktivierung – Förderung – Zuteilung* (Stuttgart: Kohlhammer).

Knegt, R. (ed.) (2008) *The Employment Contract as an Exclusionary Device. An Analysis on the Basis of 25 Years of Developments in The Netherlands* (Antwerp: Intersentia).

Kocka J. (1981) *Die Angestellten in der deutschen Geschichte 1850-1980: Vom Privatbeamten zum angestellten Arbeitnehmer* (Göttingen: Vandenhoeck & Ruprecht).

Kohl, H. and H-W. Platzner (2007) 'The Role of the State in Central and East European Industrial Relations: The Case of Minimum Wages', *Industrial Relations Journal*, 386, 614–635.

Kristensen, P. H., M. Lotz and R. Rocha (2011) 'Denmark: Tailoring Flexicurity for Changing Roles in Global Games', in P. H. Kristensen and K. Lilja (eds) *Nordic Capitalisms and Globalization* (Oxford: Oxford University Press), 86–140.

Leonardi, L. (2012) *La società europea in costruzione* (Florence: Firenze University Press).

Lukes, S. (1974; 2nd edition 2005) *Power: A Radical View* (Basingstoke: Macmillan and Palgrave Macmillan).

Mackenbach, J. P. (2006) *Health Inequalities: Europe in Profile* (Brussels: UK Presidency of the European Union).

Mackenbach, J. P. and C. W. N. Looman (2013) 'Life Expectancy and National Income in Europe, 1900–2008: An Update of Preston's Analysis, *International Journal of Epidemiology*, 42(4), 1101–10.

Mau, S. and R. Verwiebe (2010) *European Societies: Mapping Structure and Change* (Bristol: Policy Press). (Originally published as *Die Sozialstruktur Europas* (Konstanz: UVK Verlagsgesellschaft, 2009)).

Meardi, G. (2012) *Social Failures of EU Enlargement. A Case of Workers Voting with Their Feet* (London: Routledge).

Naldini, M. (2003) *The Family in the Mediterranean Welfare States* (London: Frank Cass).

OECD (2011) *Divided We Stand: Why Inequality Keeps Rising* (Paris: OECD).

OECD (2013) *Health at a Glance* (Paris: OECD).

OECD (2013a) 'Cohabitation Rate and Prevalence of Other Forms of Relationship', http://www.oecd.org/els/soc/SF3_3_Cohabitation_rate_and _prevalence_of_other_forms_of_partnership_Jan2013.pdf, date accessed 7 April 2015.

OECD (2014) *OECD Factbook 2014* (Paris: OECD).

OECD (2015a) 'Inequality', https://stats.oecd.org/index.aspx?queryid=66670, date accessed 18 December 2015.

OECD (2015b) 'Decile Ratios of Gross Earnings', https://stats.oecd.org/Index .aspx?DataSetCode=DEC_I, date accessed 7 April 2015.

Oesch, D. (2006a) *Redrawing the Class Map* (Basingstoke: Palgrave Macmillan).

Oesch, D. (2006b) 'Coming to Grips with a Changing Class Structure: An Analysis of Employment Stratification in Britain, Germany, Sweden and Switzerland', *International Sociology*, 21(2), 263–88.

Oesch, D. and J. Rodríguez Menés (2011) 'Upgrading or Polarization? Occupational Change in Britain, Germany, Spain and Switzerland, 1990–2008', *Socio-Economic Review*, 9(3), 503–31.

ONS (2012) *Official Yearbook of the United Kingdom 2012* (London: ONS).

Ost, D. (2000) 'Illusory Corporatism: Tripartism in the Service of Neoliberalism', *Politics and Society*, 28(4), 503–30.

Palier, B. (ed.) (2010) *A Long Goodbye to Bismarck? The Politics of Welfare Reform in Continental Europe* (Amsterdam: Amsterdam University Press).

Piketty, T. (2013) *Le capital au XXI siècle* (Paris: Seuil).

Saxonberg, S. and D. Szelewa (2007) 'The Continuing Legacy of the Communist Legacy? The Development of Family Policies in Poland and the Czech Republic', *Social Politics*, 4(3), 351–79.

Schmidt, V. A. (2002) *The Futures of European Capitalism* (Oxford: Oxford University Press).

Schmidt, V. A. (2006) *Democracy in Europe* (Oxford: Oxford University Press).

Schneider, F. and A. Buehn (2012) 'Shadow Economies in Highly Developed OECD Countries: What Are the Driving Forces?', IZA Discussion Paper 6891 (Bonn: IZA).

Schneider, F., A. Buehn and C. E. Montenegro (2010) 'Shadow Economies all over the World', Policy Research Working Paper 5356, World Bank Developing Economics Group (Washington DC: World Bank).

Scott, J. (1994) 'Class Analysis: Back to the Future', *Sociology*, 28(4), 933–42.

Sinzheimer, H. (1921) *Grundzüge des Arbeitsrechts* (Berlin: Fischer).

Standing, G. (1999) *Global Labour Flexibility: Seeking Distributive Justice* (Basingstoke: Palgrave Macmillan).

Standing, G. (2011) *The Precariat: The New Dangerous Class,* London: Bloomsbury.

Statistics Denmark (2012) *Statistical Yearbook 2012* (Copenhagen: Statistics Denmark).

Statistics Japan (2015) *Statistical Yearbook of Japan 2015* (Tokyo: Statistics Japan), Table 2.8.

Statistisches Bundesamt (2013) *Statistical Yearbook of Germany 2013* (Wiesbaden: Statistisches Bundesamt).

Statistik Austria (2014) *Statistisches Jahrbuch Österreich 2012* (Vienna: Statistik Austria).

Swiss Central Statistical Office (2012) *Statistical Yearbook of Switzerland 2012* (Bern: Swiss Central Statistical Office).

UNECE (2013) *Economic Survey of Europe* (New York: United Nations Economic Commission for Europe).

UNECE (2015) 'Mean age of women at first marriage', http://w3.unece.org/PXWeb/en/Charts?IndicatorCode=303&CountryCode=196, date accessed 15 December 2015.

United Nations (2013) *Statistical Yearbook, 57th Edition* (New York: United Nations Organization).

UN Population Division (2015) *World Population Prospects. The 2015 Revision* (New York: United Nations Organization).

Van Bavel, J. (2012) 'The Reversal of Gender Inequality in Education, Union Formation and Fertility in Europe', *Vienna Yearbook of Population Research,* 10, 127–154.

Weber, M. (1922) *Wirtschaft und Gesellschaft,* Tübingen: Mohr.

Winkler, H. A. (2015) *Geschichte des Westerns. Die Zeit der Gegenwart* (Munich: C. H. Beck).

World Bank (2015a) 'GDP per capita (current US$)', http://data.worldbank.org/indicator/NY.GDP.PCAP.PP.CD?order=wbapi_data_value_2012+wbapi_data_value+wbapi_data_value-last&sort=desc, date accessed 8 December 2015.

World Bank (2015b) 'Death rate, crude (per 1,000 people)', http://www.data-worldbank.org/indicator/SP.DYN.CDRT.IN., date accessed 11 December 2015.

World Bank (2015c) 'Labor force participation rate, female (% of female population ages 15+) (modelled ILO estimate)', http://data.worldbank.org/indicator/SL.TLF.CACT.FE.ZS, date accessed 7 April 2015.

World Health Organization (2015a) 'Life Expectancy', http://www.who.int/gho/mortality_burden_disease/life_tables/situation_trends/en/, date accessed 8 December 2015.

World Health Organization (2015b) 'Crude birth and death rate: Data by country', pps.who.int/gho/data/node.main.CBDR107?lang=en, date accessed 8 December 2015.

World Wealth and Income Database (2015) http://www.wid.world, date accessed 21 December 2015.

Index